While drawing on lessons from past faith giants, to enrich missional practices and mission practi model. Nicholl's audience is the Lausanne Move constituency. Her presentation leaves no doubt ......uvation of spirituality will enrich Lausanne's programs and make them more effective. Nicholl's proposal goes beyond Lausanne. All Christian organizations will benefit by her clear and compelling call. A prophetic message for the church today.

J. Daniel Salinas, PhD
International Partnership Coordinator for the Theological Education Initiative,
United World Mission

Like a dramatic symphony, Dr. Sarah Nicholl has brought the music of Scripture and the theology of Minority and Majority and older and contemporary "worlds" together in a missional spirituality. This work is a corrective challenge to aspects of global evangelicalism and the Lausanne Movement, bringing hope that present-day mission will be a more integrated endeavour with sustained outcomes for strengthening the church and bringing God's shalom to the world.

Charles R. Ringma, PhD
Emeritus Professor,
Regent College, Canada

If mission is participation in the life and mission of the triune God, then spirituality is in mission and mission in spirituality. This is the integrated life that overcomes the perceived tension between contemplation and action. Sarah Nicholl has expressed this beautifully in this book.

Ross Hastings, PhD
Sangwoo Youtong Chee Chair of Theology,
Regent College, Canada

Sarah Nicholl seeks to integrate voices from the Majority and Minority world to challenge the Lausanne Movement regarding the need for a more articulated missional spirituality that fits global Christianity. While situating the voices of Segundo Galilea, Orlando Costas, Ignatius of Loyola, and John Wesley in their own contexts, she aptly incorporates their voices to form a rich tapestry that informs missional practices in our global world.

Athena Gorospe, PhD
Biblical Studies Department Chair,
Asian Theological Seminary, Philippines

Integrated Mission

Integrated Mission

Recovering a Christian Spirituality for
Evangelical Integral Transformation

Sarah Nicholl

Langham

ACADEMIC

© 2024 Sarah Nicholl

Published 2024 by Langham Academic
An imprint of Langham Publishing
www.langhampublishing.org

Langham Publishing and its imprints are a ministry of Langham Partnership

Langham Partnership
PO Box 296, Carlisle, Cumbria, CA3 9WZ, UK
www.langham.org

ISBNs:
978-1-83973-762-6 Print
978-1-83973-979-8 ePub
978-1-83973-980-4 PDF

Scriptures taken from the Holy Bible, New International Version®, NIV®. Copyright © 1973, 1978, 1984, 2011 by Biblica, Inc.™ Used by permission of Zondervan.

British Library Cataloguing-in-Publication Data
A catalogue record for this book is available from the British Library

ISBN: 978-1-83973-762-6

Cover & Book Design: projectluz.com

Contents

Abstract

This book argues for the integration of missional and spiritual practices into what is defined as "integrated mission," with a particular focus on the evangelical Lausanne Movement. Integrated mission is a practice that is beneficial for both mission and the missioner as it ensures both are centred in God.

Employing the practical theological method of Don Browning (appropriately adapted), the first chapter introduces the subject matter and the second chapter describes my method and hermeneutic. In chapter 3, the first movement of Browning's method provides a thick description and critique of Lausanne's three congressional documents which inform its mission. Here I argue that the Lausanne Movement's practice, although implicitly referring to spiritual themes, lacks an explicit missional spirituality.

Chapters 4 and 5 form the historical or second movement of Browning's method. I employ a Gadamerian hermeneutic to draw on the writings of two well known historical Christians, each of whom was involved in mission and formed structured communities that benefited the participants and their contexts. The texts examined in these chapters are the sermons of John Wesley (who formed the Methodist societies) and the writings of Ignatius of Loyola (who formed the Company of Jesus, better known as the Jesuits).

The third movement (chapters 6 and 7) looks at two contemporary theologians, namely, Orlando Costas, and Segundo Galilea. Costas was a missiologist who served also as a Baptist pastor and was a significant member of the radical evangelical movement in Latin America. Galilea was a Roman Catholic priest who was influenced by the liberation movement and whose writings advocate for a spirituality of liberation for those involved in the work of liberation. He lived and wrote from Latin America. The choice of theologians is intentionally ecumenical and attends to voices from the Majority World.

The final two chapters of the book form my strategic practical theology. Chapter 8 takes the form of a round table; here, through a dialogical format, questions exploring the concept of integrated mission are "posed" to all the participating theologians and the Lausanne Movement. The answering "discussion" reveals that mission practice is a sanctifying and sacramental practice that is spiritually forming for the missioner. Further, such integration enriches the practice of mission by enabling the missioner to fully participate with the Triune God in the *missio Dei* through the development of an experiential, cognitive and mutually loving relationship with God. This relationship is formed through traditional practices of prayer, meditational biblical reading, and sacramental practice that are missionally and contextually grounded. This integrated practice is biblically based in the concept of "loving God and neighbour" and the parable in Matthew 25:31–46 where Christ identifies with the marginalized; it is also grounded in the spiritual concept of "following Jesus."

In the concluding chapter, the book proposes various practices for the Lausanne Movement to employ in moving towards a practice of integrated mission.

Acknowledgements

I am indebted and thankful to: my advisers, Dr. Neil Pembroke and Dr. Charles Ringma, for their continual support and advice; the staff at the University of Queensland library, the Richard Allison Library, Regent College, and the Dr. John Micallef Library, St. Marks College, who supplied me with books and journals both in tangible and digital form; Father Balthasar and Father Angel who shared their knowledge of Father Segundo Galilea, together with Charles Goff who introduced and interpreted for me; friends who encouraged and supported me, in particular, Melody Mazuk, Ann-Marie Ellingthorpe, Wendy Pitt-Brooke, Ann Bartley, Vic and Sherri Coulthard, and members of my running group; and finally my husband, Alan, and my son, Joel, who were generous, gracious, and supportive, particularly when wife and mum was MIA.

1

Introduction

> Mission without spirituality cannot survive any more than combustion without oxygen. It must be a spirituality of engagement and not of withdrawal . . . cultivated in obedience and discipleship, and not in the isolated comfort of one's inner self.[1]

The radical evangelical, Orlando Costas, made this statement in 1982 eight years after the birth of the evangelical mission organization, the Lausanne Movement (Lausanne), of which he was an active member. In this book, I am engaging this call for a missional spirituality, particularly for Lausanne, and arguing that any such spirituality is best combined with the context of its mission, in this case, Lausanne's mission guidelines, so that the benefits of a spirituality integrated with mission are revealed.

Lausanne is one of the primary evangelical movements that influences current evangelical global missional theory and practice.[2] It was established in 1974 by the Billy Graham Evangelistic Association and the British theologian, John Stott. Today, it continues to have a large global following among evangelicals; for example, the last international congress held in Cape Town in 2010 had four thousand mission leaders attend from 198 countries.[3]

---

1. Orlando Costas, *Christ Outside the Gate: Mission beyond Christendom* (Maryknoll: Orbis Books, 1992), 172.

2. There are others, for example, there were those that objected formally to Lausanne's description of mission at its first Congress, the radical evangelicals, primarily from Latin America who are still prominent today and as a group are now global. Many founding members of the radicals continued within Lausanne, such as the late theologian, René Padilla from Argentina and Orlando Costas, whose texts are part of this book. Another example, prominent today, that has a similar structure to Lausanne is the World Evangelical Alliance (formally the World Evangelical Fellowship).

3. https://lausanne.org/cape-town-2010-the-third-lausanne-congress-on-world-evangelization.

The documents resulting from its congresses together with its papers from various sub-committees on particular mission topics form the basis of its missional platform. Lausanne pursues implementation of its missional stance through its networks of like-minded evangelical mission organizations and churches. In its current format, Lausanne is an evangelical think-tank, a voice to those connected with it, and a movement that forms leaders as "catalysts" to encourage Christian missional transformation both in geographical regions, and areas of concern. However, despite its missional dynamic, Lausanne is yet to explicitly acknowledge the need to integrate mission practice with a spirituality. It is this lacuna that I seek to challenge.

I am engaging with this issue now for various reasons. First, various works published over the last decade argue for a missional spirituality.[4] Some of this thinking is evolving in North America as a critical response to The Gospel and Our Culture Network – which is seeking to provide structural, strategic and theological analysis and guidance for mission – and which, like Lausanne, has not seen fit to attend to an overall missional spirituality for its proposed missional congregations.[5] The critical voices promoting a missional spirituality for the missional church concept come from both evangelical and mainline churches.[6] Other advocates for a missional spirituality include pastors in

---

4. L. Paul Jensen's *Subversive Spirituality: Transforming Mission through the Collapse of Space and Time* (Eugene: Pickwick, 2009) is an interesting study. Based upon cultural, social, and field research of generations X and Y and the rise of the technological era, Jensen records the loss of discretionary time and public social space that these generations are challenging. Through an analysis of the biblical narrative of Jesus's life, the early church, and subsequent historical movements, Jensen argues that the church ought to spend more time encouraging a spirituality that embraces spiritual disciplines, both in isolation and community; that is, the church should slow down and spend more time with God. He proposes that traditional disciplines may take fresh and flexible forms. His findings reveal a positive correlation (rather than a causal relationship) between spirituality and mission. He suggests there is a link between the inward and outward rhythm of the Christian life and advocates his belief that the church, when its life is based upon spending more time with God, will move out with mission practices that will reach these current generations.

5. See, for example, Nathan A. Finn and Keith S. Whitfield, eds., *Spirituality for the Sent: Casting a New Vision for the Missional Church* (Downers Grove: IVP Academic, 2017). In their chapter "The Missional Church and Spiritual Formation," Finn and Whitfield advocate for the melding of the spirituality of the Protestant Renovare Movement, the spirituality of the New Calvinist Movement , and the mission concepts from the Missional Church.

6. Dwight J. Zscheile, ed., *Cultivating Sent Communities: Missional Spiritual Formation.* Missional Church Series, (Grand Rapids: Eerdmans). This is a collection of papers originally presented at the sixth Annual Missional Consultation sponsored by Luther Seminary in St Paul, Minnesota. The various papers are from a Lutheran perspective.

North America[7] and evangelical "missioners" around the globe.[8] However, none to date have engaged with Lausanne: this being the case, I am choosing to participate in the ongoing conversation regarding missional spirituality.

Second, *The Cape Town Commitment* (Lausanne most recent document resulting from its most recent international congress) contains changes that may make Lausanne more open to integrating an explicit spirituality within its mission. These changes are at both theological and practice levels; I highlight these in chapter three of this book.

Third, scholars are calling for more integration between areas of theory and practice. In bringing together missiology, mission practice, and spirituality, I am participating in reversing a long historical theological approach that has academically separated the study of theology, practice, and spirituality into theoretical and practical elements.[9] This division commenced in the thirteenth century when, influenced by Greek philosophy, scholars began to categorize theology into various disciplines for study. Before this, all theology had a spiritual/practical focus, for example, patristic theology consisted primarily of biblical exegesis for the purposes of understanding and living the Christian

---

7. Roger Helland and Len Hjarlmarson, *Missional Spirituality: Embodying God's Love from the Inside Out* (Downers Grove: InterVarsity Press, 2011), Kindle. These two Pastors are Canadian: Helland is a Baptist and Hjalmarson is a Mennonite in the Missionary Alliance. They argue that sound, biblical, spiritual formation will lead to missional engagement. However, this is not a knowledge-based spiritual formation but a practice-based spirituality in which ideas are moved from the head to the heart. They ground such a spirituality in Jesus's command to "Love the Lord your God with all your heart and with all your soul and with all your mind and with all your strength" and to "love your neighbour as yourself" (Mark 12:30–31). Thus, spiritual formation is an inner to outward movement.

8. John Amalraj, Geoffrey W. Hahn, and William D. Taylor, eds., *Spirituality in Mission: Embracing the Lifelong Journey* (New York: World Evangelical Alliance Mission Commission, 2018), Kindle. In this volume, a number of mission practitioners from eighteen countries reflect on what mission spirituality means in various contexts. It is written primarily for other practitioners.

9. Even within the academic pursuit of spirituality, there are those such as Simon Chan who separate spiritual theology (the theory) from spirituality (the lived experience). For Chan, a spirituality arises out of a particular spiritual theology. The theology comes first and then is applied. See *Spiritual Theology: A Systematic Study in the Christian Life* (Downers Grove: InterVarsity Press, 1998), 16. However, there are those who integrate both, such as Bradley Holt and Sandra Schneiders. Schneiders argues that for academic writing to be relevant to today's understanding of spirituality, it is better to place them together. Her definition of spirituality is therefore broad: "the experience of consciously striving to integrate one's life in terms not of isolation and self-absorption but of self-transcendence towards the ultimate value one perceives." She argues that when one's ultimate concern is "God revealed in Jesus Christ and experienced through the Holy Spirit within the life of the Church, one is dealing with Christian Spirituality." She affirms that, for a Christian spirituality, theology is intrinsic. Sandra Schneiders, "Spirituality in the Academy," in *Exploring Christian Spirituality: An Ecumenical Reader* (Grand Rapids: Baker Books, 1991).

faith, rather than expounding doctrine. Today, this trend of re-integrating theology and practice is evident in such movements as liberation theology and radical evangelicalism.[10]

Philip Sheldrake, in speaking to this division of theology from spirituality, notes that there was also a second consequence, namely that the subject of spirituality became an inner faith journey, no longer about an integrated life in the Spirit involving reflective social practice and ethics. Thus, it became an inner journey isolated from practice, similar in many ways to some of the contemporary secular spiritualities that deal with the self. The natural consequence of this was that Christian spirituality also became individualized, rather than a communal enterprise.[11] By arguing for the re-integration of mission and spirituality, involving both inner and outer dimensions of life and the individual and the church community, I am also participating with those seeking to reverse these trends. As Sheldrake argues:

> Spirituality is understood to include not merely techniques in prayer but more broadly a conscious relationship with God in Jesus Christ through the indwelling of the Holy Spirit and the context of the community of believers. Spirituality is concerned with the conjunction of theology, prayer, and practical Christianity.[12]

Practical and spiritual theologian, Claire Wolfteich, agrees with this integrated approach. She argues that while spirituality and practical theology are separate academic arenas, they are useful partners in seeking solutions to issues.[13] Therefore by addressing the issue of Lausanne's lack of an explicit spirituality in mission through a practical theological methodology, this book refuses this unfortunate divide.

My interest in this subject matter derives from various junctures in my life to date. My concern for Lausanne dates from my early days as an evangelical

---

10. Liberation theologians such as Gustavo Gutiérrez have authored books on theology and spirituality. Gutiérrez has sought to show how the Liberation Movement is an integration of theology and spirituality. See Gustavo Gutiérrez, *A Theology of Liberation* (London: SCM, 1974); and Gustavo Gutiérrez, *We Drink from Our Own Wells: The Spiritual Journey of a People* (Maryknoll: Orbis Books, 1984). Similarly, radical evangelicalism purports to integrate missiology and practice. Orlando Costas notes that "Radical evangelicals have been basically concerned not with a theoretical view of the Bible (the doctrine of inspiration) but with its content and implication for life." *Liberating News: A Theology of Contextual Evangelization* (Grand Rapids: Eerdmans, 1989), 11.

11. Philip Sheldrake, "What is Spirituality?," in Collins, *Exploring Christian Spirituality*, 32.

12. Sheldrake, "What is Spirituality?," 40.

13. Claire Wolfteich, "Spirituality," in *The Wiley-Blackwell Companion to Practical Theology*, ed. Bonnie J. Miller-McLemore (Malden: Wiley-Blackwell, 2012), 334–35.

Christian in the UK during the 1980s; at that time, John Stott and similar evangelical voices informed my experience of Christianity. My involvement in mission and spirituality comes from my studies at Regent College in Vancouver, a hub of Christian spirituality.[14] From an academic perspective, I am interested in juxtaposing historical, missional, and spiritual sources of a global and ecumenical nature in suggesting an integrated practice of mission and spirituality for a global, international, evangelical, missional organization such as the Lausanne Movement. My current field of practical theology enables me to do this. Generally, as an evangelical, also I want to critique and contribute to my own heritage.

In this study, I argue that Lausanne would benefit from incorporating an approach in which mission practice and spirituality are closely integrated ("integrated mission"). I specifically contend that mission is empowered and informed by spiritual practices, it is a means of sanctification, and it has a sacramental dimension. I further contend that leaders in Lausanne need to revise their theoretical framework, giving far greater emphasis to the incorporation of spiritual practices with those of mission. This will highlight for evangelical missioners the centrality of practice that is animated by, rooted in, related to, and participatory with the Triune God in God's mission to the world. I make this argument using Don Browning's practical theological method (albeit in a slightly adapted form).[15]

Definitions

It is necessary to define the terms used frequently in this book, particularly when some of those terms are open to interpretation. For the purposes of clarity, I will define my meaning of the following terms: "spirituality," "missional spirituality," "spiritual practices," "integrated mission," and "evangelical," as they are used in the context of my study.

---

14. Finn and Whitfield, "The Missional Church," 38–39. In relation to Regent College, they specifically note the work of Dr. James Houston and the late Eugene Peterson. I had the honour of sitting in both their respective classrooms. I am particularly influenced by the work of Dr. Houston and the work of former Regent Mission and Spirituality Professor, Dr. Charles Ringma.

15. Don S. Browning, *A Fundamental Practical Theology: Descriptive and Strategic Proposals* (Minneapolis: Fortress, 1991). In this volume, Browning establishes his preferred methodology.

Spirituality

Spiritualities that give persons inner strength, understanding and sense of meaning and purpose, whether related to a religion or not, are now broadly recognized in our Western society. George Hunsberger notes that such secular spiritualities tend to relate to a dimension of the human designated "spiritual." He quotes from *Psychology Today*:

> Spirituality means something different for everyone. For some, it is about participating in organized religion: going to church, synagogue, a mosque, and so on. For others, it's more personal: some people get in touch with their spiritual side through private prayer, yoga, meditation, quiet reflection, or even long walks.[16]

Hunsberger then indicates that, while he is not denying that there is a spiritual aspect to people, Christian spirituality's focus is not upon the human spirit but the Spirit of God, the Holy Spirit.[17] I consider this insight helpful in our contemporary age in distinguishing Christian spirituality from many others. It is also important to note that Christian spirituality as a concept (not a term) is not something new; it has a long history as evidenced in the Bible, the traditions of the church, and in Christian experience.

The term, "Christian spirituality," was first used by Roman Catholics in the seventeenth century but was only adopted by Protestants in the last fifty years. It is defined in the *Westminster Dictionary of Christian Spirituality* as "those attitudes, beliefs and practices which animate peoples' lives and help them to reach out towards super-sensible realities."[18] Contemporary Christian spiritual theologians define it in various ways. Bradley Holt describes it as the "lived experience" of the Christian, in terms of a Spirit-filled and guided life, lived in the context of a community of believers.[19] Philip Sheldrake states that it "seeks to express the conscious human response that is both personal and ecclesial. In short, life in the Spirit."[20] For Lawrence Cunningham and Keith Egan, "it is the lived encounter with Jesus Christ in the Spirit."[21] While each definition has

---

16. George R. Hunsberger, "Journey in the Spirit," in *Spirituality for the Sent: Casting a New Vision for the Missional Church*, eds. Nathan A. Finn and Keith S. Whitfield (Downers Grove: IVP Academic, 2017), 332–33.

17. Hunsberger, "Journey in the Spirit," 335.

18. Quoted in Bradley Holt, *Thirsty for God: A Brief History of Christian Spirituality* (Minneapolis: Fortress, 1993), 6.

19. Holt, *Thirsty for God*, 6.

20. Sheldrake, "What is Spirituality?," 25.

21. Lawrence S. Cunningham and Keith J. Egan, *Christian Spirituality: Themes from the Tradition* (New York: Paulist, 1996), 7.

slightly different emphases, the essence of them all is that Christian spirituality is about how Christians live in Christ, aided by the Holy Spirit, and it is this shared view of Christian spirituality that I have used in this book.

Missional Spirituality

In recent literature, the concept of missional spirituality is also variously defined. Roger Helland and Len Harljmarson define it integrally, as "an attentive and active engagement in embodied love for God and neighbour expressed from the inside out."[22] Nathan Finn and Keith Whitfield define missional spirituality by defining both missional and spirituality separately; "being missional" is living directed, shaped, and sent on the mission of God.[23] They define spiritual formation as "the cultivation of grace-motivated spiritual practices and habits, drawn from the authoritative Scriptures and the best of the Christian tradition, that the Holy Spirit uses to foster spiritual maturity in the life of the believer for the glory of God, the health of the church, and the sake of the world."[24] They advocate that the process of bringing missional and spiritual formation together leads to "missionally formed Christians." Kirk Franklin describes spirituality in mission as "fundamentally connected with examining the foundations for mission such as discerning the work of the Holy Spirit, discovering what God is doing in the world, and joining with him. Missional spirituality is "lived in and fuelled by awareness of the *Missio Dei* as the Holy Spirit enlivens it."[25] Father Segundo Galilea, writing at the end of the twentieth century, describes missional spirituality as "Christian spirituality" because he considers that the essence of all Christian spirituality is "the process of following Christ, under the direction of the Spirit"[26] and "to follow Jesus is to collaborate with him in the liberating salvation of the world, which is the extension of the Kingdom of God."[27] Thus for Galilea, God's nature is missionary as revealed in the incarnation, and therefore Christians by "following Jesus" are becoming missionary as they participate with God in how God calls them to live. It is clear just from these four definitions alone that

---

22. Helland and Hjarlmarson, *Missional Spirituality*, Loc. 284 of 2615, Kindle.

23. Finn and Whitfield, "The Missional Church," 40–41.

24. Finn and Whitfield, "The Missional Church," 43.

25. Kirk Franklin, "Mission and Spirituality," in *Spirituality in Mission: Embracing the Lifelong Journey*, eds. Amalraj, Hahn, and Taylor, Loc. 1003 of 8929, Kindle.

26. Segundo Galilea, *The Way of Living Faith: A Spirituality of Liberation*, trans. John W. Diercksmeier (San Francisco: Harper & Row, 1988), 4.

27. Galilea, *The Way of Living Faith*, 157.

the term "missional spirituality" is viewed somewhat differently, with some definitions more specific than others. So how am I using the term?

In this book, I am defining missional spirituality simply. "Missional" is used by many as an adjective of the word that follows, and I am using the term in the same way.[28] I define missional spirituality as how Christians live a mission focused life aided by the Holy Spirit. I aver that a missional spirituality is contextual in nature; that is, its spiritual practices will vary depending on the nature of the Christian denomination or the location within which it is formed. For example, Anglican practice may vary from that of a Roman Catholic one, or a practice within the inner city of Sydney will differ from one established within rural Africa. However, I also consider that there are basic elements common in many missional spiritualities. Therefore, in this book I seek to uncover the elemental practices of a missional spirituality that could be tailored to a particular situation.

Spiritual Practices

In Anglican parlance of the eighteenth century, spiritual acts such as prayer and Bible reading were called "acts of piety." I have sought to contemporize the term by using "spiritual practices" instead. I use the term "spiritual practice" to mean an act that can bring a Christian into the presence of the Triune God so that God may speak through experiential or cognitive means to the Christian. When I speak of a missional spirituality, I am referring to a combination of spiritual practices that enable an encounter with the Triune God that is oriented towards mission; these are the elemental practices referred to in the previous definition.

Integrated Mission

In this book, I am arguing for what I term "integrated mission." This means combining spiritual and missional practices in a practice of mission. I emphasise the integration of such practices, arguing that there are essential benefits to such a synthesis that are lost if missional and spiritual practices are divided. My research reveals that when such practices are brought together

---

28. Christopher J. H. Wright, *The Mission of God: Unlocking the Bible's Grand Narrative* (Downers Grove: InterVarsity Press, 2006), 24. Wright notes that: "Missional is simply an adjective denoting something that is related to or characterized by mission, or has the qualities, attributes or dynamics of mission."

in relationship, they ground mission in the Triune God, inform mission, and empower the missioner, that is, they become sacramental and sanctifying acts through the Triune God's presence. Mission is both outreach to the world and transforming for the missionized and the missioner.

While integrated and integral are similar words, my choice of the former is specific. Radical evangelicals have promoted the term "integral mission" to suggest that all acts of mission, whether evangelism, social care, or social action are equally mission. They use this terminology to distinguish their view from those of Lausanne which until recently gave priority to evangelism. In order to distinguish my approach from that of radical evangelicals, I have chosen "integrated." My term implies the synthesis of spiritual and missional practice.

"Integral" also infers the idea of completeness or wholeness which I am not assuming in my approach. I am seeking to highlight the importance of spiritual practices combined with the missional task for mission. In my view, this is an essential, not a complete way of mission.

Finally, as a note to the reader, this book predominately explores the nature of integrated mission. While I use this term wherever possible, I do use other phrases to explain the richness of this integration, such as "the synthesis of mission and spirituality" and "the interdependence of encountering God and the shape of mission." In all such terms, I am highlighting the varied dynamic of integrated mission.

Evangelical

Today, evangelicalism has an "institutional" presence within Christianity and is also a global movement. Evangelicals are found in all the major Christian denominations; consequently, evangelicals can have broad theological differences. Today, evangelical presence is also shifting, with the majority of evangelical Christians residing in Africa, South America, and Asia rather than North America and Europe. Consequently, it is notoriously difficult to establish a comprehensive definition of the movement. In this book, I have adopted a minimal definition of evangelicalism proposed by David Bebbington. He uses a quadrilateral to establish four cornerstones of evangelical identity. In this conception evangelical/evangelicalism means those who adhere to the importance in the Christian life of conversion, biblical authority, the atonement provided by Christ, and mission activity.[29]

---

29. David W. Bebbington, *Evangelicalism in Modern Britain: A History from the 1730s to the 1980s* (Abingdon: Routledge, 1989), 16–42.

Book Outline

In order to make the argument for integrated mission, particularly for Lausanne, this book proceeds as follows. There is an explanation of my chosen method and hermeneutic in the next chapter. This leads to the first movement in chapter three which is a thick description and critical survey of Lausanne's three main congressional documents: *The Lausanne Covenant* (1974), *The Manila Manifesto* (1989), and *The Cape Town Commitment* (2010). These documents shape Lausanne's proposals for evangelical mission practice. My aim is to show to what extent (if any) Lausanne's missional practice incorporates either an explicit or implicit integrated mission. As the intent of this book is to make suggestions towards a contemporary practice for Lausanne, I will give more weight in my analysis to Lausanne's latest document, *The Cape Town Commitment*.

The book's second movement is historical as my intent is to root my proposed integrated mission in previous Christian practice. I have two chapters in this section. Chapter four focuses on the sermons and practice of John Wesley who, during the eighteenth-century evangelical revival in Britain, established the Methodist movement that became known for its socially transformative practices and holiness. In chapter five, I research the spiritual theology and practice of Ignatius of Loyola; Ignatius founded of the Jesuit Order during the fifteenth century in Europe, and is widely known as a "contemplative in action." My aim is to examine to what extent these men pursued integrated mission.

In the third movement of the book, I seek to ground integrated mission in more contemporary missiology and spirituality. I have two chapters in this area. Chapter six explores the missiology and practice of the radical evangelical, Orlando Costas, and chapter seven focuses on the spiritual theology of Fr. Segundo Galilea, a Roman Catholic and proponent of liberation theology, who promoted a spirituality of liberation. Both men wrote in the context of Latin America in the 1960s to 1980s. I interpret their respective texts through a lens focusing on the extent to which a missional and spiritual dynamic is at work in their theories and suggested practices.

Chapters eight and nine comprise the fourth movement, "strategic practical theology." Chapter eight is my theological reflection using the tool of a round table. My goal is to create a meaningful understanding of integrated mission through asking questions of and noting the various "similarities in difference" in my respective theologians' texts. My final chapter formalises my findings and, shaped by them, I make proposals for a scheme of integrated mission for Lausanne. This is not a detailed model; rather, it takes the form of suggestions that, if utilized by Lausanne, could significantly benefit its missioners and enrich its mission.

The Choice of Theological Participants

In choosing my historical and contemporary voices, it is clearly important that each participant was part of a missional movement and spoke of a spirituality or a way of life with God that was pivotal to their activities in mission. I have also chosen a Roman Catholic as well as evangelical participants from both historical and contemporary periods, as my intention is to be ecumenical. While evangelicals need to maintain their critical stance in relation to the theology and practices of other Christian traditions, they need to also be active and constructive participants in the movement for Christian unity and to humbly learn from other communions.

My approach is not without precedent. As examples: from 1974 to 1984 evangelicals dialogued with Roman Catholics on matters relating to mission; in the 1990s a group named "Evangelicals and Catholics Together" emerged calling for common understanding and joint working in areas of mission;[30] and most recently, suggesting that dialogue between Roman Catholics and Protestants on mission may be fruitful, Stephen Bevans published an article comparing the recent mission documents from the World Council of Churches (WCC), Pope Francis in *Evangelii Gaudium*, and Lausanne's *Cape Town Commitment*.[31] Overall, I consider that Roman Catholics have a rich heritage of spirituality that is also useful for the proposed dialogue.

Finally, I intentionally chose contemporary voices from the majority Christian world.[32] For too long those of us in the global North have failed to take seriously enough the experience and theological insights of our sisters

---

30. Stephen B. Bevans and Roger P. Schroeder, *Constants in Context: A Theology of Mission for Today* (Maryknoll: Orbis Books, 2004), 326–27. They also consider that Pope John Paul II's *Redemptio Missio's* Christocentric stance is similar to that of the *Lausanne Covenant. Constants in Context*, 325. This provides another reason why such ecumenical dialogue is useful.

31. Stephen B. Bevans, "Life, Joy, and Love: Together towards Life in Dialogue with *Evangelii Gaudium* and *The Cape Town Commitment*," *International Review of Mission* 104, no. 2 (2015): 200–202.

32. By Majority World, I refer to the fact that most Christians now live in the Global South. Philip Jenkins notes that in 1900, eighty-three percent of the world's Christians lived in Europe and North America. It is projected that by 2050 seventy-three percent of the world's Christians will live in Africa, Asia and Latin America. He states: "If we want to visualize a "typical" contemporary Christian, we should think of a woman living in Nigeria or in a Brazilian *favela*." Philip Jenkins, *The Next Christendom: The Coming of Global Christianity*, third edition, (New York: Oxford University Press, 2011), preface and 2–3.

and brothers in the global South. In the Majority World many local theologies are formed by indigenous scholars – liberation theology being one example of this. These theologies can have a global impact if the minority world turns its ear and attention to their theologians. Therefore, I consider it vital to engage persons from the Majority World when considering a significant theological issue upon which they have a knowledgeable voice. By attending to Galilea's work on spirituality, I am enabling this process to take place. Further, as I engage with Costas, who has experience of both Latin America and North America, I am giving voice to an evangelical missiologist with global experience and perspective.

Finally, the choice of these theologians is a result of my research journey to date. Regarding the contemporary voices, prior to this book my research was in liberation spirituality in Latin America. Here Galilea gained my attention. His focus on a missional spirituality for those Christians working for social transformation resonated with me, particularly in relation to my thoughts regarding the lack of an explicit spirituality within Lausanne's evangelical mission. I have also previously studied the work of the radical evangelicals in Latin America. I consider Costas a good candidate as an evangelical missiologist, who participated in Lausanne and was willing to challenge it. Further, he was ecumenical and towards the end of his life championed the integration of spirituality with mission.

Historically, I regard a voice that represents the original evangelical revival important. John Wesley, an early evangelical missioner and a pastoral theologian who founded the Methodist movement, known for its transformational work within society in eighteenth century Britain, was a clear candidate. When looking for a Roman Catholic voice, Ignatius of Loyola, the founder of the Jesuits (which was originally a missionary order) and the author of spiritual exercises still used today for spiritual formation, seemed appropriate.

I realise that in choosing these theologians, I exclude the input of other Christian traditions and Protestant denominations. Nonetheless, this is necessary within the boundaries of this book's method; in my view, the book's outcome endorses the choice made.

2

Methodology and Hermeneutic

Brief Overview of the Discipline of Practical Theology

Friedrich Schleiermacher in his *Kurze Darstellung des Theolgischen Studium (Brief Outline on the Study of Theology)* of 1811 famously described practical theology as the crown of all theology. Analogically, describing theology as a tree, he considered theology had three parts: its roots were philosophical, its trunk historical, and its crown practical. The crown represented the practical outworking of the historical and philosophical theory.[1] Even though his description gives a positive view of practical theology, as a relative newcomer to the academic realm it has struggled to gain academic support. Its relegation in academia was partly due to the perception that its main concern was training clergy.[2] This reductionist view, known as the "clerical paradigm," was critiqued by Edward Farley in his 1983 treatise, *Theologia*.[3]

Since then, practical theology has grown and developed. Farley began its expansion by arguing that it involved both the concept of "habitus" and theological teaching.[4] In other words, practical theology was interested in the

---

1. See Gerben Heitnik, *Practical Theology, History, Theory, Action, Domains: Manual for Practical Theology.* Reinder Bruinsma, trans. (Grand Rapids: Eerdmans, 1999) and for further details of Schleiermacher's contribution to Practical Theology, 22–28.

2. Bonnie Miller-McLemore notes that many practical theologians bemoan that practical theology is still marginalized within academia. She argues that this is not a theological issue but one within academia. She opines that practice remains subservient to theory. See Bonnie J. Miller-McLemore, "Five Misunderstandings about Practical Theology," *International Journal of Practical Theology* 16, no. 1 (2012): 5–26.

3. Edward Farley, *Theologia: The Fragmentation and Unity of Theological Education* (Philadelphia: Fortress, 1983).

4. In *Theologia*, Farley undertook a critique of clerical education. During his research, he apprehended that the cause of the failing clerical system was not a necessarily faulty curricula but a loss of a unifying structure, namely *"theologia,"* or theological understanding, For Farley, part of this loss was an understanding of theology as "habitus," an historical term that he

connection of faith with human life and the teaching thereof.[5] Alongside such developments, practical theologians began to encompass the use of human and social sciences in their methodologies to improve their understanding of persons and respective contexts.

In 1991, the International Academy of Practical Theology was founded together with various regional associations, providing a significant milestone in practical theology's academic journey.[6] In this manner, practical theology has expanded its purview and established itself as a worthwhile academic pursuit.

Today, practical theology primarily examines the relationship between theory and practice. However, scholars in the field define it variously. Don Browning states that practical theology "is the mutual critical correlation of the interpreted theory and praxis of the Christian faith with the interpreted theory and praxis of the contemporary situation."[7] For Browning, it is an enterprise that at all stages must be thoroughly theological.[8] Bonnie Miller-McLemore, in her introduction to *The Wiley-Blackwell Companion to Practical Theology*, contends that practical theology is multivalent and a pursuit of an embodied faith. It involves four distinct enterprises: first, it is "an activity of believers seeking to sustain a life of reflective faith in the everyday"; second, "it is a method or way of understanding or analysing theology in practice used by religious leaders and by teachers and students across the theological curriculum"; third, it is "a curricular area in theological education that focuses on ministerial practice and sub-specialties"; and fourth, it is "an academic discipline pursued by a smaller sub-set of scholars to support and sustain these

---

defines as "a cognitive disposition and orientation of the soul, a knowledge of God and what God reveals . . . habit having the primary character of wisdom." In other words, theology is not only a theoretical discipline, it also has a sapiential quality, one that is practical and relates to a salvific knowledge of God, 35.

5. Miller-McLemore notes that Farley, in a footnote, states it was not his intention to undermine the importance of ministerial education, although the treatise is portrayed by many practical theologians as such. She argues that "the clerical paradigm" was not the only reason for practical theology's marginalization; another issue was the problem of intellectualism that "distorts how religious knowledge is learned, conveyed, and practiced." She argues that to overcome this anti-intellectual view there is a need for practical theology to promote other ways of "knowing" within academia. Miller-McLemore, "Five Misunderstandings," 13.

6. Examples are the Association of Practical Theology (APT), the British and Irish Association of Practical Theology (BIAPT), and the Association of Practical Theology in Oceania (APTO).

7. Browning, *A Fundamental Practical Theology*, 47. The late Don Browning, a North American, is considered an important contributor and member of the discipline in its current form.

8. Browning, *A Fundamental Practical Theology*, 47.

first three enterprises."[9] Furthermore, Kathleen Cahalan and James Nieman assert that the "basic task that orients practical theology is to promote faithful discipleship . . . rooted in Christian tradition, practical theology focuses on a called people who manifest a particular faith through concrete ways of life."[10] With such varied definitions, there are many different aspects to practical theology involving both lay and academic theologians; however, all focus on Christian practice with a view to improving it in alignment with a theological perspective through a process of theological reflection. This book, as it seeks to improve the practice of mission by integrating it with spiritual practices, falls within academic practical theology.

Richard Osmer suggests that different approaches to academic practical theology are a consequence of the researcher's views at a meta-theoretical level. He argues practical theological research involves four basic areas: descriptive/empirical, interpretative, normative, and pragmatic. How a researcher incorporates these into her research, however, is dependent upon her views of the theory-praxis relationship, the sources of justification, and on the theological rationale of her work. These views will lead to divergence in practical theological work. For Osmer, what is important is that practical theology continues to focus on practice that is beneficial to both the church and the world.[11]

I agree with Osmer. I realize that as an evangelical, I have certain views regarding the relationship between theory and practice. I recognize that my methodology and reflective theological process are affected by this stance. However, the focus of this book is to generally improve evangelical missional activity and assist those that are involved in such work for the benefit of society and the church. I intend to do this through using Don Browning's well-accepted method suggested in his *Fundamental Practical Theology*, although adapted to suit the particularity of my book.

---

9. Bonnie J. Miller-McLemore. "Introduction: The Contributions of Practical Theology," in Miller-McLemore, *The Wiley-Blackwell Companion to Practical Theology*, 5.

10. Kathleen A. Cahalan and James R. Nieman, "Mapping the Field of Practical Theology," in *For Life Abundant: Practical Theology, Theological Education and Christian Ministry*, eds. Dorothy C. Bass and Craig Dykstra (Grand Rapids: Eerdmans, 2008), 67.

11. Richard R. Osmer, "Practical Theology: A Current International Perspective," *HTS Theological Studies* 67, no. 2 (2011): 1–7, https://doi.org/10.4102/hts.v67i2.1058.

Method

Based on its history, method is important in the realm of practical theology because it is tied to its credibility as an area of academic research.[12] Browning's method encompasses four movements: descriptive theology, historical theology, systematic theology, and strategic or fully practical theology.[13]

Browning describes each movement as follows. Descriptive theology is a full description of the theory-laden practices that are the subject of the research; this leads to the questions that generate the theological reflection. Historical theology involves researching the normative texts from history, including the Bible, in order to provide insights with which to confront current practice. Systematic theology brings the latent visions within the practices together with contemporary theologizing to discover whether both are aligned. The fourth movement, strategic practical theology, brings all the findings of the first three movements together with the concrete situation under study and, in an organized, structured way, asks various questions of it.[14]

Browning's method resonates with me for various reasons. First, its use of both historical and contemporary theological perspectives for a comprehensive approach aligns with my own. As noted previously, my argument draws upon both historical and contemporary spiritual and pastoral theological work from a range of Christian traditions. Second, even though I am researching within a practical theological framework, my work also falls within the discipline of Christian spirituality. I therefore am seeking a methodology acceptable to both academies. Practical theologian Claire Wolfteich, who often works within such an interdisciplinary area, suggests that Browning's practical theological method encapsulates a methodology that is very acceptable as it examines historical theology, contemporary theology, and context using hermeneutical theories – all important factors in spiritual theological research.[15] Third, as my

---

12. Neil Pembroke, "Outsiders and Insiders: Personal Reflections on Methodology in the Studies of Religion at The University of Queensland, 1986–2010," *Crossroads* 5, no. 2 (2011): 123–26, https://61UQ_eSpace. Pembroke notes how method historically and currently is important to the development of practical theology work within the School of History and Philosophical Inquiry at the University of Queensland, Australia.

13. Browning uses "strategic" and "fully" interchangeably. Browning, *Fundamental Practical Theology*, 8.

14. Browning, *Fundamental Practical Theology*, 49, 55–56.

15. Claire Wolfteich, "Animating Questions: Spirituality and Practical Theology," *International Journal of Practical Theology* 13 (2009): 138. In this article she notes three main theological methods within spirituality: anthropological/hermeneutical, historical/contextual, and biblical and theological. She also strongly argues that practical theology and spirituality in certain circumstances could form a fruitful research partnership. See also Claire Wolfteich, "Spirituality," in McLemore, *The Wiley-Blackwell Companion to Practical Theology*, 328–336.

work involves the interpretation of written texts of theologians, Browning's method also appeals because of its foundation in hermeneutics. Browning's methodology involves aspects of the hermeneutical theory of Hans-Georg Gadamer, and consequently I employ a Gadamerian hermeneutic in my four interpretative chapters on Wesley, Ignatius, Costas and Galilea.

Finally, David Tracy, at the meeting of the International Practical Theological Academy in 2008, argued for the importance of the use of a spiritual dynamic within practical theology.[16] He proposes that Browning's method can incorporate this by involving a spiritual aspect in both the second and third movements. I have adopted his suggestion in my method because both Ignatius and Galilea, as spiritual theologians, bring these components to this argument. (This does not prevent them having other contributions, nor does it prevent Wesley or Costas from providing spiritual insight.)

My Strategic Practical Theology takes the form of a round table in which I will address questions relating to the formation of integrated mission to the texts of the chosen participants, including those of Lausanne. For me, this process as a form of theological reflection, is a means of interconnecting the written thoughts and statements of all my chosen participants on the themes of this book. In this way, their contributions to the emergence of an integrated mission become apparent.

The last chapter of this book forms the second part of the Strategic Practical Theology, whereby I take the findings from my theological reflection and seek to re-fashion them into proposals which could help form an integrated mission for Lausanne.

Hermeneutics

Hermeneutics is key to Don Browning's method; for Browning, interpretation of the past and present in a dialogical manner is fundamental to finding future ways forward. His method employs the hermeneutical theory of Hans-Georg Gadamer and, accordingly, so does this book. Gadamer is one of the first philosophers to argue that it is possible to have a universal theory of interpretation for all matters, whether theological, legal or the humanities.[17]

---

16. David Tracy, "A Correlational Model of Practical Theology Revisited," in *Religion Diversity and Conflict*, ed. Edward Foley (New Jersey: Transaction, 2008), 49–61.

17. In Gadamer's foreword to the second edition of *Truth and Method*, he denies that his theory was intended to refute the necessity of method (a critique of his first edition); it also was not intended to create a "method of understanding" in itself. Gadamer describes understanding

Building on Heidegger's concept that "understanding" is Dasein's mode of being, Gadamer argues that hermeneutics is significant because it is humanity's foundation for existence.[18] It must therefore be practice oriented.[19]

Gadamer's theory espouses that humans interpret through dialogue and that history and tradition are valuable dialogue partners.[20] One of his first definitions of hermeneutics states that interpretation allows the "alienated" and "distanced" to speak again. In other words, it is often the "forgotten" and the "far off" that give meaning today. However, this is not because they are "alienated" or "distanced" but because the past shapes or is inherent in the present.[21] Gadamer argues that humanity, consciously and unconsciously, is created by its history and traditions.[22] He describes this as "effective historical consciousness."[23] He opines that often this unconscious/conscious traditional formation of the self leads to the current questions being asked.[24] For example, it is arguable that my interest in spirituality linked to missional activities for evangelicalism lies within my evangelical and Christian formation to date. There is something that leads me to question why such integration is not effectively encouraged and developed within evangelical mission, because instinctually I consider it is in keeping with evangelical thought. Overall, Gadamer's theory highlights the importance of history and tradition and, in my view, underscores the importance of the historical movement in Browning's method, thereby giving credence to my research approach.

---

as more of an "event" than a process. Hans-Georg Gadamer, *Truth and Method*, ed. and trans. Joel Weinsheimer and Donald G. Marshall, 4th ed. (London: Bloomsbury, 2013), xxv–xxxv.

18. Gadamer, *Truth and Method*, xxvii.

19. Gadamer, *Truth and Method*, xxvii.

20. Charles Ringma notes that Paul Ricoeur does not agree that a text creates a true dialogue partner as in a real conversation. However, like Gadamer who considers tradition as a genuine partner in communication, Ringma argues: "there is no reason to posit that a text, because it transcends its own originating context, ceases to be a conversation partner. The very nature of a text is that it addresses us and the productive nature of *Zeitenabstand* allows the otherness of the text to emerge more fully." Charles R. Ringma, *Gadamer's Dialogical Hermeneutic: The Hermeneutics of Bultmann, of the New Testament Sociologists, and of the Social Theologians in Dialogue with Gadamer's Hermeneutic* (Heidelberg: University of Heidelberg, 1999), 41.

21. Ringma, *Gadamer's Dialogical Hermeneutic*, 17.

22. Gadamer, *Truth and Method*, 312.

23. For the full content of historical consciousness and its effect in hermeneutics, see Gadamer, *Truth and Method*, 311–18.

24. Gadamer, *Truth and Method*, 311. Gadamer notes regarding the effect of the historical on a human: "It determines in advance both what seems to us worth inquiring about and about what will appear as an object of investigation." He continues that often humans are unaware of this phenomenon.

As well as Browning agreeing with Gadamer on the importance of history and tradition for the present and future, Browning's method also follows Gadamer's theory in the way one approaches the reading of history; that is, it takes a dialogical approach focused on the historical texts of the author. Philosophers of hermeneutics have suggested various ways to comprehend history. For example, when looking at historical texts there are authors, their intentions and respective contexts, the written text, and the reader. Philosophers such as Schleiermacher and Dilthey argue that to interpret a text and find its true meaning a reader must understand both the author's intent and context. Gadamer critiques both philosophers, arguing that it is not the reader's task to get inside the head of the author nor can she fully understand their context.[25] Therefore, a reader must primarily apply herself to the interpretation of the text before her.[26] For Gadamer, interpretation comes out of the relationship between the reader and the text.[27] This is significant for all works that interpret text.

In following Gadamer's hermeneutic, I will focus on the texts of my respective chosen authors, not their intentions or contexts. Therefore, my chapters will only include background details regarding the historical period or context that I consider are useful in promoting understanding. Gadamer further opines that readers come to texts with what he describes as prejudices,[28] fore-structures, or pre-understandings.[29] These are the cultural, social and familial factors that have formed the human to date, shaping her worldview and, subsequently, her interpretation.[30] These factors form what Gadamer terms as the "interpreter's horizon."[31] Thus, as I read the texts of my chosen participants, I come with my own fore-structures, which I cannot put aside as

---

25. Gadamer rejects Dilthey's proposal that there is a universal life within history that an interpreter could discover. See Ringma, *Gadamer's Dialogical Hermeneutic*, 20–21.

26. Gadamer, *Truth and Method*, 307.

27. Gadamer, *Truth and Method*, 305. He argues that the process of understanding is neither objective nor subjective; rather, he describes it "as the interplay of the movement of tradition and the movement of the interpreter."

28. By prejudice, Gadamer means the legal use of the term, that is, a pre-formed judgement before all facts have been rendered. Gadamer, *Truth and Method*, 283. He also notes that the concept of prejudice only gained a negative connotation during the Enlightenment. He argues that it can have a positive and legitimate one also. Gadamer, *Truth and Method*, 284, 289.

29. Gadamer perceptively notes regarding history and prejudice that "history does not belong to us; we belong to it . . . *The prejudices of the individual, far more than his judgements, constitute the historical reality of his being*" (emphasis original). Gadamer, *Truth and Method*, 288–89.

30. Gadamer, *Truth and Method*, 288–89.

31. Gadamer makes the point that this is not a closed horizon; it is always in motion as new understanding leads to change. Gadamer, *Truth and Method*, 317.

they are who I am. All I can do is acknowledge them and know that they can potentially affect my interpretation. However, Gadamer argues that readers must remain open to those texts re-forming their perspectives; they cannot allow their prejudices to misunderstand the text. By remaining open in a reflexive process, prejudices become productive.[32]

For the record, these are my known pre-understandings that may affect my interpretation. I am a Caucasian woman in mid-life. I am married and a parent of a teenage son. I grew up in England and, after graduating from university, lived for ten years in Northern Ireland. I now live in western Canada, having been there for over twenty years. I was educated in the United Kingdom during the 1970s–1980s and in Canada from the late 1990s–early 2000s. I am a trained lawyer and formerly practised as such in both Northern Ireland and Canada. I also have a Master of Arts in Christian Spirituality. I became a Christian during my undergraduate days in England and remain so. I am interdenominational in my Christian practice, although I am influenced by attending evangelical churches, predominantly Baptist. My study in spirituality gives me an understanding and affection for Roman Catholic spirituality and sacramental practice. Generally, I am analytical and critical in my approach. I am aware of differing cultural, geographical and historical traditions, and I am open and positive towards them. This is my history and the traditions that consciously shape me; I acknowledge that there are others factors shaping me of which I am unaware.

Gadamer argues that interpretation involves the reader bringing her contemporary questions from her context to the chosen text. It is this dialogical relationship that creates new meaning and understanding.[33] Gadamer suggests that, to the reader, these texts are both familiar and strange: familiar, in the sense that some of the factors within the text have shaped the reader, and strange, in the sense that they are alien to the reader's pre-understandings. Gadamer describes this as the "in-between"; it is an intermediary location where true hermeneutics takes place.[34] For example, I understand Costas's evangelical approach because we share the same tradition. Yet, I am unfamiliar with his Latin American heritage or the poverty he describes, so this is strange. However, in being open to the "other," my prejudice is productive, as I am

---

32. Gadamer, *Truth and Method*, 282. He notes: "The important thing is to be aware of one's own bias, so that the text can present itself in all its otherness and thus assert its truth against one's own fore meanings."

33. Gadamer, *Truth and Method*, 317.

34. Gadamer, *Truth and Method*, 306.

re-formed by my understanding of Costas's text. Gadamer argues that in this dialogical experience whereby two differing horizons come together, something new is formed. Taking my example, something new is created when I read Costas's text. This is because I am not assimilating Costas's opinion in a pure or whole form; rather, I am allowing my horizon and what I understand of his text in light of my question to create something different.[35] This re-formation is what Gadamer describes as a "fusion of horizons." It is this fusion that creates new understanding. I am receiving and re-articulating a tradition that is part of me in a way that is relevant to the present. This is the hermeneutical process that takes place in the chapters of this book where I am engaging other texts. My pre-understandings and contemporary questions relating to spirituality and missional activities dialogue with the various texts to allow a fusion of horizons; this then leads to the creation of new horizons that I will then theologically reflect upon in my strategic practical theological reflection.

As noted, my strategic practical theology takes the form of a round table through which I theologically reflect upon my interpretations of Wesley, Ignatius, Costas and Galilea – both in the process of the method and through wise critical analysis. In so doing, I am opening my pre-existing horizon of integrated mission to re-formation by my interpretations of my other chosen voices in order to address and consider the nature of integrated mission for Lausanne.

---

35. Gadamer makes the point that new understanding is not new in the sense of superior but in the sense of different: "It is enough to say that we understand in a different way, if we understand at all." Gadamer, *Truth and Method*, 307.

3

The First Movement – Descriptive Theology

The Lausanne Documents

This chapter forms the descriptive theology of Don Browning's practical theological method, which he describes as the first movement in theology: a description of the source of a theological practical issue that requires further theological reflection.[1] In this case, I explore the three main documents that resulted from the evangelical Lausanne Movement's International Congresses held at Lausanne in 1974, Manila in 1989, and Cape Town in 2010. These documents delineate a particular evangelical theology and practice of mission; I consider their mission proposals and whether any elements of integrated mission, implicit or explicit, lie within them.

Based on my findings, I raise questions that require further historical and contemporary theological research and reflection. Browning describes this initial process as a hermeneutical dialogue between the researcher and the practice that is the focus of the research. Thus, this chapter is my interpretation of Lausanne's documents and practices, although it is also informed by Lausanne's formation and context, and by appropriate secondary materials.

---

1. Browning, *A Fundamental Practical Theology*, 47.

The Lausanne Movement's Birth

The Lausanne Movement was formed because evangelicals, unhappy with the direction taken by the World Council of Churches (WCC) at Uppsala in 1968, wanted to clearly distinguish their own position on various areas, including their own biblical understanding of missional practice. Evangelicals, prior to Uppsala, had already begun to separate themselves as a group within Protestantism. They arranged two meetings in Berlin, West Germany, and Wheaton, USA, in 1966 to consolidate their presence within Protestantism.[2] In 1974, sponsored by the Billy Graham Evangelistic Association, the International Congress on World Evangelization took place in Lausanne, Switzerland. This is considered a watershed event in evangelicalism: 2,700 participants attended from 150 nations,[3] a third of whom were from today's Majority World. This meeting led to the formation of the evangelical Lausanne Committee for World Evangelization and the birth of the Lausanne Movement.

At the time Lausanne represented the second largest mission movement within Protestantism.[4] Bevans and Schroeder, commenting on its establishment, considered it a landmark in the history of Protestant mission in the twentieth century, noting its development resulted in two distinct forms of Protestant mission in the latter part of that century, namely the Conciliar Protestants represented by the WCC, and Lausanne evangelicals and Pentecostals.[5]

A decade or more passed between each international congress; it was fifteen years between Lausanne and Manila, and just over twenty years between Manila and Cape Town.[6] These Congresses met in differing world circumstances; so, to properly understand the relevant documents, it is important to garner some knowledge of their respective contexts.

---

2. Bevans and Schroeder, *Constants in Context*, 260.

3. It was described by Time Magazine as "possibly the widest ranging meeting of Christianity ever held." Quote taken from John Stott, ed., *Making Christ Known: Historic Mission Documents from the Lausanne Movement, 1974–1989* (Grand Rapids: Eerdmans, 1996), xi.

4. The WCC was the first. Henning Wrogemann, *Theologies of Mission*, trans. Karl E. Bohmer (Downers Grove: InterVarsity Press, 2018), 117.

5. Bevans and Schroeder, *Constants in Context*, 283–84. These authors identify three forms of mission practice rooted in differing theological thought towards the end of the twentieth century: those of Vatican II and the Eastern Orthodox Church based in communion with the Trinitarian God; the WCC and Pope Paul VI's *Evangelii Nuntiandi*, 1975, focused on establishing God's reign; and John Paul's encyclical *Redemtoris Missio*, 1991, and Lausanne evangelicals focused upon the centrality of Christ. Owing to the limitations on the length of this book, I am only engaging mission and spiritual practice within a focused area of Roman Catholicism and evangelicalism.

6. The Lausanne Movement continued to meet in various sub-committees during the intervening years.

I review these documents in two sections. First, I deal with *The Lausanne Covenant* (*The Covenant*) and *The Manila Manifesto* (*The Manifesto*) that were published in the last century and then I look at *The Cape Town Commitment* (*The Commitment*) (the most recently published document reflecting Lausanne's current perspective).

The Covenant and *The Manifesto*
The Covenant's *Context: The 1960s-70s*

The 1960s in the Western world was generally an upbeat decade with much hope placed in the movements of secularism, urbanization and new technologies – so much so that the WCC indicated that it considered God was working in these movements to extend God's kingdom. When taking this stance, the WCC was significantly influenced by the missiology of Johannes Hoekendijk.[7] Bevans and Schroeder succinctly capture his theological view in the following statement: "[M]ission should shift from the church to the world, which is in need of shalom; and that the church was important, but only as God's instrument and not as the focus of God's intention."[8] In other words, mission ought to focus on the world rather than the growth of the church; this theme was the focus of the WCC's mission at Uppsala in 1968.

The 1970s is generally considered a more subdued decade than the 1960s. Wrogemann points out that the spirit of the WCC's 1973 meeting in Bangkok was very different from that of upbeat Uppsala. The early 1970s brought reports of ecological challenges created by the recently developed industrial technologies. An increase in desertification gave rise to increased famine. The oil crisis of 1973 and the consequent surge in price caused economic crisis. There were escalating acts of war, the Vietnam conflict was ongoing, and harsh military dictatorships were taking over various Latin American countries. There were also challenges stemming from the dependency of developing economies on the developed world.[9] All of this led to more uncertainty and less hope.

The anger of those living in former colonized countries spilled over into the Bangkok WCC meeting. Many Christians from such countries felt that the dependency model created by colonialism was also evident in the new

---

7. For a good summary of Hoekendijk's theology, see Wrogemann, *Theologies of Mission*, 71–80.

8. Bevans and Schroeder, *Constants in Context*, 260.

9. Wrogemann, *Theologies of Mission*, 105–7.

churches within those countries. Consequently, there was a call for a reduction in missionaries to these places so that these new churches could establish themselves within their own cultures.

Being significantly influenced by both the struggle for justice and demands for independence by these new churches, the Bangkok meeting sought to define "salvation" broadly and holistically and to incorporate their missional focus on the ills of the world. The meeting spoke of salvation as a process and aligned it with the struggle for justice in terms of human dignity, solidarity with the poor against alienation, and the idea of bringing hope amid despair. The WCC grounded such mission on Jesus's statement in Luke 4:18–19 that he had come to preach good news to the poor, freedom for prisoners, sight for the blind, and release for the oppressed. The WCC also established that mission was to use a contextual hermeneutic; in each situation the church was to determine its mission based on its circumstance, with the view that missional practice was formed from "below." Furthermore, it argued for a liberation theological model for mission rather than that of dependency.[10] These WCC policies were subject to criticism and objection from within but the critiques were insufficient to alter the WCC's direction. Many of the objectors were those who found their alternate voices heard at Lausanne.[11] *The Covenant* therefore takes a very different position from the WCC's position.

The Manifesto's *Context: The 1980s–1990s*

Lausanne's Second International Congress occurred in Manila, the Philippines, in 1989. Many world issues had changed since the first Lausanne Congress. Thatcherism in the UK and Reaganomics in the US with their tight monetary policies had contributed to high interest rates in the developed world. This economic change took place alongside a slump in the price of commodities produced from the poorer, developing countries. In an effort to increase their domestic income, many developing countries increased the supply of commodities on the market, increasing the imbalances between supply and demand and leading to further price erosion. As income fell in these poorer countries and the cost of borrowing money increased, Third World debt became a major cause of concern. Consequently, tensions increased between

---

10. Wrogemann, *Theologies of Mission*, 107–15.

11. Re Bangkok, see also Bevans and Schroeder, *Constants in Context*, 262–63, and David J. Bosch, *Transforming Mission:Paradigm Shifts in Theology of Mission* (Maryknoll: Orbis Books, 1991); on despair with the church, 384–85; and, regarding its concept of salvation, 396–98.

the "developed" countries and the "developing" countries: this spilled over into the church with the newer churches questioning how Christians in the developed world could support such governments and whether they should tie themselves with such churches.

There was also increased global nuclear concern due to the US placing more nuclear weapons in Europe: nuclear disasters in Three Mile Island, USA (1979), and Chernobyl, USSR (1986), only added to global unease.

In terms of global conflict, the Shah of Iran was removed from power in 1979 and replaced by the Ayatollah Khomeini and the theocratic Islamic Republic of Iran. This was followed by the Iran–Iraq war (1980–88) and the invasion of Afghanistan by the USSR – both seeking to circumvent any expansion of the theocracy beyond Iran's borders. Within the USSR itself, Mikhail Gorbachev came to power in 1985 and his series of economic reforms known as *Perestroika* ultimately led to the break-up of the USSR and the end of the Cold War. The Berlin Wall came down in November 1989, leading to the re-unification of Germany. Within China that same year, students protesting for democracy and free speech were massacred by the Communist Party-led Chinese Government.[12]

When the WCC met in Melbourne in 1980 the delegates were very aware of the changes in the world around them, particularly the worsening plight of the poor. The WCC affirmed the liberation theology's preferential option of the poor and considered that, with the increasing shift in Christian populations towards the developing world, the church was now moving towards being poor, rather than just being for the poor. The poor were thereby perceived as the bearers of mission.[13] Melbourne established a theology that critiqued the powerful authorities who cause poverty through unjust systems and structures. This theology was based on the cross, kenosis, and the kingdom of God.[14]

The Manila Congress was entitled, "Proclaim Christ until He Comes: Calling the Whole Church to Take the Whole Gospel to the Whole World." The location of the Philippines was significant as it was a country in which the division between rich and poor was highly visible. Radical evangelicals hoped this would draw attention to the need for the integration of evangelism and

---

12. Wrogemann, *Theologies of Mission*, 130–33.

13. David Bosch notes that Emilio Castro, reflecting on the conference, stated that in affirming the poor, the conference had made them the "missiological principle par excellence" and the church's relation to the poor was "the missionary yardstick." *Transforming Mission*, 435.

14. Bevans and Schroeder also note that the WCC at Melbourne consolidated their mission perspective from an understanding of the kingdom of God. It also affirmed that "proclamation" included both words and deeds. *Constants in Context*, 263.

social responsibility within mission. However, *The Manifesto* continued with *The Covenant's* missiological direction of giving priority to evangelism. It did acknowledge the poor and the devastating poverty through endorsing the need for social service to the poor and denunciation of unjust situations.[15] However, unlike the WCC, it did not affirm the preferential option for the poor and made it clear that poor persons, like everyone else, received salvation through God's grace by faith in the Lord Jesus.[16] As with *The Covenant*, the world context had little explicit impact on the document.

Contents of The Covenant *and* The Manifesto

Lausanne did not use the term "mission" within *The Covenant* or *The Manifesto*; it preferred the term "evangelization."[17] In this section, I will do the same to avoid confusion. By using this term, Lausanne distinguishes itself from the WCC.[18] Its direction in evangelization also differs: the WCC focuses on the world, arguing that God's purpose for it is bringing God's reign and shalom to the world and its people; in contrast, Lausanne's attention is the church and its growth, arguing that the creation of a "saved" people is God's ultimate purpose, and he sends such persons into the world to be witnesses and servants.[19] Similarly, while the WCC grounds its missiology in the kingdom of God inaugurated by Jesus, Lausanne evangelicals remain focused on the atonement achieved by Jesus in his death and resurrection bringing in an era of

---

15. Lausanne, *The Manifesto*, Affirmation 8 and 9. See also section A, paragraph 4: On "Social Responsibility," https:// www.lausanne.org/content/manifesto/the-manila-manifesto. All references to this document are from this source unless otherwise stated.

16. *The Manifesto*, section A, paragraph 2: on "Good News for Today."

17. David Kirkpatrick notes that the term "evangelization" as used by Lausanne is a synonym for evangelism. This was done by way of verbal proclamation. *A Gospel for the Poor: Global Social Christianity and the Latin American Evangelical Left* (Philadelphia: Pennsylvania University Press, 2019), 21.

18. Wrogemann, *Theologies of Mission*, 117. Roman Catholics also use the term "evangelization"; however, its meaning differs from Lausanne's meaning. It is an integral approach to mission. Pope Paul VI in 1975 defined the term in *Evangelii Nuntiandi* as a process whereby the Church seeks to transform "solely through the divine power of the message she proclaims, both the personal and collective consciences of people, the activities in which they engage, and the lives and concrete milieu of their lives." Quoted in Bevans and Schroeder, *Constants in Context*, 8. The quote is from *Evangelii Nuntiandi*, paragraph 18, see: https://www.vatican.va/content/paul-vi/en/apost_exhortations/documents/hf_p-vi_exh_19751208_evangelii-nuntiandi.html for the full document.

19. Lausanne, *The Covenant*, covenant one, in Stott, ed. *Making Christ Known*, 9. There are other views on God's ultimate purpose. Pope Paul VI in *Evangelii Nuntiandi*, paragraph 8 stated that the kingdom of God was the basis of God's plan and everything else was relative. See also Bevans and Schroeder, *Constants in Context*, 7.

human salvation. Further, the Lausanne evangelical approach to evangelization remained unchanged despite the various significant issues in the world during the times of the respective two Lausanne Congresses; these were not a major focus of either *The Covenant or The Manifesto*.[20]

There are commonalities of missional understanding in *The Covenant* and *The Manifesto*. In my view, these common threads undergird Lausanne's missional practice. These commonalities are: the nature of God, the uniqueness of Christ, the biblical source of evangelization, the contents of evangelization, the role of the church, and Lausanne's view of eschatology. These also remain the same in *The Commitment*. Within these threads there are also explicit references to spiritual matters such as the role of prayer and implicit references to an incarnational kenotic way of life with Jesus as its model.

The Nature of God

In *The Covenant*, God is declared as Trinitarian. Each person of the Godhead is involved in evangelization and this is described throughout *The Covenant*.[21] However, there is no direct mention of the Trinity in *The Manifesto*. Interestingly, both documents are more Christological than Trinitarian. In the documents, God is also described as Lord, Creator, Judge, Evangelist and the sender of the church into the world for the purposes of evangelization.

The Unique Status of Christ

Lausanne's practice is highly Christological. In evangelization the status of Christ as Lord, and the importance of Jesus's atonement through his death and resurrection are significant. To become a Christian, a person must repent and receive in faith the grace provided through the atonement and accept God's lordship over their life. Through this process, God gives such persons forgiveness from sin and the gift of the liberating Holy Spirit.[22]

Lausanne is clear that it does not accept universalism, nor does it affirm that a person is "saved" through any other religion; Jesus is the only mediator between God and humanity.[23] It is this message that the church is called to proclaim to those yet to become Christians. *The Manifesto* states: "([T]he

---

20. *The Manifesto* does mention the effects of modernization on evangelization. See section C, paragraph 10, in Stott, ed. *Making Christ Known*, 244.

21. *The Covenant*, covenant one, in Stott, ed. *Making Christ Known*, 9.

22. See also *The Manifesto*, paragraph 2: "Good News for Today," in Stott, ed. *Making Christ Known*, 234.

23. *The Covenant*, covenant three, in Stott, ed. *Making Christ Known*, 16; *The Manifesto*, paragraph 3: "The Uniqueness of Christ," in Stott, ed. *Making Christ Known*, 236.

apostles) boldly affirmed the uniqueness, indispensability and centrality of Christ. We must do the same."[24]

The Source of Evangelization

Lausanne also grounds all its understanding of God, Christ, and God's purpose in its interpretation of the Bible. In covenant two of *The Covenant*, entitled "The Power and Authority of the Bible," Lausanne emphasises that evangelization is rooted in the biblical text since the Bible is the "infallible rule of faith and practice."[25] Stott noted that, while it was "strange" for a mission organization to include a statement about the authority of the Bible and to lay such emphasis on it, it was done because it is a faithful reflection of the Congress's programme.[26] The content of the gospel is what Lausanne intends to preach, and the content's source is the biblical narrative. No other resource is mentioned; there is no appeal to tradition, experience or the Holy Spirit. This clearly affirms that Lausanne has a high view of the biblical narrative and its ability to interpret it. From my perspective, this statement also hermeneutically implies that, for Lausanne, mission practice is not construed from a contextual approach from below; rather Lausanne establishes its missional practice on an interpretation of the Bible that is then applied to each circumstance.[27] This approach is another way that Lausanne evangelicals distinguish themselves from the WCC.

The Contents of Evangelization

Lausanne considers there are three objectives of evangelization, namely: the extension of God's kingdom, the building up of Christ's body, and the glorification of God's name. Within evangelization, it considers there are two main tasks: evangelism and social responsibility. The Christian is thus called to witness and serve.

Evangelism is defined in *The Covenant* as:

---

24. *The Manifesto*, paragraph three, in Stott, ed. *Making Christ Known*, 235.

25. *The Covenant*, covenant two, in Stott, ed. *Making Christ Known*, 13; *The Manifesto* in its second affirmation states: "We affirm that in the Scriptures of the Old and New Testaments God has given us an authoritative disclosure of his character and will, his redemptive acts and their meaning, and his mandate for mission," in Stott, ed. *Making Christ Known*, 231.

26. Stott, ed. *Making Christ Known*, 13.

27. Wrogemann affirms this view. He also states that in his opinion evangelicals view the gospel as a unit of the biblical text. It is not found in society and therefore must be translated into society by the church. The world is thus an alien place without hope. He argues that this evangelical view underscores the primacy of the gospel over the context. *Theologies of Mission*, 117–18.

> To evangelize is to spread the good news that Jesus died for our
> sins, was raised from the dead according to the Scriptures, and that
> as the reigning Lord he now offers the forgiveness of sins and the
> liberating gift of the Holy Spirit to those who repent and believe . . .
> Evangelism itself is the proclamation of the historical, biblical
> Christ as Saviour and Lord, with a view to persuading people
> to come to him personally and so be reconciled to God . . . The
> results of evangelism include obedience to Christ, incorporation
> into his church and responsible service in the world.[28]

Lausanne's early view of the gospel is narrow – focusing on the atonement
rather than all of Jesus's incarnation and his message of the inbreaking of
God's kingdom.[29]

Social responsibility is defined as:

> We affirm that God is both the Creator and the Judge for all men.
> We therefore should share his concern for justice and reconciliation
> throughout human society and for the liberation of men from
> every kind of oppression. Because mankind is made in the image
> of God, every person . . . has an intrinsic dignity because of which
> he should be respected and served, not exploited . . . Although
> reconciliation with man is not reconciliation with God, nor is
> social action evangelism, nor is political liberation salvation,
> nevertheless we affirm that evangelism and social-political
> involvement are both part of our Christian duty.[30]

The relationship between social responsibility and evangelism was further
defined at a sub-committee of Lausanne in 1983: the former is a consequence,

---

28. This quote is only part of the full covenant four, but I consider that it conveys its essential parts. *The Covenant*, covenant four, in Stott, ed. *Making Christ Known*, 20.

29. Robert Schreiter affirms this position. Commenting on *The Covenant*, he notes how it is rooted in Reformed theology, i.e. there is an emphasis on sin and God's provision of forgiveness through Christ's atonement. "From the Lausanne Covenant to the Cape Town Commitment: A Theological Reflection," *International Bulletin of Missionary Research* 35, no. 2, 88–91, https://doi.org/10.1177/239693931103500205.

30. Again, this quote is my abbreviation of *The Covenant*, covenant five, in Stott, ed. *Making Christ Known*, 24.

bridge, and partner to the latter.[31] Despite criticism of this "two-mandate" approach,[32] these two tasks remain the basis of evangelical evangelization.[33]

Another subject that has caused much tension within Lausanne is the priority given to evangelism over social responsibility. This is stated in *The Covenant's* covenant six.[34]

> We affirm that Christ sends his redeemed people into the world as the Father sent him . . . We need to break out of our ecclesiastical ghettos and permeate non-Christian society . . . In the church's mission of sacrificial service evangelism is primary . . .[35]

---

31. At this subcommittee, "The Consultation on Evangelism and Social Responsibility" (CESR), in Stott ed., *Making Christ Known*, 181–82, Lausanne clarified its definition of social responsibility. It divided the term into two sub-areas: social service and social action. Social service includes those activities that relieve human need, are philanthropic, aim at individuals and families, and are described as "works of mercy." Pursuits of social action are those actions that seek to remove the causes of human need and are described as political and economic activities; they attempt to change the structures of society and pursue justice. CESR stated that Jesus preached and went out and about doing good, implying that Jesus partook in both evangelism and social service, so that both of these are Christian obligations. It did not state that Jesus conducted social action. A full copy of the Statement is found in Stott ed., *Making Christ Known*, 165–213.

32. David Bosch, while noting that the two mandate approach is better than one mandate i.e. evangelization is only evangelism, is still critical of Stott's approach. Bosch notes that Stott's view of evangelism plus social responsibility "was under pressure from the beginning." Bosch notes that once you create two mandates, you are asserting that each one has a life of their own and can stand independently, i.e. one can do evangelism without any social obligation. Further once you give priority to one, you are saying in effect, one is essential, the other optional. *Transforming Mission*, 405.

33. See also *The Manifesto*, paragraph 4: "The Gospel and Social Responsibility," in Stott ed., *Making Christ Known*, 236. Both social responsibility and the priority of evangelism are reaffirmed.

34. Al Tizon notes that prioritizing evangelism ensured that the pre-Lausanne dichotomy between evangelism and social responsibility among evangelicals remained. It also highlighted division in the Lausanne membership over the content of mission practice. He notes there were three groups of evangelicals at Lausanne, with varying views: the first group took the same view as that held in the earlier part of that century, that personal evangelism and conversion of individuals is the only object of mission; the second group, then known as "the new evangelicals," led by Billy Graham, held the same view as *The Covenant*, that Christian personal evangelism is primary over social responsibility; the third group, the radical evangelicals, advocated that there should be no dichotomy between evangelism and social activity, that both inhere within one another. Tizon comments that to a certain extent these distinct mission approaches remain within the evangelical movement today. *Transformation after Lausanne: Radical Evangelical Mission in Global-Local Perspective* (Eugene: Wipf and Stock, 2008), 28–31. Wrogemann is of the same opinion as Tizon regarding the continuation of the division. *Theologies of Mission*, 120.

35. Stott ed., *Making Christ Known*, 28. This is my précis that highlights the main points.

At Lausanne, a sub-group of evangelicals met and produced a document to publicly object to the priority given to evangelism.[36] This group known as the radical evangelicals, who at the time predominantly came from Latin America, were pleased that Lausanne affirmed social responsibility as the task of mission; however, they did not think it went far enough. While the radical evangelicals were not able to alter Lausanne's direction, they continued to press for change within Lausanne. While this issue remains to this day, it is less prominent.[37] The radical evangelicals remain a significant evangelical group, and their vision has broadened to other Majority World countries. Orlando Costas, whose views form part of this work, was a significant member of this group.

Lausanne's emphasis on evangelism is based on its understanding of God's "great commission" in the gospel of Matthew 28:18–20, where Jesus commands the disciples to go and make disciples of all nations, and in Matthew 24:14, where Jesus states that the end of this age (interpreted as Christ's return and the coming of the eschatological kingdom) will only come after the gospel is preached to all nations. The meeting at Manila underscored the importance of this effort. With the end of the millennium then approaching, much of the document referred to strategies to evangelize the world by 2000. *The Manifesto* declared:

> Now the year 2000 has become for many a challenging milestone. Can we commit to evangelize the world during the last decade of the millennium? There is nothing magical about this date, yet

36. Radical evangelicals met separately at Lausanne and formed a document known as *The Response to Lausanne*. Stott comments that the idea of the church being marked by the cross came from this document, *Making Christ Known*, 30. Samuel Escobar was both a member of *The Covenant's* drafting committee and the radical group. The first radical group emerged from Latin America in 1970 when the Latin American Theological Fraternity was formed. As Orlando Costas was a significant member of this group, chapter 5 of this book highlights its development. The radicals were extremely pleased that Lausanne affirmed that social responsibility was a task of mission. However, they opined that it did not go far enough. *The Response to Lausanne* articulated the radicals' concerns and argued, among other matters, that in their view the gospel was broader and more communitarian than espoused by Lausanne, and that evangelism and social responsibility should not be divided but viewed integrally as mission. A copy of the Statement is available in A. Tizon, *Transformation after Lausanne*, 239–40, Appendix 1. This book traces the work of radical evangelical mission after Lausanne. For further commentary on the radical evangelical Movement in Latin America, see Sharon E. Heaney, *Contextual Theology for Latin America: Liberation Themes in Theological Perspective*, Paternoster Theological Monographs (Eugene: Wipf and Stock, 2008). A recent publication documenting the history of the radical evangelical movement in Latin America and its influence on global evangelicalism is David C. Kirkpatrick, *A Gospel for the Poor*.

37. *The Commitment* sets out evangelism and social responsibility as separate paragraphs in that order but does not use the word "priority." *The Commitment*, part I, 10, B. 45. https://www.lausanne.org/content/ctc/ctcommitment.

should we not do our best to reach this goal? Christ commands us to take the gospel to all peoples. The task is urgent.[38]

The importance of evangelism for Lausanne was further underscored in both *The Covenant* and *The Manifesto* with both detailing the numbers of unevangelized and unreached peoples across the globe.[39]

The Role of the Church

Lausanne affirms that the church is called to the task of world evangelization; as God sent Christ, so Christ sends God's redeemed people into the world.[40] For Lausanne, the church is not an institution but rather the people of God.[41] It is the community of God's people which is biblically mandated to undertake evangelism and social responsibility; Christians are to witness to the gospel and serve the world.

Lausanne declares that the work of evangelization is that of the Holy Spirit working with and through Christians.[42] While such declarations are valuable, they are minimal within the documents. I contend Lausanne's overall emphasis is upon the practice of mission; it does not underscore that pivotal to mission practice is a missioner's connection, cooperation, and participation with the Triune God. Neither does Lausanne clarify ways that this may be done.

The church is also a sign of God's kingdom and therefore it must live with integrity and in accordance with the values and attributes of God. Lausanne

---

38. *The Manifesto*, section C, paragraph 11, in Stott ed. *Making Christ Known*, 246.

39. *The Covenant*, covenant nine states that in 1974, 2,700 million people "have yet to be evangelized." in Stott ed. *Making Christ Known*, 33. *The Manifesto* categorizes persons into: committed Christians, the uncommitted, the unevangelized, and the unreached. It notes that in 1989 there were some 2000 peoples or nationalities that were without a "vital indigenous church movement." Section C. paragraph 11, in Stott ed. *Making Christ Known*, 245. A leading evangelical missiologist of the 1970's to 1980's was the dean and founder of Fuller Theological Seminary in California, Donald A. McGavran. He was also the founder of the Church Growth Movement that underscored the importance of evangelism and church growth in terms of numbers. Wrogemann considers that McGavran's influence on Lausanne was limited. *Theologies of Mission*, 213. However, George G. Hunter notes that the use by Lausanne of "reached" and "unreached" persons as categories in *The Covenant* and *The Manifesto* is clearly a consequence of McGavran's influence. McGavran gave a paper at Lausanne and attracted the criticism of the radical evangelicals. George G. Hunter, "The Legacy of Donald G. McGavran," *International Bulletin of Missionary Research* 16, no. 4 (October 1992): 160.

40. *The Covenant*, covenant six. See also *The Manifesto*, affirmation 12, in Stott ed. *Making Christ Known*, 28, 232.

41. This concept of the Church as a people rather than an institution is also found in Vatican II. For the full impact of this communal image on the Roman Catholic Church, see Bevans and Schroeder, *Constants in Context*, 56.

42. *The Manifesto*, section B, paragraph 5, in Stott ed. *Making Christ Known*, 238.

underscores the importance of embodiment – in individual Christians and the church – for witnessing to the gospel and the kingdom.[43] Quoting Samuel Escobar from a presentation at Lausanne, Stott affirms that the church is called to be "a radically different community" from the society in which it lives.[44] Stott also submits that the church is to be marked by the cross, such that if the church preaches "Christ crucified," it must also show the same characteristics, namely self-denial, self-humbling, and self-giving. For Lausanne, the only specified preparation for Christians and the church pursuing these tasks of mission is that of education. It underscores didactic methods rather than those of spiritual formation. Lausanne calls for the establishment of more Christian seminaries and encourages the leaders of churches to equip the laity through their teaching.[45]

The Role of Eschatology

Lausanne's eschatological view is that when Christ returns a new kingdom in its fullness will arrive, and the old world will disappear. While Jesus inaugurated a period of salvation, only persons are "saved" in this time of the "now" and "not yet"; that is, not social structures. I consider that this perspective significantly affects Lausanne's approach to evangelization.[46]

This eschatological conviction gives insights into Lausanne's prioritization of evangelism and its categorization of social responsibility. It seeks to remind WCC-aligned Christians that structural and systemic change, while valuable, is not significant for the coming kingdom, and does not and cannot constitute salvation. The Covenant states that "reconciliation with man is not reconciliation with God, nor is social action evangelism, nor is political liberation salvation."[47] This approach contradicts the view of the WCC and leads Lausanne to de-emphasize the importance of this work for the church. Instead, it promotes prophetic denunciation and social service over social action: it also prioritises evangelism.

---

43. The Manifesto, section C, paragraph 8, in Stott ed. Making Christ Known, 241–42.

44. Stott, ed. Making Christ Known, 30. Pope Paul VI in Evangelii Nuntiandi, paragraph 21, also emphasized the church should be counter-cultural. He considered the presence of such a church community within society was evangelizing in itself: "Such a witness is already a silent proclamation of the Good News and a very powerful and effective one. Here we have an initial act of evangelization." See also Bevans and Schroeder, Constants in Context, 305–307.

45. The Covenant, covenant eleven, The Manifesto, section B, paragraph 6, in Stott ed. Making Christ Known, 39, 239.

46. The Covenant, covenant fifteen, in Stott ed. Making Christ Known, 49.

47. The Covenant, covenant five, in Stott ed. Making Christ Known, 24.

This perspective potentially creates dualisms in Christian thinking. Lausanne's emphasis on creating a "saved" people has given rise to a "world-denying" attitude: Christians are to be in the world but need to distinguish themselves from it. This approach can naturally lead to non-involvement in the world by the laity (a point which *The Commitment* later acknowledges). This emphasis leads to spirituality becoming focused on personal "inner" matters rather than focusing on attributes that God might give to a Christian for activity in "the world" and consequently undermines thoughts toward the relevance of integrated mission. Therefore, it is no surprise that there are only scant references to spirituality in Lausanne's documents.

Explicit and Implicit References to a Missional Spiritual life and Practice

This book espouses that a spiritual life is one connected to the Holy Spirit and thereby the Triune God – in all life's dimensions. I argue that if Lausanne is concerned with providing evangelical missioners with theological direction for mission practice, it should also provide spiritual formation for such Christians, so that inner, outer and communal dimensions of their lives are in synthesis; mission thereby becomes integrated for the missioner. The question is whether these documents in any way explicitly or implicitly refer Christians towards connecting with God in their missional practice.

An explicit spiritual practice mentioned in *The Covenant* is prayer. Although there is no specific section on prayer, it does encourage prayer within certain areas: to ask God what missioners should do in relation to younger churches in developing countries that no longer needed help;[48] for salvation of the unreached;[49] against the principalities and powers of evil;[50] for freedom to preach the gospel where it is not permitted;[51] and for a "visit" of the Holy Spirit upon the church in renewal.[52]

From my perspective, while it is important that Christians intercede for God's help, this is only one means of prayer in terms of relating to God in a personal way. There are many forms of prayer, some more contemplative than intercession. Such ways of prayer focus on the Christian knowing and experiencing God leading to an intimate relationship with God, and the

---

48. *The Covenant*, covenant eight, in Stott ed. *Making Christ Known*, 33

49. *The Covenant*, covenant nine, in Stott ed. *Making Christ Known*, 33

50. *The Covenant*, covenant twelve, in Stott ed. *Making Christ Known*, 44.

51. *The Covenant*, covenant thirteen, in Stott ed. *Making Christ Known*, 44.

52. *The Covenant*, covenant fourteen, in Stott ed. *Making Christ Known*, 49. There is no reference to a practice of prayer in *The Manifesto*.

benefits of godly direction and nourishment.[53] I suggest that it would be better if Lausanne's direction on prayer encompassed both intercession and contemplative modes; this would enable missioners to source and integrate their witness and service in their relationship with the Triune God. God thereby becomes the centre of mission rather than the God who is called to aid missioners' tasks.

I note that there are implicit signs of a missional spirituality within *The Covenant* and *The Manifesto*. Both documents encourage an evangelization practice based on Jesus's life as a model. Both speak of a kenotic and incarnational approach. *The Covenant* states that the people of God are the bearers of mission, they are witnesses and servants, and these roles are based on those of Jesus.[54] This is not just a concept for the individual missioner, but also for the church. *The Manifesto* underscores the theological pattern of incarnation, which Lausanne defines as: "[M]oving humbly into other people's worlds, identifying with their social reality, their sorrow and suffering, and their struggles for justice against oppressive powers." It notes that such work cannot be undertaken without sacrifice.[55] Such themes are common within many historic spiritualities and provide a starting point upon which an interaction with Lausanne in this arena is possible.

A Short Critique

The Covenant and *The Manifesto* form a long list of what Lausanne evangelicals ought to do missionally founded on Lausanne's biblical interpretations. Lausanne's focus in these documents is on the task of evangelism, based on the proclamation of the atonement, and the primary call to make Christian converts, grounded in their focus on the great commission in Matthew's gospel. Social responsibility, primarily in the form of social service, is an obligation of the Christian life. The Christian is called to serve the world; Lausanne through a prescriptive approach encourages work in this arena.

Lausanne recognizes the role of God the Creator, Jesus, and the Holy Spirit in the work of mission, and yet to this reader, the plans and strategies of

---

53. For example, Richard J. Foster in his book entitled *Prayer: Finding the Heart's True Home* (New York: HarperCollins, 1992) lists the various forms of prayer that can be practised by a Christian, intercession being only one such practice.

54. *The Covenant*, covenant one, in Stott ed. *Making Christ Known*, 11. The biblical reference to Jesus as "witness" is John 18:37 and to "servant" is Mark 10:45.

55. *The Manifesto*, section A, 4: "The Gospel and Social Responsibility," in Stott ed. *Making Christ Known*, 237.

the church take precedence in the documents. Lausanne creates a top-down approach, placing most of the burden of evangelization on the leaders of the church who are supported through education and training. I consider the lack of recognition of the need for a form of spirituality interconnecting Christians with God through the Holy Spirit is a serious lacuna in Lausanne's approach to mission. This thought is supported by, among other works, a recent book by evangelical missioners calling for a spirituality as mission's foundation and wellspring.[56]

I consider that any potential and adequate spirituality for Lausanne must link with its general ethos of missions. In other words, the spiritual theological foundations of any proposed spirituality should marry with Lausanne's theology of evangelization.[57] For me, one of the disappointments *of The Covenant* and *The Manifesto* is their failure to adopt some of the Protestant missiology of the era, such as the *missio Dei*.[58] There is no apparent reason for this failure other than Lausanne's aim to distinguish itself from the WCC. Consequently, any references to participation with, and relatedness to, God are muted in Lausanne's approach. This is unfortunate, because if God is the author of mission, through Jesus, and in connection with the Holy Spirit, then a missioner's spirituality is significant for evangelization.

---

56. This was referenced in this book (chapter 1, "Introduction"). John Amalraj, Geoffrey W. Hahn, and William D. Taylor, eds. *Spirituality in Mission.*

57. Evangelical Simon Chan notes in *Spiritual Theology* that before the systemization of theology, all theology was focused on Christian growth in godliness. Now with theologies separated into differing areas, spiritual theology which seeks to define and give direction for life lived in the Holy Spirit must interrelate with systematic theology to draw out the practical implications from its theological concepts so that they are lived out. Chan's approach in forming a spirituality is to start with the biblical theology and move towards practice, this is described as a method from "above." In my view this approach is in keeping with Lausanne's missiological approach. Not all spiritual theologians follow this approach. Sandra M. Schneiders argues that the academic study of spirituality should commence with the experience of the Christian and then move back towards the theological concepts; this method is described as a "method from below." Schneiders, "Spirituality in the Academy," in *Exploring Christian Spiritualities*, 249–69. However, whether from "above" or "below" both interrelate with theology. These are interesting thoughts when thinking of a spirituality for Lausanne which prefers a top-down approach in mission.

58. At a meeting of the International Missionary Congress at Willingen in 1952, the idea of the *missio Dei* emerged. This theological concept expresses the view that the Christian Triune God is a missionary God; mission is endemic to God's character as trinity, and God is the source of all mission. As such, the church is not the instigator of mission (which at the time, it was thought to be), merely the participant. It is God's design and purpose that is at the helm of all missionary endeavour. See Wrogemann for a full description of the nature of the *missio Dei, Theologies of Mission*, 66–70. See also: Bosch, *Transforming Mission*, 389–90; Bevans and Schroeder, *Constants in Context*, 289–91.

Lausanne's preference for "the great commission" as its main missional text, in my view, limits its view of mission. By choosing such a text, it diminishes other missional texts of great import, for example, Luke 4 (which was adopted by the WCC). In preferring the great commission text, Lausanne justifies its prioritization of evangelism over social service. As I shall note, there is a change in its main missional text in the later *Commitment,* one that in my opinion provides an opportunity for a comprehensive approach.

I consider that in its early documents Lausanne did not have an explicit missional spirituality, as defined in this book. However, in terms of an implicit missional spirituality, there are concepts inherent within Lausanne's proposals for evangelization (namely incarnation, kenosis and Jesus as a pattern or model) which provide suggestions for spiritual practice in alignment with other historical spiritualities. It is these implicit building blocks that suggest a path of missional spirituality that could embrace and affect Lausanne's evangelization and support missioners in connecting with the Triune God as a means of empowerment and in particular, for spiritual formation.

While the theological themes above have remained largely unchanged for almost fifty years, there are several elements within Lausanne's understanding that are changing. The changes are apparent in *The Commitment*; in my view, some of these changes are helpful in the building of a spirituality.

The Cape Town Commitment
Context

The most recent international congress was held in post-apartheid South Africa in Cape Town in 2010. It was titled "God in Christ, Reconciling the World to Himself" and the document resulting from that Congress was *The Commitment*.[59] In a new century and at the beginning of a second decade, circumstances were very different to those in 1989. The interim period had experienced global violence and conflict. The world had witnessed genocides in Rwanda and Burundi; wars in the Balkans; and the destruction of the twin towers in New York, leading to an era of fundamental Islamic terrorism throughout the world, and the US/Iraq war. The balance of economic powers had also changed with continents and countries like China, India and Brazil coming to the fore and the arena of technology shaping the world. The shift

---

59. https://www.lausanne.org/contents/ctc/ctcommitment. This is the source for this document unless otherwise referenced.

towards the majority of Christians living in the global South was now a reality, with the new minority slowly coming to terms with its position.

Contents

The architect of *The Commitment* was Christopher J. H. Wright, a good friend of Stott's who had taken over his role.[60] As a consequence, the format and content of the document differs. It takes an essay-like form and is a much lengthier document. It has two parts. The first part establishes Lausanne's biblical convictions; these are more expansive than in its previous documents. This part takes the form of a confessional statement that establishes evangelical mission in the context of God's love for humanity and the world, together with the reciprocating love of Christians for God. The second part is a call to action and is divided into six sections. As in previous documents, it is prescriptive of the mission activities in which the church might work.

The Commitment affirms both *The Covenant* and *The Manifesto* and views itself as a continuation of them.[61] Certainly its main theological contents align with the common threads noted above. However, I consider that *The Commitment* also differs as it seeks to progress the thinking of Lausanne.[62] Its direct references to God's love, and the reciprocal love of humankind, convey a greater sense of compassion not evident in the former documents and ground mission on a broader basis. It is also more world attentive, acknowledging changes in its current context, namely globalization, the digital revolution, the changing balance of economic and political power, and the shift of the majority Christian world to the South and the East.[63] It evidences this approach in its biblical and theological statements: "Love is the language of covenant. The

---

60. Stott still had some influence as alluded to by Wright in his various videos about the writing of *The Commitment* on Lausanne's website. Wright states that *The Commitment* was read to Stott who approved all its contents. See Additional Resources, Videos by Chris J. H. Wright under Cape Town Commitment at https://www.lausanne.org.

61. *The Commitment*, "Preamble," 11–15.

62. I am not alone in perceiving a difference. Robert Schreiter, commenting on *The Commitment*, perceives some positive "movement" in Lausanne's approach. He opines that the confessional statement has a more comprehensive theological basis than either *The Covenant* or *The Manifesto*. He also suggests that the inclusion of love and a greater embrace of the world may signal a move away from the early reformed theological roots of Lausanne. However, he is not definitive on this point and notes that this requires further theological reflection. "From the Lausanne Covenant to the Cape Town Commitment," 91.

63. *The Commitment*, "Preamble," 12.

biblical covenants, old and new, are the expression of God's redeeming love and grace reaching out to lost humanity and *spoiled creation*."[64]

It admits to the many differing theological views within Lausanne and so notes that *The Commitment* works within the "breadth and boundaries" of the Movement.[65] It tries to draw the breadth together by emphasizing that the major incentive for mission is "the glorification of God" over all other matters, and not just obedience to the great commission or the love of sinners perishing, even though these retain importance.[66]

I will now highlight some of the expanded areas that I consider important in considering integrated mission for Lausanne.

Love

The Commitment's grounding of evangelization in love is a significant change from the previous documents. *The Commitment* defines world evangelization as: "the outflow of God's love to us and through us."[67] This new frame is cultivated through an emphasis on Jesus's command in Matthew 22:37–40 to love God and neighbour. *The Commitment* identifies Lausanne's commitments as follows: to love God, to love the neighbour, to love each other, and to love the world.[68] This emphasis on loving God and neighbour is also central to some

---

64. *The Commitment*, "Preamble," 14. (Emphasis is mine.) To me, this more open acknowledgement towards creation rather than just humanity reveals a difference in theological perspective from previous documents. The reason for this is apparent in a new edition of *Christian Mission in the Modern World*, which is a revised edition of John Stott's original book (published just after the Lausanne meeting in 1975). This expanded version has a reflective chapter by Christopher J. H. Wright after each of Stott's original chapters. In Wright's chapter on salvation, he shows discrepancies in Stott's argument regarding social mission and physical healing. While Stott held that both were important and would finally be accomplished in God's coming kingdom, he denied they were part of salvation in this world. This was Stott's reaction to liberation theology and that of the WCC. Wright argues that a better argument regarding social change and physical healing would be not to separate salvation in terms of content received now and in the future; rather, it would recognize the biblical wholeness of salvation achieved through Christ – all of which is assured and some of which is experienced in this world. Stott and Wright, *Christian Mission in the Modern World* 2nd ed. (Downers Grove: InterVarsity Press, 2015), 164–81.

65. *The Commitment*, "Forward," 8.

66. *The Commitment*, part 1, 2, B, 20–21. A quote from John Stott is inserted in the document here. Henning Wrogemann also suggests that the basis of a contextual missiology ought to be a Christian's call to praise and glorify God. He argues that "mission has to do with imparting a doxological impulse with a broad ecumenical impact, one that permeates the household of the entire creation." *Theologies of Mission*, 381. Based on the Greek word for household (*oikos*), he entitled it, "Mission as Oikoumenical Doxology." He outlined his thinking in Part IV of *Theologies of Mission*, 377– 407.

67. *The Commitment*, part 1, 1, 17.

68. *The Commitment*, part 1, 1, C, 18.

of the spiritualities researched in this book; therefore, Lausanne's alternate biblical foundation for mission augurs well for the formation of an adequate missional spirituality for Lausanne and provides a promising foundation for an integrated mission practice

The document has a stronger Trinitarian emphasis. In the first part, each person of the Trinity is separated out and Lausanne's particular love for each is established: Father, Son, and Holy Spirit. In particular, the role of the Holy Spirit is given much more attention than in previous documents. *The Commitment* states:

> There is no true or whole gospel and no biblical mission, without the Person, work, and power of the Holy Spirit. We pray for a greater awakening to this biblical truth, and for its experience to be reality in all parts of the worldwide body of Christ.[69]

The Commitment acknowledges that there is a need for skills of discernment when working with the Spirit. It therefore calls for more biblical teaching, preaching and prayer. The concept of spiritual formation or spiritual direction is not included and, as with its predecessors, I consider this is a missed opportunity.

The Commitment also highlights the role of the Holy Spirit when expressing Lausanne's commitment to the Bible. While noting that the Bible is the primary witness to Jesus Christ, it affirms that Jesus is encountered in the Bible through the Holy Spirit.[70] Again, this identification of the breadth of the work of the Spirit is encouraging as an integrated missional approach will promote differing ways of reading the Bible beyond historical interpretation. (In later sections in this book I highlight alternate ways of reading the biblical text.)

In keeping with a higher profile for the work of social responsibility that is noted later, there is a section expressing love for God's world, particularly creation. This is a more affirming approach to the world than in previous documents. For the first time, Lausanne speaks of integral mission.[71] It defines it as:

> Discerning, proclaiming, and living out, the biblical truth that the gospel is God's good news, through the cross and resurrection of Jesus Christ, for individual persons, and for society, and for creation. All three are broken and suffering because of sin; all

---

69. *The Commitment*, part 1, 5, C, 28.

70. *The Commitment*, part 1, 6, A, 29.

71. *The Commitment* uses the term in a similar way to the radical evangelicals.

three are included in the redeeming love and mission of God; all three must be part of the comprehensive mission of God's people.[72]

There is an attempt to bring evangelism and social responsibility closer together under the umbrella of love. There is no use of the word "priority" in the document. However, the two mandates remain distinguished, and the relationship of each is described as a consequence of the other.[73]

The *Missio Dei*

While the term *missio Dei* is not used in *The Commitment*, the essence of it is clearly stated: "[O]ur mission is wholly derived from God's mission, addresses the whole of God's creation, and is grounded at its centre in the redeeming victory of the cross." God's people are called to "participate" in this venture, "to be a blessing and light to the nations," "a community of holiness, compassion, and justice," "to bear witness," "to worship and glorify God . . . and to participate in the transforming mission of God within history."[74] I consider this declaration that mission is God's and that the people of God are participants in it is helpful as a building block for integrated mission. There is, however, an unanswered question of how this process operates: how do the people of God discern where God desires missional work and in what manner is this to be achieved contextually? I suggest that this unanswered question gives an opportunity to introduce spiritual practices for missioners to connect individually and corporately with God in their participatory task.

Dualism

I highlighted earlier that within both *The Covenant* and *The Manifesto* there is an implicit dualism between the sacred and the secular that is problematic for establishing an integrated mission. In its section on the workplace, Lausanne admits to this dualism and confesses how "a falsehood of a 'sacred–secular divide' has permeated the church's thinking and action. This divide tells us that religious activity belongs to God, whereas other activity does not."[75] For Lausanne, such thinking demeaned secular occupations and was an obstacle to mobilizing the laity. Lausanne's public rejection of this dualism should enable all people to see their secular work as part of their Christian life and,

---

72. *The Commitment*, part 1, 7, A, 33.
73. *The Commitment*, part 1,10, B, 45–46.
74. *The Commitment*, part 1, 10, A, 45.
75. *The Commitment*, part IIA, 3, A, 59.

consequently, their spirituality. It also suggests that Christians should view all of life, and not just prayer and other religious practices, as "spiritual."

Social Responsibility

The Commitment further extends the area of evangelization to the workplace. Lausanne acknowledges that it has "failed to regard work in itself as biblically and intrinsically significant, as we have failed to bring the whole of life under the Lordship of Christ." It reinforces the importance of all Christians evangelizing in their respective workplaces and particularly notes "works of service."[76] It also names public areas of interest where Christians ought to be involved and have a voice, such as: the media, arts, science and emerging technologies, government, business, academia, ethnic conflict, slavery and human trafficking, and poverty.[77] The call is not only for "prophetic denunciation" but also positive action, for example, "to promote authentically Christian responses and practical action in the arena of public policies," "to form national or regional think tanks,"[78] and "to be actively engaged . . . in order to shape societal values and influence public debate."[79] In summary, *The Commitment* advocates for much more Christian involvement in the world so that Christian ideas and understanding are engaged.

Prayer

The Commitment has a small section on prayer. It encourages two types of prayer. First, there is intercession: for more missioners in full time ministry; for the "lost" (that is, those who do not know Christ) to be drawn to God by the Holy Spirit; for God's glory to be revealed and Christ's name to be known and praised; and for God's kingdom to come, that God's will may be done on earth as it is in heaven. Second, there are prayers of thankfulness for God's work among the nations.[80] However, as mentioned previously, practising only prayers of intercession and thankfulness is not a practice of prayer that necessarily leads to an attentive relationship with God, so there is still a formative lacuna here. I contend that, without a directive towards incorporating a missional spirituality within Lausanne's practice, any individual spiritual practices that a missioner may participate in, while helpful, would not create the unity required among

76. *The Commitment*, part IIA, 3, 58; and part IIA, 3, B, 59
77. *The Commitment*, part IIA, 4, 5, 6, 7, 60–64.
78. *The Commitment*, part IIA, 6, 62, 63
79. *The Commitment*, part IIA, 7, A, 63.
80. *The Commitment*, part II, D, 6, A and B, 92–93.

missioners in relation to their task. I suggest that what is required is a specified way of practice that is both spiritual and missional and which is founded in God's relationship with God's missioners. Subsequent chapters highlight historical and contemporary situations with such a focus; these reveal how God uses such practices to empower and sanctify missioners.

Embodiment

While the concept of embodying the gospel in the way of Jesus is present in the former documents, it is underscored in *The Commitment*. Lausanne advocates strongly for Christian discipleship within the world as bearing witness to Jesus Christ. It calls for consistency between Christian proclamation and lifestyle. It advocates that the Bible:

> portrays a quality of life that should mark the believer and the community of believers . . . we learn that such a biblical lifestyle includes justice, compassion, humility, integrity, truthfulness, sexual chastity, generosity, kindness, self-denial, hospitality, peace-making, non-retaliation, doing good, forgiveness, joy, contentment and love all combined in lives of worship, praise and faithfulness to God.[81]

Discipleship is performed in obedience to Jesus, who continues to serve as the model for the Christian life, bringing together both character and activity. *The Commitment* states:

> Jesus calls us to discipleship, to take up our cross and follow him in the path of self-denial, servanthood and obedience . . . We are called to live as Christ lived and to love as Christ loved.[82]

> In his life Jesus walked in perfect faithfulness and obedience to God. He announced and taught the kingdom of God and modelled the way his disciples must live under God's reign.[83]

This concept of discipleship in *The Commitment's* "Call to Action" is fleshed out with the biblical metaphor of "walking in the ways of the Lord."[84] It calls for "prayerful, prophetic discernment" regarding idols that keep Christians from

---

81. *The Commitment*, part 1, 6, D, 31.
82. *The Commitment*, part 1, 4, B, 25.
83. *The Commitment*, part 1, 4, A, ii, 24.
84. *The Commitment*, part IIE, 93.

such a walk.[85] In terms of the path of Christian living, it encourages distinctive biblical living in areas of sexuality,[86] humility[87], integrity,[88] and simplicity.[89]

While *The Commitment* does not use the term, I aver that Lausanne is explicitly acknowledging the importance of an integrated mission practice for the missioner, as understood in this book. Lausanne is reinforcing that missioners must be concerned about the character of their lives as disciples as well as their missional tasks. However, while Lausanne describes the nature of such missional discipleship, I consider that it fails to provide practical ways of enabling one. Its top-down approach of educating and training leaders who can then do the same in their respective churches is inadequate.[90] In my view, a description of discipleship is not the same as a spirituality. The characteristics of the latter are not achieved by teaching and self-discipline, but rather require the gifts of the Holy Spirit given through means of a missioner having an intimate relationship with God. From my perspective, Lausanne lacks an understanding of missional spiritual formation; however, this aspect of Lausanne's missional direction does provide an explicit opportunity to guide it towards a better approach that supports integrated mission.

A Critique of The Commitment

There is much to commend in *The Commitment*. It is a lengthy document with such diversity therein that I expect most evangelical views are accommodated. The highlighted changes from the earlier documents provide a broader and more comprehensive approach within society than its previous documents rendered. Whether Lausanne's evangelicals will engage the guidelines to have a positive and impactful voice regarding world issues remains to be seen. While other Protestant Christian groups, such as the WCC and radical evangelicals, have implemented a more involved missional practice in global issues by basing their mission on a kingdom theology, Lausanne remains focused on a

---

85. *The Commitment*, part IIE, 1, A, 94.

86. This section emphasizes that healthy sexual relationships are those within marriage. (This assumes marriage between a man and a woman.) Anything else is considered disordered sexuality. *The Commitment*, part IIE, 2, 94–97.

87. This section emphasizes submission and reciprocal love rather than assuming power. *The Commitment*, part IIE, 3, 97–98.

88. This section underscores honesty and integrity over success. *The Commitment*, part IIE, 4, 98–99.

89. This section is critical of the "prosperity gospel." *The Commitment*, part IIE, 5, 99–102.

90. *The Commitment*, part IID, 3, 87–89.

salvation approach, although it does now mention that Jesus preached about the kingdom.[91] Overall, its focus remains on Christ, salvation, and service. That said, Lausanne is seeking to overcome its world-denying attitude by confessing to its former dualistic approach and expanding the areas in which Christians can minister.

The Commitment's inclusion in its missional approach of godly love, the missio Dei (in substance, if not in name), an increasing role for the Holy Spirit, and an embodied life engaging the attributes and characteristics of God and godly action are helpful additional building blocks for an integrated mission. However, like The Covenant and The Manifesto, I do not believe The Commitment expresses an explicit spirituality; it moves in the direction of one, but it does not go far enough.

Conclusion

Both The Covenant and The Manifesto focus on giving evangelicals a practice of evangelization that distinguishes the Lausanne Movement from the way of the WCC. For Lausanne, evangelism of individuals and thereby the growth of the church is God's intention for mission; this view is based on its reading of the biblical text, particularly the great commission. It affirms that God also wants the church to serve the world and that these two mandates, evangelism and social service, are good partners. There is some indication that for missioners to carry out such a life, they should model it on Jesus's life. I hold that this is Lausanne's only implicit inclination towards a type of spirituality in these documents. Lausanne's only explicit reference to a spiritual practice is to prayer and this has a restricted focus.

The Commitment gives more credence to the world and the laity ministering within it. It also guides missioners to the type of life that they ought to live. For me, this expansion of practice within the world increases the burden of mission on the laity without providing a way of formation or direction based on a life under God the Creator, in Christ, and through the power of the Holy Spirit, that is, with the Triune God. I consider that Lausanne's proposals of more education for Church leaders, though helpful, is inadequate. In my view, the lack of a formative spirituality for leaders and laity alike is a significant lacuna that needs challenging.

---

91. John Stott considered that the kingdom and salvation were synonymous terms. Stott and Wright, Christian Mission in the Modern World, 161.

I contend that Lausanne must comprehend the necessary experiential element of Christianity and the practices that will support leaders and laity in living such a life. It is these rhythms of practice together with a continued relationship and encounter with God that nourish and develop a Christian's life so that she can participate with God in mission. This is a spiritual life that encompasses individuals and Christians corporately.

Taking into account Lausanne's implicit references, to living like Jesus, incarnational and kenotic practices, love, and participation in God's mission, through the following research, I seek to establish a way rooted in both historical and contemporary practices for Lausanne to move toward integrated mission.

4

Second Movement – Historical Theology Part 1

John Wesley's Pastoral Theology

The second movement in Browning's methodology is historical. He notes that the purpose of looking back is to ask: "What do the normative texts that are already part of our effective history *really* imply for our praxis when confronted honestly?"[1] Therefore, having examined the Lausanne evangelical documents highlighting the theory and practice driving its current evangelical mission, I now turn to examine the theological writing of one of the early evangelicals, John Wesley. Specifically, I will consider whether his texts promote anything of an integrated missional practice that can provide some helpful perspectives in furthering this concept. My reason for choosing Wesley is that, as a significant participant in the evangelical revival in Britain, his texts provide some of the earliest and most insightful evangelical theological thinking on mission and the Christian life.

Wesley was an intelligent, well-read and prolific writer on pastoral, theological, and spiritual matters.[2] He kept a journal and diary, he penned many

---

1. Browning, *Fundamental Practical Theology*, 49. (Emphasis is Browning's.)

2. Overall, Wesley's theological method gave priority to the rule of Scripture, but he also allowed tradition, reason, and experience to have influence. This use of Scripture, tradition, reason, and experience was subsequently labelled the Wesleyan Quadrilateral (although the method itself was not his invention) and is the subject of much debate. The Anglican interpretative method of the eighteenth century asserted that: Scripture was foundational and pre-eminent; tradition, especially that of the early church, was doctrinally dependable; reason and tradition could be utilized for ecclesial law and practice unless prohibited by Scripture; and sermons and liturgy were used in such a manner so that they were "experienced" by worshippers.

letters to various correspondents, and he wrote many significant sermons for publication.[3] It is within these texts that one gains insight into his theological views. Due to Wesley's extensive writings and the myriad of secondary material written about him and early Methodism, I have chosen to limit my discussion in this book primarily to Wesley's sermons that deal with issues related to the search for an integrated mission.

I argue that Wesley promoted a Christian life that is integrated, that is, it is missional and lived in a relationship with God, in Christ, through the Holy Spirit. He rooted this way of life in Jesus's biblical injunction to love God and neighbour, or in the parlance of eighteenth-century Anglicanism, in "works of piety" and "works of mercy."[4] Further, Wesley viewed these "works" as interdependent and interrelated through the Holy Spirit. Moreover, from a theological perspective, Wesley also argued that "works of mercy" as well as "works of piety" were also a means of sanctification, that is, that service to one's neighbour is a source of spiritual formation, alongside prayer and participation in the sacraments. In this way, Wesley advocated for an integrated Christian life, one that is outwardly focused and lived in Christ and the Holy Spirit.

As an early evangelical, Wesley's biblical and theological interpretation of the Christian life revealed how an intentional and participatory relationship with Christ through the Holy Spirit is required for a Christian to appropriately

---

For Anglicans of the period, Scripture was authoritative only to matters related to salvation – not for everything. (The dissenters took the opposite view.) Wesley, as an Anglican, was familiar with this interpretative method. See W. Stephen Gunter et al. *Wesley and the Quadrilateral: Renewing the Conversation* (Nashville: Abingdon, 1997), 130. The authors of this book suggest that Wesley determined that the main purpose of Scripture was soteriological, but Scripture had to be read as a whole, and this led to salvation as persons gained knowledge of the "saving reality of God." In terms of tradition, Wesley tended to use it to support his renewal programmes in the church. He also used the tradition of the early church, for example, where it was closest to its "apostolic roots," particularly in his endeavour to encourage moral and spiritual purity. Reason, for Wesley, was a tool for understanding Scripture, tradition, and experience; it was not a source of knowledge itself. While Christianity was a reasonable faith according to Wesley, reason had its limits; for reason to function required faith and Scripture. Regarding experience, Wesley viewed evaluating experience in community important to avoid skepticism and heresy. He advocated learning from historical experience by publishing books of the lives of respected Christians. He used experience to determine doctrine when Scripture, tradition, and reason were unclear and to discern what was relevant at any given time in terms of teaching. Wesley demonstrates that in theological method, Scripture, tradition, reason, and experience are interdependent, but Scripture is primary. Gunter et al., *Wesley*, 129–42.

3. There are two collections of Wesley's works: The Jackson Edition and The Bicentennial Edition. All references in this chapter to Wesley's Works are taken from *The Works of John Wesley: The Bicentennial Edition*, ed. Albert C. Outler (Nashville: Abingdon, 1984–1992) unless otherwise stated.

4. Outler notes that these works of mercy and piety were commonplace in Anglicanism rather than being Wesley's creation. Wesley, "The Repentance of Believers," *Works*, 1:343n65.

live a mission-oriented life. Consequently, I consider his texts to be historical sources that are helpful in engaging the questions that arise from Lausanne's failure to employ an explicit integrated mission. However, I aver it is important to know something of Wesley's context and his journey to faith in Christ to understand his writings.

John Wesley's Context: Eighteenth-Century Britain

Wesley lived during a significant time of change in Britain. Born in England in 1703, his life spanned much of the eighteenth century. Many historians mark this century as the beginning of "modern Britain." It was marked by significant change, including the period known culturally as the Enlightenment. Many of these developments affected Wesley as an itinerant Anglican minister.

The Monarchy, Establishment, and Church of England

The relationship between the monarchy, the established Church of England (CoE), and the English Parliament was complex. Laws were introduced to cultivate this tripartite relationship.[5] The CoE was protected over dissenting religious groups; for example, it was the only church that could legally officiate over Holy Communion. *The Book of Common Prayer* was revised so that loyalty to the monarch became an article of faith, and clergy were required to take an oath of allegiance to the monarch. Anyone unwilling to do so was removed from their parish and became known as a non-juror. Furthermore, the church's bishops were members of the House of Lords. The British monarchy, Parliament and the church were thus interrelated. Consequently, Anglican bishops, clergy, and their congregations tended to be royalists and supported the constitutional parliament. Wesley, as an Anglican minister, was also a royalist, and this accounts for his support of the British government during the colonial unrest of the period.

The state of the CoE in the eighteenth century is contested. Historians wrote of the following: lax, non-resident clergy who left their parishes vacant or in the hands of inexperienced curates; bishops focused on politics rather than their

---

5. In the 1530s, Henry VIII created the Church of England as a substitute for the Roman Catholic Church in England. Howard A. Snyder in his "Pietism, Moraviansim, and Methodism as Renewal Movement: A Comparative and Thematic Study" (PhD diss., University of Notre Dame, 1983) notes that the Church of England mediated the Catholic tradition: "it was the middle way between Catholicism and Protestantism," 238. Due to the crisis of the Glorious Revolution and thereafter, there was a general anti-Roman Catholic sentiment in Britain.

clergy; an increasingly gentrified clergy out of touch with their parishioners; and a church that preached a rational faith and decried "enthusiasm" or miracles.[6] However, other historians through new research now argue that the state of the CoE was not as problematic as originally thought.[7] Regardless, Wesley considered it was in need of reform, which was one of the reasons he created the Methodists.[8]

Economics and Society

During this period, British rule was expanding globally, and Great Britain was becoming a major mercantile nation. It is generally thought that the slave trade was a significant contributor to British economic growth.[9] British society also began to change as artisans and industrialists challenged the feudal system and aristocracy. With increasing industry came increasing urbanization and poverty. There were no government-led social welfare, education, or health systems in the country; however, Christian involvement in these areas was significant.

This colonial expansion of the British empire gave rise to the modern concept of overseas mission. As countries became colonies, churches also sought to establish themselves among these new people, and this gave rise to the nineteenth-century overseas mission agencies, many of which continue to the present. David Bosch submits that the period of the Enlightenment

---

6. Gregory Leonard, "The Long Eighteenth Century," in *The Cambridge Companion to John Wesley*, eds. Randy L. Maddox and Jason E. Vickers (Cambridge: Cambridge University Press, 2010), 25–26; David Lyle Jeffrey, "Introduction," in *English Spirituality in the Age of Wesley*, ed. David Lyle Jeffrey (Vancouver: Regent College, 2000), 2–4; Mark A. Noll, *The Rise of Evangelicalism: The Age of Edwards, Whitefield and the Wesleys* (Downers Grove: InterVarsity Press, 2003), 39–42.

7. Dean Norman Sykes at the beginning of the twentieth century argued that not all clergy were as previously characterized nor were all bishops disconnected from their parishes. His research was based on correspondence between bishops and their clergy, and clergy with their congregants. Gregory Leonard, "The Long Eighteenth Century," 33. Frank Whaling also supports this revised view of the clergy, although he argues that the problem with the Church at that time was its lack of structure. "Introduction," in *John and Charles Wesley: Selected Writings and Hymns*, ed. Frank Whaling, The Classics of Western Spirituality (New York: Paulist, 1981), 25.

8. Howard Snyder notes that Wesley considered that the Church overall was in a fallen state; however, he still held it as a true church because it had a structure, liturgy, and true believers within it. "Pietism, Moravianism," 242.

9. Most politicians at that time believed that if the slave trade was abolished, it would weaken Britain's economic prowess. Irv Brendlinger, *Social Justice: Through the Eyes of Wesley: John Wesley's Theological Challenge to Slavery*, (Peterborough: Joshua Press, 2006), 51.

had a "profound influence" on Protestantism, particularly in terms of mission thinking and practice.[10]

Cultural Change

Culturally, the Enlightenment period elevated the importance of human reason and the ideas of such men as Locke, Voltaire, and Kant. Locke, for example, argued for more reasonable beliefs and questioned those arising from passionate and enthusiastic sources, expressing disdain for ideas of the miraculous and emotional. Thus, traditional concepts and ways of knowing were questioned and with these came the onset of secular society.[11]

The Evangelical Revival in Britain

This was also the era of Christian revival and the beginnings of evangelicalism.[12] In a context where religious ceremony and life were performed almost by rote and nominalism was rife, preachers such as George Whitefield and Wesley took to the streets and fields of Britain, urging persons to heartfelt conversion, to place their faith in God, who had saved them by grace through the work of Jesus Christ. The response to this preaching was overwhelming and touched many Protestant denominations, both Anglicans and Dissenters. Hundreds of men and women, regardless of social class, were convicted of their sin and need for salvation. As a consequence, these converts sought to transform their lives in order to live in a godly way.[13]

Such transformation was both personal and social. Mark Noll notes that while the emphasis in these revivals was primarily focused upon individual personal conversion and transformation, converted evangelical Christians

---

10. Bosch, *Transforming Mission*, 274.

11. Jeffrey, "Introduction," 2. Methodism was often criticized by persons within the Anglican Church for its enthusiastic nature. Wesley did not deny the experience of his fellow Methodists but also challenged Methodism's critics with the reasonableness of Methodism's doctrine. See John Wesley, "An Earnest Appeal to Men of Reason and Religion," in *John Wesley*, ed. Albert C. Outler (New York: Oxford University Press, 1964), 384–424.

12. Some scholars argue that evangelicalism also had antecedent stirrings among the German continental pietists and the Moravians in Europe. Mark A. Noll, *The Rise of Evangelicalism*, 50–75. See W. Reginald Ward, *The Protestant Evangelical Awakening* (New York: Cambridge Press, 2006).

13. Noll, *The Rise of Evangelicalism*, 100. For a summary of the various explanations of the sudden rise of the evangelical movement see chapter 5, 136–54.

also looked to live out their faith in their work environments and vocations.[14] Consequently, transformation began to take place in society, with evangelicals starting to work and advocate for social reform where there were inadequate and unjust circumstances.

Wesley's Early Life and Christian Conversion[15]

Wesley was born into a large Christian family; his father, Samuel, was an Anglican priest. Despite the family's modest income, John was well educated. He attended Christ Church College, Oxford, and became a Fellow of Lincoln College in 1726 where he taught until 1735.

The year 1725 marked Wesley's serious turn towards Christianity and an earnest focus on inner purity. Wesley's decision to become a committed Christian was a consequence of the influence of two spiritual books: Bishop Taylor's *Rules and Exercises of Holy Living and Dying* and Thomas à Kempis's *The Imitation of Christ*. Writing of this decision, Wesley commented regarding Taylor:

> In reading several parts of this book I was exceedingly affected, by that part in particular which related to "purity of intention." Instantly I resolved to dedicate all my life to God, all my thoughts and words and actions, being thoroughly convinced there was no medium, but that every part of my life (not some only) must be a sacrifice to God.

Regarding à Kempis, he noted:

> The nature and extent of inward religion, the religion of the heart, now appeared to me in a stronger light than ever it had done before. I saw that giving even all my life to God (supposing it possible to do this and go no further) would profit me nothing unless I gave my heart, yea, all my heart to him.[16]

---

14. Noll, *The Rise of Evangelicalism*, 233–35.

15. For the various content of this section, I am indebted to the following sources: Outler, "Introduction," *John Wesley*; D. Bruce Hindmarsh, *The Spirit of Early Evangelicalism: True Religion in a Modern World* (New York: Oxford University Press, 2018); Noll, *The Rise of Evangelicalism*; Whaling, "Introduction"; Jeffrey, "Introduction"; Kenneth J. Collins, "Wesley's Life and Ministry," in *The Cambridge Companion to John Wesley* eds. Randy L. Maddox and Jason E. Vickers (Cambridge: Cambridge University Press, 2010), 43–59; Howard A. Snyder, *The Radical Wesley and Patterns for Church Renewal* (Downers Grove: InterVarsity Press, 1980); Brendlinger, *Social Justice*.

16. Wesley, "A Plain Account of Christian Perfection," *John and Charles Wesley*, 299.

For Wesleyan scholar, Albert C. Outler, 1725 marks Wesley's "conversion" to Christianity, as from this point onwards, Wesley devoted himself to biblical study and theology, reading widely on the subject.[17]

Our first insight into Wesley's own spiritual practices is found in his involvement in a group that became known as the "Oxford Methodists."[18] On his return to Oxford in 1729, John joined his brother Charles and several other Christians to regularly pray, study the Bible, take Holy Communion, fast, and carry out work among the poor in Oxford. The latter activity included visiting prisoners in the local prisons and starting educational classes for poor children. They all kept diaries of their daily devotions, social service, and reflections, and lived as minimally as possible so that they could give as much as they could to the poor.[19] Bruce Hindmarsh describes this Oxford Methodist lifestyle as "living by rule" and likens it to former monastic groups, particularly Jesuit spirituality. Here is evidence of Wesley cultivating a spiritual life in his context.[20]

In 1735, following the death of his father, Wesley travelled to Georgia, America, then a British colony. Wesley went primarily as a missionary to the indigenous and colonists, and to establish "the Methodists" in Georgia.[21] Wesley stayed for two years but his time there did not go well. Outler describes the mission as a "fiasco."[22] Wesley did not see any conversions, and although the "Oxford Methodists" continued their communal living "by rule" and sought to create similar groups in Georgia, they were not welcomed by the colonists.[23] He returned demoralised to London in 1738.[24]

---

17. Outler, "Introduction," *John Wesley*, 7. In contrast Frank Whaling is not willing to pinpoint Wesley's conversion. However, about 1725, he states: "It was clearly an important stage in his spiritual development and heralded his entry into a life of genuine spirituality," "Introduction," 9.

18. After calling themselves by several names, "The Methodists" was the name that finally attached itself although Wesley did not like it. Wesley, "The Character of a Methodist," *Works*, 9:39.

19. Snyder indicates that such a religious group was not new. In the late 1600s, similar groups had started in the Church of England and had formed a mini-renewal movement. Samuel Wesley had organized such a society in his parish in 1702 and was a supporter of them. Wesley and his friends were aware of such groups when they formed their own community. *The Radical Wesley*, 14–18.

20. Hindmarsh, *The Spirit of Early Evangelicalism*, 15–21.

21. Snyder, *The Radical Wesley*, 22.

22. Outler, "Introduction," *John Wesley*, 11.

23. Wesley was accused of being either a Roman Catholic or a Puritan Separatist. Snyder, *The Radical Wesley*, 21.

24. Outler, "Introduction," *John Wesley*, 11–13. This gives details of a romantic affair that ended in a defamation lawsuit.

Notwithstanding, there were several positive highlights from the Georgia mission. One of these was Wesley's formation of a relationship with a German Moravian group, whom he first met on his outbound journey.[25] He was particularly challenged by his conversations with their leader, Augustus Spanenberg, regarding the nature of faith. (Spanenberg questioned Wesley as to whether he had personal assurance from God that he was a Christian.[26])

On his return to Britain Wesley, reflecting on his time in Georgia and with the Moravians, wrote the following in his journal:

> I who went to America to convert others, was never myself converted to God . . . The faith I want is, "a sure trust and confidence in God, that through the merits of Christ my sins are forgiven, and I am reconciled to the favour of God." . . . [T]hat faith which enables everyone that hath it to cry out, "I live not, but Christ liveth in me; and the life which I now live, I live by faith in the Son of God, who loved me and gave himself for me."[27]

In February 1738, Wesley befriended the German Moravian missionary, Peter Bohler. Bohler continued to emphasise to Wesley that God's justification was not achieved through a Christian's works but was given by God's grace through a Christian's faith alone and that, when received, a Christian would gain assurance of it. With a desire to have such confirmation, Wesley attended a Moravian religious society meeting on 24 May 1738. During this service Wesley underwent a religious experience that gave him an assurance of his salvation. He wrote the following in his journal about this experience:

> In the evening, I went very unwillingly to a society in Aldersgate Street, where one was reading Luther's preface to The Epistle to the Romans. About a quarter before nine, while he was describing

---

25. The Moravians were a part of the Pietist movement in Europe. In the eighteenth century, they were led and renewed in form and practice by Count von Zinzendorf. Zinzendorf was a Lutheran but committed to the practical life of the church, the poor, the oppressed, and the persecuted. He established a large Christian community on his estate in Herrnhut, Germany, which was Moravian rather than Lutheran. There one lived in "a Christian fellowship and household where the personal, economic, social and religious dimensions of life were integrated into one common system." Snyder, "Pietism, Moravianism," 102. As well as the community, its focus was also missionary, with many leaving Herrnhut to establish similar communities elsewhere. Moravian communities were founded in other parts of Europe, England, Israel (Nazareth, Bethlehem) and the USA (Pennsylvania). Snyder further notes that "Moravianism under Zinzendorf became an intensive but highly mobile missionary order" before later assuming a more traditional denominational pattern. 109, 217.

26. Collins, "Wesley's Life and Ministry," 4.

27. Wesley, "Journal Entry, Sunday January 29, 1738," *Works*, 18:214–16.

the change in the heart that God works through faith in Christ, I felt my heart strangely warmed. I felt I did trust in Christ, Christ alone for salvation; and an assurance was given me that he had taken away my sins, even mine, and saved me, from the law of sin and death.[28]

Much is made of this "Aldersgate experience," evangelical scholars in particular consider this event to mark Wesley's "real" conversion to Christianity. Kenneth Collins notes that early scholars tend to identify 1725 as the point of Wesley's conversion. However, he contends that subsequent research has cast doubt about 1725 being the date of Wesley's conversion, stating that the event in 1738 "represented an important actualization of saving grace." He further notes that, after Aldersgate, Wesley "never repudiated the standard of the new birth and the assurance that commonly accompanies it, an assurance that marked his own conversion to the *proper* Christian faith."[29] Bruce Hindmarsh, while not perceiving this event as the only conversion experience of Wesley, views Aldersgate as Wesley's "momentous evangelical conversion."[30]

Outler notes that while this experience is one of the most well-known passages in Wesley's works, Wesley himself only referred to it on two other occasions. Outler states, "it simply drops out of sight in the whole of Wesley's subsequent writings."[31] He also highlights that prior to 1738, Wesley wrote about other situations where he had similar "spiritual exaltations" and, shortly after Aldersgate, wrote of times where he experienced "spiritual depression." His opinion is that in reviewing his Christian life, "it is as if Wesley came to realise that 'Aldersgate' had been *one* in a *series* of 'turning points' in his passage from don to missionary to evangelist."[32]

However one characterizes "Aldersgate," Outler underscores that one cannot understand Wesley's theological thought without taking it into account.[33] I agree with Outler that it was a pivotal moment in Wesley's life. It also provided

---

28. Wesley, "Journal Entry, May 24, 1738," *John Wesley*, 66.

29. Collins, "Wesley's Life and Ministry," 48. (Emphasis is mine).

30. Hindmarsh, *The Spirit of Early Evangelicalism*, 90. W. Reginald. Ward considers neither the 1725 nor 1738 experiences to be Wesley's true conversion experience. He argues this to have been in the spring of 1739 after Wesley read Jonathan Edwards's, *The Surprising Work of God* and reflected upon his new-found success in outdoor preaching amongst the Kingswood colliers. W. Reginald. Ward, *Early Evangelicalism: A Global Intellectual History, 1670–1789* (New York: Cambridge University Press, 2006), 127–29.

31. Outler, "Introduction to the Aldersgate Experience," *John Wesley*, 51.

32. Outler, "Introduction to the Aldersgate Experience," *John Wesley*, 52. (Emphasis original.)

33. Outler, "Introduction to the Aldersgate Experience," *John Wesley*, 52.

a watershed in his ministry, with Wesley thereafter becoming an open-air preacher, evangelist and prominent leader in the evangelical revival in Britain.

The Christian Life and Perfection

Wesley's life was mission oriented.[34] Interestingly, the terms "evangelism," "mission," and "social mission" were not part of Wesley's vocabulary; rather, he framed his concerns as Christian salvation and the practice of Christianity. Wesley's role in the evangelical revival saw him leading hundreds of persons to faith in Christ Jesus. However, his missional concern went beyond conversion to ensure that such new Christians pursued their Christian lives and grew to maturity. For him, the Christian life had two parts, "justification" and "sanctification."[35] He described the former as what God does for us through Christ, enabling persons to become Christians: he described the latter as what God does in us through restoration, that is, growing us through sanctifying grace into Christlikeness.[36] Wesley's chief pastoral concern was this process of sanctification which he termed "the way of perfection."[37] To be clear at the outset, Wesley's focus on sanctification did not mean he was preaching salvation through "works."[38] For him, a person became a Christian through their initial conversion and then grew as a Christian, all through God's grace alone. His continued focus on growing in Christ through God's means of grace reveals that Wesley wanted to make certain that Christians remained on God's path after conversion and received all the grace that God had for them. In other words, Wesley's missional focus went beyond conversion into making great disciples.

---

34. Jeffrey, *English Spirituality*, 31.

35. Wesley, "The Scripture Way of Salvation," *Works*, 2:157. In his sermon, "On Working Out Our Own Salvation", *Works* 3:204. Wesley succinctly defines what he means by these two terms: "By justification, we are saved from the guilt of sin, and restored to the favour of God: by sanctification we are saved from the power and root of sin, and restored to the image of God."

36. Outler's note as editor. Wesley, "Justification by Faith" in *Works*, 1:187n3.

37. Kenneth J. Collins affirms this view, "John Wesley's Assessment of Christian Mysticism," *Lexington Theological Quarterly* 28, no. 4 (Winter 1993): 299.

38. Some of Wesley's contemporaries argued that his instruction on the way of perfection sounded as though he was promoting salvation by "works." In response, he asserted that this was not the case: "I have continually testified in private and in public that we are sanctified as well as justified by faith." Wesley, "The Scripture Way of Salvation," *Works*, 2:163.

For Wesley, the goal of the Christian was what he described as "perfection"[39] or "entire sanctification" or "[l]oving God with all our heart, mind, soul, and strength. This implies that no wrong temper, none contrary to love, remains in the soul and that all the thoughts, words and actions are governed by pure love."[40] Further, this state is "in subjection to the obedience of Christ. The will is entirely subject to the will of God and the affections are wholly fixed on him."[41] He emphasized that the focal point of perfection was the gift of pure love for God and the ability to purely love one's neighbour according to God's will.[42] Thus Wesley described the goal of the Christian life as being able to love God and neighbour in pure unadulterated love. [43]

Wesley opined that sanctification was received as a gracious gift from God in faith through God's grace.[44] For him, God can give sanctification to a Christian through a life process so that a Christian can "grow in grace" and attain holiness over her lifetime. He also held that God can give the gift in its entirety immediately, enabling a Christian to be sanctified – made sinless and perfected in love – in a moment. This latter view is more controversial, but various Methodists maintained they had received such a gift. While Wesley himself did not receive sanctification in a moment, he submitted that as God grants sanctification as a gracious gift, it is entirely conceivable that God can grant immediate and complete sanctification:

> Perhaps it may be gradually wrought in some – I mean in this
> sense, that they do not advert to the particular moment wherein
> sin ceases to be. But it is infinitely desirable, were it the will of
> God, that it should be done instantaneously, that is that the Lord
> should destroy sin "by the breath of his mouth" (Job 15:30), in a

---

39. The text for Wesley's use of the term "perfection" was Paul's comment that "Not as though I have ready attained all this or have been already made perfect" (Phil 3:12). He was criticized by his contemporaries for the use of this term, but he defended its use by arguing it was used in the Bible. Wesley, "Christian Perfection," in *John Wesley*, 252.

40. Wesley, "Thoughts on Christian Perfection," *John Wesley*, 284.

41. Wesley, "Thoughts on Christian Perfection," *John Wesley*, 286.

42. Wesley, "Christian Perfection," *Works*, 2:100–105.

43. Lyon Hynson notes that the theme of Christian perfection was always of concern to Wesley even prior to his evangelical conversion in 1738. His interest in the subject prior to 1738 was grounded in his false belief that he had to live the sanctified life in order to gain God's acceptance (salvation through works). After 1738, when he realized justification and sanctification were received through grace, his concern turned to others, that all might receive God's entire grace. *To Reform the Nation: Theological Foundations of Wesley's Ethics* (Grand Rapids: Francis Asbury Press, 1984), 37.

44. Wesley, "The Scripture Way of Salvation," *Works*, 2:157.

moment, in a twinkling of an eye. And so he generally does; a plain fact of which there is evidence enough to satisfy any unprejudiced person.[45]

The contemporary theologians, Irv Brendlinger and Randy Maddox, argue that Wesley's overall description of sanctification points to more of a process than a particular state. Brendlinger describes it as a relationship between God and the Christian that requires a constant connection.[46] Maddox prefers the image of a responsive or progressive journey with God.[47] I agree with both scholars that Wesley underscores a way of sanctification that has a trajectory towards perfection. However, for me, the important point is that the way of perfection is made with God, in Christ, through the Holy Spirit. In other words, Wesley's Christian life was a spirituality in accordance with the definition of the term in this book. Wesley's Christian life was a journey or a relationship with the Triune God.

While acknowledging that sanctification was a gift Wesley, in challenging the Quietism of his day which was practised by the Moravians, urged Christians not to wait for this gift[48]

> In careless indifference or indolent inactivity, but in vigorous and universal obedience; in a zealous keeping of all the commandments; in watchfulness and painfulness; in denying ourselves and in taking up our cross daily; as well as in earnest prayer and fasting and a close attendance on all the ordinances of God . . . It is true we receive it by simple faith; but God does not,

---

45. Wesley, "The Scripture Way of Salvation," *Works*, 2:168–169. Various scholars argue that Wesley fluctuated in his opinion about whether sanctification was given instantly or was obtained through a process of growth. Maddox opines that for the first twenty years of the revival, Wesley highlighted growth in grace but he began to emphasize immediate sanctification after 1760. When this emphasis caused controversy, Wesley moved to accommodate both positions. Randy L. Maddox, *Responsible Grace: John Wesley's Practical Theology* (Nashville: Abingdon, 1994), 180–87. Brendlinger indicates that Rob Staples, in *John Wesley's Doctrine of Christian Perfection*, submits that from 1725 to 1738 Wesley argued exclusively for a gradual sanctification; from 1738 to 1758 he held for both, sometimes emphasizing one over the other; and from 1758 he argued for a synthesis of both. See Brendlinger, *Social Justice*, 112.

46. Brendlinger, *Social Justice*, 110–15.

47. Maddox, *Responsible Grace*, 190.

48. Quietism required "stillness" and "inner waiting" for assurance of salvation before any activity was undertaken – including participation in God's ordinances. Wesley opposed this. He believed that Christians ought to serve throughout the differing stages of the Christian life. This was a primary reason he parted ways with the Moravians.

will not, give that faith unless we seek it with all diligence in the way in which he hath ordained.[49]

In other words, Christians were to continue to live in accordance with God's will, even if imperfectly.

In living such a life, Wesley had confidence that the Holy Spirit would enable a Christian to perform tasks, whether ones of devotion to God or serving one's neighbour. He often spoke that "faith worketh by love" based on Galatians 5:6, that is, "The only thing that counts is faith expressing itself through love." If persons have faith, they will obey God's call even though not yet sanctified. Moreover, if Christians are perfected gradually over time, they will grow in their love through these actions as love is received through the Holy Spirit and sin is conquered.[50] Wesley therefore encouraged Christians to view the commandments of God as promises, arguing that God's request to "love one's neighbour" is, in effect, a promise from God that they can love their neighbour through the power of the Holy Spirit.[51] For Wesley, one practises loving neighbours as one continues to await the gift of "perfection," as it is part of the process of growing into it.[52]

For Christians, in pursuit of perfection, it was important to know the sources of sanctifying grace from God. In his sermon, "The Scripture Way of Salvation," Wesley described two particular types of Christian activity: the first is "works of piety," "such as public prayer, family prayer, and praying in our closet; receiving the Supper of our Lord; searching the Scriptures by hearing, reading, meditating; and using such a measure of fasting or abstinence as our bodily health allows"; second is "works of mercy," such as:

> feeding the hungry, clothing the naked, entertaining the stranger, visiting those that are in prison, or sick, or variously afflicted; such as endeavouring to instruct the ignorant, to awaken the stupid sinner, to quicken the lukewarm, to confirm the wavering, to comfort the feebleminded, to succour the tempted, or contribute in any manner to the saving souls from death.[53]

---

49. Wesley, "Thoughts on Christian Perfection," *John Wesley*, 294.

50. With regard to sin, Wesley, like Augustine, believed in original sin and that the power of original sin was broken when a Christian was justified. To quote Wesley, sin "no longer reigned but it did remain." Wesley, "Thoughts on Christian Perfection." As such, a person could sin after justification and so repentance was still necessary.

51. Brendlinger, *Social Justice*, 116.

52. Brendlinger, *Social Justice*, 103.

53. Wesley, "The Scripture Way of Salvation," *Works*, 2:166.

These two types of activity are in keeping with the focus of loving God and neighbour; "works of piety" centre on devotion to God (with social and personal aspects) and "works of mercy" aim at loving one's neighbours.[54] Works of piety were readily accepted within the church as means of sanctification, and Wesley affirmed this position.[55] He considered such works were all sacramental in nature, placing a person in the presence of God to receive blessing. Within his context, he also included participation in forms of Methodist worship, such as the band meeting and the love feast, as "works of piety." For Wesley, the sacraments, particularly Holy Communion, were not simply an acknowledgement of what Christ had done to provide salvation; they were also a means of nourishing and empowering grace for the participant from God. Thus, participating and receiving grace from God through the sacraments was considered a significant part of the process of sanctification.[56]

While the CofE endorsed "works of piety" as means of grace in sanctification, Wesley went further and argued that service in the form of "loving one's neighbour," that is, works of mercy were also means of grace, which was a novel view. Wesley, in "On Visiting the Sick" (1786), stated:

> It is generally supposed that "the means of grace" and "the ordinances of God" are equivalent terms . . . But are they the only means of grace? . . . Surely there are works of mercy, as well as works of piety, which are real means of grace. [57]

Therefore, Wesley argued that both "works of mercy" and "works of piety" are channels of God's grace in Christ through the Holy Spirit and thus are modes towards perfection; so, both are necessary for sanctification.

"On Visiting the Sick" is a sermon specifically on Matthew 25:36. However, in Wesley's description of "works of mercy" as a means of grace, he referred to the whole parable on "the sheep and the goats" recorded in the gospel of Matthew, arguing that all of the matters listed therein are examples of such means: providing for the hungry, thirsty, those lacking clothes; taking in the

---

54. Wesley also describes these acts as ways of repentance and humility lived after justification as an acknowledgement of a Christian's dependence on God. Wesley, "The Repentance of Believers," Works, 1:343.

55. Wesley, "The Means of Grace," Works, 1:396. Wesley affirms in this sermon that works of piety are means of grace. He emphasizes that it is not the work itself that provides the grace but states that "In using all means, seek God alone. In and through every outward thing, look singly to the power of his Spirit; and the merits of his Son . . . Nothing short of God can satisfy your soul. Therefore, eye him in all, through all, and above all."

56. See Maddox, Responsible Grace, 197–201.

57. Wesley, "On Visiting the Sick," Works, 3:385.

stranger; and visiting the prisoner as well as the sick.[58] For Wesley, all service in society was a means of grace and sanctification. Wesley emphasised that in order to benefit from the gift of sanctification Christians were called to undertake such service themselves; they would not experience God's sanctifying grace by sending a doctor, proxy or money. He stated that:

> If you do not [go yourself], you lose a means of grace; you lose an excellent means of increasing your thankfulness to God . . . as well as of increasing your sympathy with the afflicted, your benevolence, and all social affections.[59]

Further, Wesley affirmed that, as God is present, the Christian in performing the service ought to pray to God who participates with the Christian and provides all that is required for the task:

> Whenever, therefore, you are about to enter upon the work, seek his help by earnest prayer. Cry to him for the whole spirit of humility, lest if pride steal into your heart, if you ascribe anything to yourself, while you strive to save others, you destroy your own soul. Before and through the work, from the beginning to the end, let your heart wait upon him for a continual supply of meekness and gentleness, of patience and longsuffering, that you may never be angry or discouraged at whatever treatment, rough or smooth, kind or unkind, you may meet with.[60]

This prayer to God before and during the task acknowledges God's presence, but also that there is a need to connect with God throughout as the source of empowerment for the work. I consider this exhortation to prayer highlights the level of interconnectivity that Wesley understood between "works of mercy," "works of piety," and the presence of God in Christ through the Holy Spirit.

I consider that there are two levels of interconnectivity or relationship described within Wesley's integration of works of mercy and works of piety. First, there is a general relationship, that both works of mercy and works of piety are required within a Christian's life with each supporting the other. Wesley referred to this relationship between the two in various texts. For example, in relation to the link between the necessity to love God in order to

---

58. Matthew 25:31–46.
59. Wesley, "On Visiting the Sick," *Works*, 3:387.
60. Wesley, "On Visiting the Sick," *Works*, 3:390.

love neighbour Wesley commented, "But it is that love of our neighbour which springs from the love of God; otherwise itself is nothing worth. It behooves us therefore to examine well upon what foundation our love of neighbour stands; whether it is really built upon the love of God."[61]

This view of the interdependence of works of piety and mercy is affirmed by Maddox, who also argues that there is an interconnectedness between loving God and neighbour and, therefore, between works of piety and mercy. He describes this link as dialectical:

> On the one hand he (Wesley) would insist (in contrast with deism) that we can truly love other humans only in conjunction with love for God. On the other hand, he denied that anyone who failed to love their neighbour could truly love God. On such terms, works of piety like worship – which express responsive love for God – would deepen our love for others, while works of mercy would deepen our love for God.[62]

In this first level of interconnectivity, Wesley argued that a Christian requires both a pious and an active Christian life and that one without the other is deficient; a Christian's works of mercy are grounded in works of piety and vice versa. However, I would go further than this first level and argue that there is a second level within the act of mercy itself. In the above quotation from "On Visiting the Sick," Wesley indicated the necessity to be in relationship with the Holy Spirit throughout the work of mercy. In other words, a Christian's life integrates works of mercy and piety with the Holy Spirit in the tasks themselves. Wesley argued for the need to wrap the act in prayer or communication with God because a Christian needs to be in relationship with the Holy Spirit to perform these tasks. Referring to what is meant by "the grace of God" in his sermon "On the Witness of Our Own Spirit" (based on 2 Corinthians 1:12), he stated:

> Here it means that power of God, the Holy Spirit, who works in us, both to will and to do His pleasure. As soon as God's grace in

---

61. Wesley, "Upon Our Lord's Sermon on the Mount III," *Works*, 1:510. Maddox also references "Advice to the People Called Methodists," *Works*, 9:124 and others. See Maddox, *Responsible Grace*, 215n149.

62. Maddox, *Responsible Grace*, 215. Maddox also notes that in three of Wesley's major sermons, "The Character of a Methodist" (1742), "The Scripture Way of Salvation" (1765), and "On Working Out Our Own Salvation" (1785), Wesley respectively links love of God and neighbour and works of piety and mercy in a reciprocal relationship and notes both are required for sanctification. Randy L. Maddox, "Visit the Poor: Wesley's Precedent for Wholistic Mission," *Transformation* 18, no. 1 (January 2001): 41, https://www.jstor.org/stable/43052502.

the former sense of pardoning love is manifested to us, His grace in the latter sense is given. The power of the Holy Spirit makes it possible for us to perform, through grace, what was impossible to man. Now we can order our conversation correctly. We can do all things in the light and power of that love through Christ who strengthens us. We now have the testimony of our conscience which we could never have by fleshly wisdom. Now "in simplicity and godly sincerity we have our conversation in the world."[63]

Commenting on this text, Wesley indicated that it is the Holy Spirit abiding in and with Christians that enables them to be and act in the world. For me, Wesley is speaking of "abiding in Christ," the idea that within the Christian there is a mysterious interconnectivity between the Holy Spirit and the Christian in the performance of tasks. In loving our neighbour, Christians are participating with God the Holy Spirit in this work and therefore continual communication in the form of prayer is necessary. For Wesley, this is more than mental assent to the reality of this participatory relationship; the Christian is conscious of the Holy Spirit within, that is, it is about experience. Outler notes that by the term, "experience," Wesley means "religious intuition."[64] In Wesley's sermon, the "Witness of the Spirit: Discourse 2" (based on the text Romans 8:16), and speaking of the Holy Spirit witnessing to a Christian's spirit that a Christian is a child of God, he commented:

> I observed many years ago. it is hard to find words in the language of men, to explain the deep things of God. Indeed, there are none that will adequately express what the Spirit of God works in his children. But perhaps one might say . . . by "the testimony of the Spirit," I mean, an inward impression on the soul whereby the Spirit of God immediately and directly witnesses to my spirit, that I am a child of God.[65]

Wesley, in bringing together a Christian life of piety and mercy, loving God and neighbour, through the reality of the experience of the indwelling of Christ through the Holy Spirit, subscribed to an integrated Christian life. For him, such a life was important; he argued vehemently that throughout history

---

63. Wesley, "On the Witness of Our Own Spirit," *Holy Spirit and Power*, ed. Clare Weakley (Alachua: Bridge-Logos, 2003), 210.

64. Outler, *John Wesley*, 209.

65. Wesley, "Witness of the Spirit, Discourse 2," *John Wesley*, 211.

Christian integrity was constantly challenged, in so far as either inwardness or activity were given precedence, one over the other.

> It has been the endeavour of Satan from the beginning of the world to put asunder what God has joined together; to separate inward from outward religion; to set one of these at variance with the other. And herein, he has met with no small success among those who are ignorant of his devices.[66]

Wesley contested the division and did so by arguing for an integrated Christian life.[67] From my perspective, Wesley coherently established that the Christian life is integrated by combining "works of piety" and "works of mercy" in relationship with God in Christ and through the Holy Spirit. Furthermore, he grounded this life within a theological understanding of spiritual formation or sanctification. Christian life is lived loving God and neighbour empowered by the Holy Spirit. It is one that has a missional posture towards the world.[68]

The Practical Reality of Wesley's Christian Life

Wesley was not primarily a theoretician, rather he was a pastoral theologian and preferred simple words so everyone could understand him. Therefore, while he grounded the Christian life biblically and theologically, he was most concerned that it was practised. Wesley encouraged and supported the practice of this life in several ways.

In his "Fourth Discourse on the Sermon on the Mount" Wesley described Christianity as a "social religion."[69] By "social" he meant a Christianity that was both relational and practised in the world.[70] Wesley encouraged Christians to

---

66. Wesley, "Sermon on the Mount IV," *Works*, 1:592 –593.

67. Outler, "The Repentance of Believers," *Works*, 2:343n65 notes how Wesley always kept works of piety and mercy together and neither were given priority. He references the following sermons where this takes place: "Sermon on the Mount 2," *Works*, 1:493, and "Sermon on the Mount 4," *Works*, 1:548.

68. Randy Maddox also affirms this view, suggesting that the missional task becomes a form of spiritual formation. "Visit the Poor," 42.

69. Wesley, *Works*, 1:533. Wesley published thirteen discourses on the Sermon on the Mount, and they are considered a general statement of his social ethic. Wesley, *Works*, 1:531–549. Outler notes that these discourses contain material from 1725 onwards; each is readable on its own or as a whole. Wesley intended both styles of reading. Outler, "Introductory Comment," in Wesley, *Works*, 1:466.

70. Theodore Runyon argues that in Wesley's context, the term "social" had a different meaning from that of today. He notes: "Wesley is not using the term in the full-blown twentieth century meaning of the social gospel – that is, the application of the Christian message to

love the neighbour through works of mercy.[71] Many of his sermons focused on practical issues like "On Visiting the Sick"[72] or "On the Use of Money."[73] In his sermon, "On the Character of a Methodist,"[74] he described a Methodist practising such a Christian life as one who did good to all humanity.[75] He affirmed that Methodists carry out such tasks by attending to the hungry, naked, sick and imprisoned. They also sought to "awaken those that sleep in death; to bring those who are awakened to the atoning blood, that being justified by faith they may have peace with God; and to provoke those with peace with God to abound more in love in good works."[76] In other words, a Christian's call to love one's neighbour involves caring for all their needs. For Wesley, there is no dichotomy between physical and spiritual matters; one cares for a person's relationship with God and their need for food, education and shelter without giving priority to either.[77] In today's vocabulary, both evangelism and service are equally mission.

---

social, political and economic institutions and the structures of corporate life." "Wesley and the Theologies of Liberation," in *Sanctification and Liberation: Liberation Theologies in the Light of the Weslyan Tradition*, ed. Theodore Runyon (Nashville: Abingdon, 1981), 42. Irv Brendlinger also reminds us that Wesley lived prior to Emile Durkheim and the latter's theories regarding social structures, so Wesley would not have thought about sin in relation to institutions and other human structures. Brendlinger, *Social Justice*, 138.

71. Such a view challenged the antinomianism of Wesley's day, which he considered heresy. Antinomianism stated that through Christ's coming all biblical law was abolished and therefore there was no need to follow or obey it. For Wesley, salvation was entirely merciful grace through Christ's death and resurrection extended by the Holy Spirit to those who had faith in this event, but Christ's coming did not abolish the law and Christians still had to heed it. Wesley argued, "Whereas now all good works, *though as necessary as ever*, are not antecedent to our acceptance, but *are consequent upon it*. Therefore, the nature of the covenant of grace gives you no ground . . . to set aside any instance or degree of obedience, any part or measure of holiness." Wesley, "The Law Established through Faith, Discourse 1," *Works*, 2:27. (Emphasis mine.) Wesley held this view as vital to Christianity. He argued that without such works, a Christian's faith was questionable. Wesley, "The Law Established through Faith, Discourse 1," *Works*, 2:28.

72. Wesley, *Works*, 3:384–387.

73. Wesley, *Works*, 2:263.

74. Wesley, *Works*, 9:32–46. Outler submits that in this sermon, Wesley was emphasizing two matters: first, a perfect Methodist was in fact a perfect Christian, for example, there was no difference between Methodism and real Christianity; second, the goal of Christianity was perfection/sanctification – the reception of God's grace through faith, of the ability to perfectly love God and neighbour. Wesley, *Works*, 9:31.

75. Wesley, *Works*, 9:41.

76. Wesley, *Works*, 9:41.

77. Maddox suggests this approach by Wesley could form the basis of a theological argument against those current evangelicals who seek to prioritize evangelism over the needs of others. He further argues that Wesley's approach also suggests a holistic view of salvation, for example, not just spiritual. See Maddox, "Visit the Poor," 37–50.

For Wesley, no part of a Christian's life, religious or secular, was limited in terms of Christian service. Wesley wrote that God requires Christians to let their light shine among people, that hiding within society is not an option.[78] Therefore, works of mercy were encouraged in all a Christian's work with the community, this included one's workplace. The result was that transformation within societal structures also took place. Irv Brendlinger gives several examples of how small changes by active Methodists led to societal improvements, for example, the Newgate prison in Bristol was known for its terrible conditions: "[S]o great was the filth, the stench, the misery and wickedness, which shocked all who had a spark of humanity left."[79] Over twenty years, the jailer, Albert Dagge, a Methodist, transformed it completely. Wesley noted the changes: it was clean; there was no fighting; disputes were reconciled by Dagge; bribery, drunkenness, and prostitution were not permitted; medicines were given freely to inmates; Bibles were provided; religious services conducted; and tools and materials were given to those able to carry out work.[80] Methodists also created a system of education for the poor where there was none before and improved systems in hospitals.

Wesley also encouraged persons to practise Christianity through his publications and correspondence. Wesley abridged and published many Christian books.[81] He encouraged all Methodists to read and often gave instruction as to the method of reading. For example, in the preface to his abridgement of à Kempis's *Imitation of Christ,* he encouraged a slow, meditative reading of the text that resembled monastic *lectio divina.*[82] His books were printed in different sizes and at different prices so that they would reach differing audiences. In particular, he wanted to ensure that poor people who could not ordinarily afford books obtained copies.[83] Wesley also corresponded extensively with many individuals who sought help in living the Christian life.

Having participated in his own "Oxford Methodists," Wesley particularly understood the value of practising Christianity with others as a way of nurture and growth. He supported this communal endeavour through his organization

---

78. Wesley, "The Scripture Way of Salvation," *Works,* 2:166.

79. A comment in Wesley's journal on January 2, 1761. Quoted in Brendlinger, *Social Justice,* 139.

80. Brendlinger, *Social Justice,* 139.

81. According to the English Short Title Catalogue, Wesley was the author, editor and publisher of more items than any other person in eighteenth-century Britain. Isabel Rivers, "John Wesley as Editor and Publisher," in *The Cambridge Companion to John Wesley,* 144–59.

82. Hindmarsh, *The Spirit of Early Evangelicalism,* 92.

83. Isabel Rivers, "John Wesley as Editor," 157.

of the Methodist movement, which was distinct from the Oxford group. Methodism started as a structure of what were termed "classes" and "bands" that met within a "Methodist Society". Classes were for those desiring to know more about Christianity and seek justification, while bands were groups of justified Christians pursuing sanctification. These classes and bands met on a weekly basis for encouragement, discipline, prayer, Scripture reading, worship, and accountability. In other words, persons gathered regularly to practise "works of piety" aided by an appointed lay leader. Wesley intended Methodism to aid the revival and to reform the Anglican Church from within, so that it could embrace the many new committed Christians. He did not expect it to form a denomination, so members were expected to attend and participate in their local Anglican church on a Sunday. Therefore, these groups of classes and bands were established to enable persons to pursue their Christian life together, to grow in grace, support, and enrich one another.

As well as encouraging others in this integrated Christian life, Wesley was also a role model. Throughout his life, he valued his own close friendships for mutual spiritual practice; these are evidenced by the "Oxford Methodists," those with whom he corresponded often, and his close friend, John Fletcher. As well as spending much of his time field preaching, he embraced other "works of mercy," such as operating an orphanage and a school for the poor and establishing knitting and spinning shops to provide employment. He practically engaged those around him in his desire to follow and be obedient to Christ.

Furthermore, Wesley actively engaged in spheres of life other than the religious. He had an active interest in science and the medical field, writing tracts on the subject.[84] He advised others on medical issues and set up medical clinics for the poor. He also sought to understand the economics and politics of his day.[85] From 1772 onwards, he was actively involved in the work to abolish slavery, which was a legal enterprise in Britain.

Wesley's concern about the slave trade and the mistreatment of slaves began with his missionary trip to Georgia, where he observed the abuse and cruelty inflicted upon slaves first-hand. Consequently, he made comments against the practice in his publications and correspondence throughout his life.

---

84. For example, Wesley wrote and published "The Desideratum: Or Electricity Made Plain and Useful. By A Lover of Mankind, and of Common Sense" in 1759 and "Primitive Physick: Or an Easy Way and Natural Method of Curing Most Diseases" in 1745. For further reading, see Hindmarsh, *The Spirit of Early Evangelicalism*, 115–24.

85. For example, in 1775 (prior to the American War of Independence) Wesley wrote "A Calm Address to our American Colonies." This was in support of British policies in the region. He also wrote various political tracts. Leon Hynson, *To Reform the Nation*, 49.

In 1762, Wesley met and helped the leaders of the abolition group: Granville Sharp in Britain and Antony Benezet, the Philadelphian Quaker. In 1764 Wesley wrote and published a tract entitled, *Thoughts Upon the Slave Trade*. Wesley's argument for the slave trade's abolition was based on natural law, pragmatics, and economics rather than religion.[86] Irv Brendlinger opines that Wesley's relationship with Sharp and Benezet and their respective endeavours was "foundational to the practical success that the succeeding generation experienced," namely, its legal abolition in Britain.[87] To that end, one of Wesley's last pieces of correspondence was a letter encouraging the Christian politician and abolitionist, William Wilberforce.

Wesley was a good example of a missioner, one who evangelized and loved his neighbour. He spent his time travelling Great Britain and preaching to its population. He also abridged and published books, organized and led the Methodist Society, involved himself in matters pertaining to economics, politics, science, and medicine, and helped fight for the abolition of the slave trade. He also took seriously reading the Scriptures, participating in Holy Communion and prayer, and encouraged accountability to others in this task. Wesley spent his life loving God and his neighbour; he lived as he preached.

Concluding Reflections

While wars of independence raged in the Americas and France during the eighteenth century, Britain, with its own vulnerable monarchy, was able to remain calm, retain its monarchy, and improve its parliamentary government. Some historians such as Elie Halvie (1870–1937) argue that Britain avoided a revolution because of the Methodist outward approach to society, instilled by its leader, Wesley.[88] While this opinion regarding the influence of the Methodists may be a little overstated, it is also true that the dynamic of the movement – 50,000 strong at the end of the century – with its societal involvement in evangelism and service made a significant impact on Britain. Methodists of

---

86. Brendlinger, *Social Justice*, 48–54. Brendlinger indicates that Wesley's arguments fit within his scriptural and theological understandings of such matters as human dignity, prevenient grace, liberty and perfect love.

87. Brendlinger, *Social Justice*, 26.

88. Theodore Runyon quotes the example of Halevy who wrote such a view in his six volume *History of the English People in the Nineteenth Century*. Runyon notes that there is continued interest in Halevy's theory because it leads to questions such as whether Wesley's theological perspectives and practices led to profound socio-economic changes which in other societies were only achieved by bloody violent revolution. **"Wesley and the Theologies of Liberation,"** 15–16.

the period were known for creating schools for the poor, improving structures of welfare within hospitals and prisons, providing occupations for the working poor, and their general care and love for persons.

For the purposes of this book, I consider that Wesley's writings and life, both as a missioner and an Anglican priest, are significant because he was interested in the whole of a Christian's life, not just conversion. His desire was that persons not only turned to Christ but abided in Christ and, through the Holy Spirit, received the gifts that God had for them. This was not a purely inward journey; it was a life lived in relationship with God, fellow Christians, and with an outward focus towards the neighbour and the world. His emphasis on "perfect love" or sanctification as gift, while controversial at the time, meant that Christians did not abandon good works. Growth in grace as a journey or relationship with God was central to his understanding of Christianity; for Wesley, Christians did not just enter the race, they were to finish well.

Wesley's concern went beyond the sermon to the practical. Through the creation of the Methodist system (the accountability and fellowship of classes and bands), his general preaching and correspondence, his advocacy of reading and publication of books, his instruction to partake in works of piety and mercy, and his guidance on how to live practically he offered a structured, integrated approach to Christians seeking this life with God.

For me, his particular attention to "works of mercy" as a means of grace, together with his heeding of the necessary relationship with God to enable such work, is significant for integrated mission. Wesley revealed the interdependence of works of piety and mercy: one must "know" who God is experientially to perceive God as one is serving others. Then, when one is serving, the connection with God remains; one serves and communes with God simultaneously. God gives the missioner the gifts she requires to perform each task as she speaks with God. In my view, Wesley endorsed a missional life that incorporates both works of piety and mercy in such ways that there are not only benefits for the missionized but also the missioner. For the Christian employed in both works of piety and mercy, there are the promises of sanctification: the gift of pure love for God and neighbour. The integrating factor in these works is the real presence of God, in Christ, and through the power of the Holy Spirit in the lives of Christians. By living such lives, Christians participate with God in changing their own lives and life around them.

Like Wesley, Lausanne in *The Commitment* is emphasizing "loving God and neighbour" as its biblically informed objective. However, unlike Wesley, Lausanne (other than intercessory prayer) primarily attends to the practice of "loving one's neighbour"; it only guides missioners in relation to half of

Jesus's equation. In my view, Wesley's contribution to Lausanne's failure to embrace integrated mission is in his ability to understand the complete picture; the missioner without loving and communing with God lacks the necessary power to perform the service. For Wesley, the relationship or journey is pivotal, missioners must always abide in Christ through the Holy Spirit. For Wesley, Christians are not asked to love their neighbour with their own love; rather in the context of a loving relationship with God, through abiding in Christ and the power of the Holy Spirit, God promises that a Christian is able to love the neighbour with God's love. It is the cultivation of this relationship with God that is ultimately important for both mission and sanctification.

5

Second Movement – Historical Theology Part 2

The Spirituality of Ignatius of Loyola

I have chosen to explore Ignatius of Loyola's life and spirituality through his published writings as the second part of Browning's historical movement because, in my view, Ignatius's spirituality provides facilitative wisdom for devising a way of integrated mission for Lausanne.

El peregrino is the Spanish word for pilgrim and the name that Ignatius of Loyola (Ignatius) ascribed to himself in his *Autobiography*.[1] As a Christian pilgrim[2] living in Europe in the first half of the sixteenth century, he sought to follow in the footsteps of Jesus and to bring continual glory and praise to God through his life of God-driven service. His friend and colleague, Jerome Nadal, described Ignatius as a "contemplative in action," a label which remains to this day because his life exemplified, and his writings advocated, a life of

---

1. I am using the Ignatian writings as translated and provided in George E. Ganss, ed, *Saint Ignatius of Loyola: The Spiritual Exercises and Selected Works*, The Classics of Western Spirituality, (New York: Paulist, 1991). All references to Ignatius's texts herein are to this volume, unless otherwise stated.

2. Ignatius lived in sixteenth-century Spain in an era where the knight and military chivalry were part of the culture. John Olin argues that a common image of Ignatius is as "a soldier of Christ." He suggests that as this metaphor is outdated, the concept of "pilgrim" (which is Ignatius's own self-description) is preferable. Therefore, I am referring to Ignatius as a pilgrim in this book. In my view, it is an appropriate paradigm for his life and work. John Olin, "The Idea of Pilgrimage in the Experience of Ignatius of Loyola," *Church History* 48, no. 4 (December, 1979): 389.

intimacy and service with and for God.[3] For Ignatius, God was his leader, a trinity of Persons whom he discernibly encountered and followed as a pilgrim in missional service.

Ignatius held the tension between the transcendence and immanence of God; he held that God is encounterable in this life and that any such encounters enable a Christian to perceive both the transcendence of God and the created from the Creator's perspective.[4] I consider that his written texts provide didactic insight into how a Christian can experience God's presence, discern God's will, and live a reciprocal relationship of love, serving God.

I argue that Ignatius's spiritual theology is a helpful source for integrated mission as it affirms that mission is a God-led activity in which Christians participate by "following" Jesus; it is an outward, integral, movement towards other persons to help them commit their lives to God and God's purposes for them. Second, it highlights that participation with God requires the cultivation of an intimate life with the Triune God so that one can "know" God, both biblically and experientially. Even though Ignatius lived in a very different historical period, his texts apprehend that Christian integrated mission is founded in a reciprocal relationship of love with God.

There are only a few Ignatian writings available today. *The Spiritual Exercises* were written to guide persons through a four-week meditative retreat so that they could draw close to God and intuit how God is calling them to serve. In their original context, *The Exercises* were used so that persons could consider whether they were called to become Jesuits.[5] *The Exercises* are still in

---

3. Ganss, "Introduction," *Ignatius of Loyola*, 44.

4. Hugo Rahner considers that Ignatius's theology is dialectical. God's downward movement to us leads us upwards to God and to see all earthly things as from God. The focus for the Christian however must be through the middle, that is, in Christ the mediator who brings the "heavens and the below" together. *Ignatius the Theologian*, trans. Michael Barry (London: Geoffrey Chapman, 1968), 1–31.

5. At the time of Ignatius, there were two states of life to which a Christian could be called. Ignatius describes these in *The Exercises* as either the "ordinary Christian" in the world, who chooses to observe and be obedient to the commandments, or "the religious," who sought evangelical Perfection. *The Exercises*, 154. Therefore, the primary choice within *The Exercises* is whether one was called to an "ordinary Christian" life or that of a "religious." Until addressed by The Second Vatican Council (1962–65) this concept naturally led to the idea of two classes of Christians. In "On the Church," the Roman Catholic Church stated that "All Christians in any state or walk of life are called to the fullness of the Christian life and to the perfection of love." Quote taken from Ganss, "Notes on The Exercises," *Ignatius of Loyola*, 404. Ganss also suggests that Ignatius may have had this "broader vision" in view at that time, as while Ignatius acknowledged the two states of life in *The Exercises*, he also noted that "we shall also think about how we ought to dispose ourselves in order to come to perfection in whatsoever state of life God our Lord may grant us to elect." Ignatius, *The Exercises*, 154.

use albeit adapted for their context by contemporary spiritual directors.[6] *The Constitutions* established the purpose of the Order of the Company of Jesus (the Jesuits), and how they were to operate as a religious order. Today, the Jesuits follow an updated version of *The Constitutions,* which remain similar to the original. *The Autobiography* was only published in 1904, although a Spanish/Italian text was available to some of Ignatius's contemporaries while he remained alive.[7] Similarly, *The Spiritual Diary* and his *Deliberation on Poverty,* both personal memoirs of his intimate life with God, were only made public in 1894 when the first copy book was published. A complete critical text was subsequently published in 1934.[8] The more recent published documents reveal a personal side of Ignatius not previously known; this revelation has led to more contemporary scholarly research.[9] Up until their publication, *The Exercises* along with hagiographies written by his colleagues, portrayed Ignatius as an active missionary. Post-publication, the contemplative side of Ignatius was re-invigorated, with many scholars concluding that Ignatius was a mystic.[10] This new knowledge of him has provided fresh insights into his character and mission-oriented life.[11]

---

6. Since the mid-twentieth century, use of *The Exercises* outside of the Jesuit Order has increased, particularly as retreats are more commonplace. Thomas H. Green, in his adaptation of *The Exercises,* opines that over the years spiritual retreats have become more moralistic and less contemplative than Ignatius originally intended. He argues that *The Exercises,* taken on their own terms, are "the means to a truly joyous and liberating encounter with a loving God." Thomas H. Green, *A Vacation with the Lord* (San Francisco: Ignatius Press, 2000), 10.

7. It remained in the archives of the Jesuit House in Rome until this time.

8. Ganss, "Introduction to the Spiritual Diary," *Ignatius of Loyola,* 230.

9. Early biographies of Ignatius were hagiographical as the authors' intents were beatification. The late publication of these more personal documents led to renewed scholarship with the intent of discovering the "real" Ignatius. Unfortunately, this research has proven inconclusive. Robert Alexsander Maryks, "Introduction: Quest for the Historical Ignatius," in *A Companion to Ignatius of Loyola: Life, Writings, Spirituality, Influence,* ed. Robert Alexsander Maryks (Leiden: Brill, 2014), 2.

10. Edward Howells notes how Henri Bremond, a Jesuit and author of the great *Literary History of Religious Thought in France,* considered Ignatius a non-mystical figure concerned with action rather than contemplation until he read *The Autobiography* and *The Spiritual Diary* in the 1920s. After this, he declared Ignatius a great mystic. "Spanish Mysticism and Religious Renewal: Ignatius of Loyola, Teresa of Avila, and John of the Cross," in *The Wiley-Blackwell Companion to Christian Mysticism,* ed. Julie A. Lamm (Malden: Blackwell, 2013), 425.

11. More recent scholars Harvey D. Egan and Janet K. Ruffing both consider Ignatius a mystic. Egan states that Ignatius's decisive influence in the world and church history flows from his mystical love of God and neighbour. Harvey D. Egan, *Ignatius Loyola the Mystic: The Way of the Christian Mystics* (Collegeville: Liturgical Press, 1987), 19. Ruffing argues that Bernard McGinn's recent definition of mysticism within Christianity "best fits Ignatius case." Janet K. Ruffing, "Ignatian Mysticism of Service" in *Mysticism and Social Transformation,* ed. Janet K. Ruffing (Syracuse: Syracuse University Press, 2001), 109. McGinn's definition of

Several scholars challenge *The Autobiography*'s authenticity because it was not written directly by Ignatius. In the preface to the original work, Luis Concalves de Camara, the Minister of the Jesuit House in Rome advised that he penned *The Autobiography* from the dictated word of Ignatius. However, he confessed that he did not write the words down verbatim; instead, he listened attentively and then immediately after the session wrote down the main points of what Ignatius had said. Later he wrote down an extended version which forms the present text and dictated them to a secretary for verbatim transcription. Scholars therefore suggest that Camara had opportunity to alter Ignatius's words or meaning. In defence of *The Autobiography*, Ganss considers it a highly reliable historical source noting that most of what is stated is corroborated by other documents. Also, copies of finished portions of this work were circulating in 1554 before Ignatius's death, so it is reasonable to assume that Ignatius saw them and had no difficulty with them. I am adopting Ganss's view in this book; I assume that all of Ignatius's writings are valid historical sources.[12] *The Autobiography* is the last document that Ignatius wrote. From my perspective, it provides valuable details and personal reflections on events that Ignatius considered significant in his life.

Ignatius's Context, Conversion, and a Brief Overview of his Life
Context

Ignatius was born in 1491 in the Basque region of northern Spain to the wealthy noble family of Loyola. The political, cultural and social aspects of Spain in fifteenth and sixteenth century Europe all impacted Ignatius's life.

At that time, Spain was a young nation – it had unified in 1496 when King Ferdinand II of Aragon married Queen Isabella of Castille. It was also a Roman Catholic country in which the Pope's influence had significant political and religious sway; the Pope's wishes were often implemented by the king and queen. Despite its youth Spain was becoming one of the most important and wealthy countries in the world having just begun its colonial expansion. The Spanish king had provided patronage to the Italian, Christopher Columbus,

---

Christian mysticism is: "that part of its belief and practices, that concerns the preparation for, the consciousness of, and the reaction to what can be described as the immediate or direct presence of God." *The Foundations of Christian Mysticism*, Vol. 1 of *The Presence of God: A History of Western Mysticism* (New York: Crossroad, 1991), xvii.

12. Ganss, "Introduction," 67.

who was soon to discover the Americas; Spain was to subsequently occupy areas in Latin America and the Indies.

The nobility was a significant class in the Spanish social structure; with the flourishing Spanish Renaissance nobles were trained not only in the arts of battle but also chivalry. Pilgrimage to Jerusalem was a popular cultural practice in late Medieval times, particularly among the nobility as it was in keeping with their understanding of chivalry and the ideology of the crusading knight. By making the dangerous and long journey, Roman Catholics believed that it aided their Christian salvation, and the church endorsed this belief by granting various indulgences to those who made the tour.[13] Many nobles became Jerusalem pilgrims so that they could embark on such adventures, in order to shape their virtuous life with bravery, honour, and protection of the weak.[14] Further, Franciscan monks (who inhabited the monastery at Mount Zion and were permitted to lead pilgrimages) knighted those nobles who promised to defend the Christian faith on the Holy Sepulchre. Thus, pilgrimage to the Holy Land enabled nobles to become knights, add titles to their personages, and obtain indulgences. Upon returning home, these knights and pilgrims were held in high esteem, gaining much societally from such endeavours.

In the early sixteenth century, the Protestant reformation was in its infancy; therefore, in most cases, becoming a Christian was synonymous with becoming a Roman Catholic. Spain resolved to keep itself as a Roman Catholic nation and, in the late fifteenth and early sixteenth centuries, expelled Jews and Muslims. The church also inaugurated the Inquisition in 1478; this institution was to prosecute *conversos*, Jews who had converted to Christianity but had lapsed into practising Jewish rituals. Such persons, if discovered, were forced to revert to solely Christian practice or face being handed over to secular authorities. If found guilty by the latter, they were burned at the stake. After the excommunication of Martin Luther from the Roman Catholic Church in 1521, the role of the Inquisition was expanded to include supporters of Martin Luther; all Lutheran writings, teachings or anything that supported ideas deemed unfaithful to the church were destroyed.

---

13. Bart Holterman, *Pilgrimages in Images: Early Sixteenth-Century Views of the Holy Land with Pilgrims' Portraits as Part of the Commemoration of the Jerusalem Pilgrimage in Germany* (master's thesis, Utrecht University, 2013), 14, info:eu-repo/semantics/open access.

14. The Ottoman Turks ruled the Holy Lands from 1517. The previous rulers were the Mamluks, Muslim slave warriors, who had ruled the area for the previous 300 years. While the Turks had gained control, the Mamluks were continuing to challenge by way of combat, consequently the area was difficult to traverse. Adam Zeiden, "Mamluk," in *Encyclopædia Britannica* (Encyclopædia Britannica Inc., 2020), https://www.Britannica.com/topic/Mamluk.

Conversion

At around the age of fifteen, Ignatius, as a young noble, was sent to the home of Juan Velazques de Cuellar, the High Treasurer of King Ferdinand and Queen Isabella, to learn the life of a courtier. Here he was exposed to novels of romantic chivalry, secular and religious songs, and loose as well as moral living. Thus, the young Ignatius gained an interest in fine clothing, personal appearance, and romantic chivalrous notions.[15] *The Autobiography* describes Ignatius at that time as: "A man given to the vanities of the world; and what he enjoyed most was warlike sport, and with a great and foolish desire to win fame."[16]

In 1521, Ignatius was involved in a battle at Pamplona against the French during which he revealed his tenacious and influential character. Unfortunately, the Spanish were ill equipped and soon surrendered, but not before Ignatius's one leg was shattered and the other badly injured by a cannon ball. The French kindly returned him home, but his legs were so badly set that he had to undergo two painful surgeries to set them straight; these were followed by a long convalescence period at Loyola.[17]

During his convalescence Ignatius read two books that deeply influenced him: a book on the lives of the saints, *The Golden Legend* by the Dominican, Jacobus de Voragine, and *The Life of Christ* by the Carthusian, Ludolph of Saxony. *The Golden Legend* was written in a style similar to chivalry-type novels of the time, portraying the saints as knightly nobles serving God. The nature of the writing is generally considered the reason Ignatius was initially attracted to it. *The Autobiography* noted that Ignatius was interested in the lives of the saints but struggled with romantic thoughts of chivalry towards serving "a certain lady." Ignatius retrospectively commented that God always led him after such "worldly thought" to those of the saints and Christ, with a desire to imitate them. Over a short period, this longing grew, and *The Autobiography* noted that Ignatius began to wonder: "If I should do what St. Francis did, and what St. Dominic did?"[18] At that time, the Pope specifically sent these religious orders to convert heathens and Muslims to Christianity.[19] Ignatius

---

15. Ganss, "Introduction," 14.

16. Ignatius, *The Autobiography*, 68.

17. Ignatius, *The Autobiography*, 69–70.

18. Ignatius, *The Autobiography*, 70.

19. Eleanor Tejirian and Reeva Spector Simon, "Disintegration, Revival, Reformation, and Counter-Reformation 1450–1800," in *Conflict, Conquest, and Conversion: Two Thousand Years of Christian Missions in the Middle East* (New York: Columbia University Press, 2012), 49–50.

acknowledged in *The Autobiography* that he wanted to do the same.[20] This was the first indication of Ignatius's missional call.

Eventually, Ignatius felt compunction for his former life, desired to do penance for it, and determined to commit his life to God and, thereafter, go on pilgrimage to Jerusalem. *The Autobiography* recounts how these thoughts about following God were confirmed in Ignatius's first "spiritual experience":

> One night while he was awake he saw clearly an image of Our Lady with the Holy Child Jesus. From this sight he received for a considerable time very great consolation, and he was left with such loathing for his whole past life and especially for the things of the flesh that it seemed to him that his spirit was rid of all the images that had been painted on it. Thus from that hour until August '53 when this was written, he never gave the slightest consent to the things of the flesh. For this reason, it may be considered the work of God.[21]

This "conversionary experience" was thorough and dramatic, affecting all of Ignatius's life. He gave up his position as a noble and took on the garb of a mendicant – sackcloth, staff, and gourd – and began his pilgrimage to Jerusalem as a beggar. His family urged him not to do this; they attested to the change in him but pleaded with him not to throw his life away. However, Ignatius did not listen to them and continued with his plan to follow God.[22]

The change in identity was significant; despite his family's remonstrations, from that point onwards, Ignatius exchanged his identity as a militaristic and chivalrous noble seeking the world's fame for that of a poor pilgrim under Christ's banner within the Roman Catholic Church. Ignatius's definitive break with his former life revealed that God had impressed upon him that he needed to live differently; I consider this change symbolized his "conversion." However, from a historical theological perspective, his new commitment was neither considered "conversion" nor "salvation." For him, as a Roman Catholic, salvation was a path entered into upon baptism. However, Ignatius's protracted description of his determination to "follow God" in a more all-encompassing manner reveals that, despite the theological position of the church at that time,

---

20. Ignatius, *The Autobiography*, 70.

21. Ignatius, *The Autobiography*, 71. For clarification, the year mentioned in the quote is 1553.

22. Ignatius, *The Autobiography*, 72–73.

Ignatius knew that the process he underwent and his subsequent meeting with God was a life-altering event in terms of his Christian faith.[23]

Ignatius's Life: Experience at Manresa

After Ignatius's "conversion," he left his home and travelled to the Dominican monastery in Montserrat. Here, he made confession to the presiding priest for his past life and then moved to a cave near Manresa where he lived for about a year as an eremitic. *The Autobiography* notes this time in the cave was significant as during it, Ignatius received "visions" and "experiences" from God who "treated him at this time just as a school master treats a child whom he is teaching."[24] Four visions relating to the Trinity, creation, Jesus in the Holy Sacrament, and Jesus in his humanity are recounted[25] followed by a comment that: "[I]f there were no Scriptures to teach us these matters of faith, he would be resolved to die for them, solely because of what he had seen."[26]

The Autobiography also records a further period of contemplation that occurred at the same time as Ignatius was resident in the cave, but took place by the river close to Manresa: "The eyes of his understanding began to be opened; not that he saw any vision, but he understood and learned many things, both spiritual matters and matters of faith and scholarship, and with so great an enlightenment that everything seemed new to him."[27] The scribe, Camara, interjected in the script at this point, noting that the outcome was so significant that Ignatius "felt like another man with another man's mind."[28] Ignatius questioned why he received such knowledge in that manner. Was it because of a lack of education, intelligence or teacher? He came to no conclusion but realized that, as much as he was challenged by this means of

---

23. Despite the rise in prominence of the Protestant Reformation, Ignatius remained faithful to Roman Catholicism throughout his life. While Ignatius was aware of the Church's weaknesses, he worked for change from within. J. Carlos Coupeau argues that nineteenth-century historians who pictured Ignatius as a Roman Catholic reformer leading a charge against Luther cannot be substantiated by Ignatius's texts or those of his companions. "Five Personae of Ignatius of Loyola," in *The Cambridge Companion to the Jesuits*, ed. Thomas Worcester (Cambridge: Cambridge University, 2008), 39–44.

24. Ignatius, *The Autobiography*, 79.

25. Ignatius, *The Autobiography*, 79–80.

26. Ignatius, *The Autobiography*, 80. It is interesting to note that, in this comment, the importance of Scripture is upheld but it also reveals that God could reveal the same knowledge in a different manner.

27. Ignatius, *The Autobiography*, 81.

28. Ignatius, *The Autobiography*, 81.

learning, it was God's way of dealing with him.[29] There are not any specifics recorded about what Ignatius learned at Manresa; however, it was during this time that he began to write *The Exercises*, and whatever Ignatius taught as a result of these experiences and lessons was upheld as in keeping with Roman Catholic doctrine when challenged by the Spanish Inquisition.

In *The Autobiography*, Ignatius was transparent about these "visions" and "consolations"; they were present from the beginning to the end of his Christian life. He recounted them as events that particularly occurred during times of contemplative prayer and taking Mass, that is, within the context of his Christian practice. I will comment further on these experiences when I discuss Ignatius's intimate relationship with God in relation to his missional activity.

Ignatius's Pilgrimage to the Holy Land

Pilgrimage to the Holy Land was the first thing that Ignatius desired to do after his "commitment" to God. In so doing, he was seeking to literally follow Christ by walking in his footsteps through Jerusalem. It was also the beginning of what he considered his missional call, as his goal was to remain there to persuade Muslims to become Christians.

As a noble, Ignatius would have understood the importance of pilgrimage; however, as a Christian, he embarked upon it in a very different way. It was not a journey of seeking honour but rather one of worshipping God through following in the footsteps of Christ, as a beggar, without money or food, entirely dependent on God and God's will. *The Autobiography* noted that: "He had a great assurance in his soul that God would provide a way for him to go to Jerusalem."[30] While not permitted to stay in the Holy Land by the Franciscans due to safety concerns (which Ignatius accepted as God's will), he made the pilgrimage and returned to Barcelona safely.[31] The entire journey took about a year. For me, the nature in which Ignatius undertook the journey is the first example of how Ignatius's commitment to God was significantly transforming his way of life.

---

29. Ignatius, *The Autobiography*, 79.
30. Ignatius, *The Autobiography*, 85.
31. Ignatius, *The Autobiography*, 88.

Ignatius's Education

Upon his return to Spain, for the next ten years, Ignatius undertook academic education in order to become an ordained priest. He learned Latin with children, attended three universities (Alcala, Salamanda, and Paris), took classes in liberal arts as well as theology, and also encouraged others to use all means to learn. Therefore, Ignatius had an interest in many methods of education, and this included academic learning for lay and theologian alike.[32]

During this time in Spain, he also taught about God and gave spiritual direction to others via *The Exercises*. Ignatius and his teachings came under the scrutiny of the Spanish Inquisition several times. While attending the university in Alcala, various individuals accused Ignatius of being an *alumbrado* because of his mystical visions and experiences (*alumbrados* were persons who designated themselves as "illuminated").[33] While Ignatius knew members of this group, he resolutely denied he was one himself. The Inquisition found in his favour. On each occasion that Ignatius or *The Exercises* came under suspicion of the Inquisition, he insisted that each matter at issue was adjudicated. Neither he, his teachings, nor *The Exercises* were ever found to run counter to the theology of the Roman Catholic Church, which was very important to him.

The Formation of the Order of the Society of Jesus

At the University of Paris he befriended a number of like-minded individuals who were ordained with him in 1537. Following Ignatius's desire to go to Jerusalem as a missionary to Muslims, Ignatius and his friends agreed to go as a group on pilgrimage to the Holy Land. However, this longing of Ignatius was once again unrealized because of continued conflict in the area. Consequently, they all travelled to Rome and, after a time of prayer and discernment, sought to form the religious Order of the Society of Jesus (the Jesuits). The Pope consented to this in 1540.

While Ignatius's initial desires about serving God as an overseas missionary to non-Catholics did not transpire personally, it was fulfilled in the formation of the Society. The Jesuits were unlike other orders in that they were entirely

---

32. Ignatius's interest in education is reflected in the work of the Jesuits. The flagship of their ministry became the establishment of colleges and universities which helped restructure and transform Christian education. Coupeau, "Five Personae," 38.

33. *Alumbrados* were persons who relinquished themselves to God's love, centred themselves in receiving spiritual visions and impulses, and were openly critical of Roman Catholic priests and certain rituals; for example, they advocated that the sacrament was unbiblical and unnecessary. Lu-Ann Homza, "The Religious Milieu of the Young Ignatius," 23–25.

missionary and were not enclosed. They likened themselves to the first apostles who followed Christ and they gave a vow of obedience to the Pope (as Christ's vicar) to go wherever he sent them to serve. The Pope instructed them to travel to many parts of the "New World" to persuade "heathens" to become Roman Catholics.

Ignatius was appointed Superior General of the Society in 1541 and spent the last fifteen years of his life predominantly in Rome, writing *The Constitutions* (rules of the Society), supervising the Order, and "helping souls" through giving his *Exercises* and other spiritual direction, and serving those in need.

Ignatius's Missional Calling and Service in Rome

David Bosch notes that Ignatius was the first person to use "mission" in the manner that it is used today in that he used it to mean a person or group of persons sent by the Pope (the vicar of Christ) to persuade persons to become Christians.[34] From early in his conversionary experience, Ignatius felt drawn to a missionary lifestyle. Throughout *The Autobiography* Ignatius describes this call from God as a desire to "help souls."[35] Ganss points out that Ignatius did not use the word "soul" with a neo-platonic understanding where the "soul" is divided from the "body"; rather, "soul" in *The Autobiography* represents the whole person.[36] So, Ignatius described his vocation as one to help persons as whole beings.

The predominant way that Ignatius did this was in guiding persons to follow and serve Jesus in their own lives, or as he described it, as resolving "to live the pilgrim's way."[37] As most Spaniards and Italians baptized into the Roman Catholic faith already considered themselves "Christian," Ignatius's "help" was not technically "mission" as he defined it, that is, he was not helping the non-Catholic person become a Catholic. Instead, his call was commensurate with a broader perspective of mission in that he was seeking to transform baptized

---

34. Bosch, *Transforming Mission*, 228. Just prior to the age of Ignatius, this "persuasion" was often done by violence, for example, via the crusades. However, this "compelled by force" approach turned to a more "prevailed upon" style of mission. During Ignatius's time the Pope used monks rather than armies, and they used sermons rather than swords to missionize. However, the concept of crusading was still part of the culture and the Inquisition's persuasion still used violent means.

35. Ignatius, *The Autobiography*, 87, 89, 99.

36. Ganss, *Ignatius of Loyola*, 392n16.

37. Ignatius, *The Autobiography*, 107. See also Holterman, *Pilgrimages in Images*, 14, and Olin, "The Idea of Pilgrimage," 369.

persons into committed followers.[38] In contemporary language, he was called to the task of "re-evangelization."

Ignatius practised this call by speaking and teaching about God whenever the opportunity arose. He also spent much of his time giving his *Exercises* to persons; for him, these were significant tools in his service to others. Their purpose was a "means of preparing and disposing our soul to rid itself of all its disordered affections and then, after their removal, of seeking and finding God's will in the ordering of our life for the salvation of our soul."[39] In other words, Ignatius's goal for *The Exercises* was to guide persons into a right relationship with God so that they could discern God's purpose for them and follow it.

Ignatius's "helping of souls" also reflected a more integral understanding of the person. He knew that while teaching, preaching and participating in *The Exercises* were significant and helped individuals find God's calling for them, this alone was insufficient. For Ignatius, one had to help the person in all areas of their life, and this meant engagement in personal and societal matters.

The Autobiography records that Ignatius helped the poor, giving away to them anything he received that was superfluous to his needs.[40] While residing in his home area in 1535, he successfully advocated for changes in various laws to: help abused women, obtain regular and official help for the poor, ban gambling, and have the bells rung at the times of the Angelus so all were called to pray.[41]

Later, in Rome, when Ignatius became Superior General of the Jesuits, he established an orphanage. In 1541, the Pope extended the work remit of the Jesuits so that they could also house and help beggars. Ignatius also worked with the prostitutes of Rome. He helped establish houses for them for their protection and education. The first house, Mary Magdalene, became a community of nuns; the second house, Saint Martha's, was a refuge for those who wanted to reform their lives and re-enter society; and the third house was established for girls who might otherwise enter the profession.

---

38. Roman Catholic theology of the period intermixed salvation and ecclesiastical theology so that in the eyes of the Church one became a Christian through infant baptism. This understanding remained the basis of Roman Catholic theology and mission until the Second Vatican Council in the twentieth century.

39. Ignatius, *The Exercises*, 121.

40. For example, Ignatius recorded that after he left home for Montserrat, he collected a debt and gave all of it away to various persons and the remainder to repair a statue of the Virgin Mary. When he changed his clothes to those of a mendicant, he gave his good clothing to a beggar. On pilgrimage, he begged for money and food and gave away to other beggars what was beyond his immediate need. Ignatius, *The Autobiography*, 71, 75, 85.

41. Ignatius, *The Autobiography*, 106.

Ignatius also took an interest in the Jewish community. He influenced the Pope such that in 1542 Pope Paul III made a proclamation that no Jew could be disinherited on becoming a Christian. Ignatius also set up two houses, one for male catechumens and the other for female catechumens. The provision of housing enabled Jews, Turks, and Moors who might be turned out of their homes for becoming Christian to receive instruction and baptism.[42]

Ignatius's work was not restricted to the poor and marginalized within society. He also influenced those within other walks of life, including providing spiritual help through his *Exercises* to those who were educated and wealthy. In this regard, his *Exercises* created a flexible framework that could be readily adapted to people's circumstances. His correspondence to kings, queens, bishops, Jesuits, lay persons, and clerics also reveal his varied concerns in his later years. Many of these powerful and wealthy persons touched by Ignatius's ministries supported the Jesuits financially and otherwise.[43]

This broad view of mission enabled Ignatius to serve all kinds of persons, from the noble, rich, and wealthy to the beggar, orphan, prostitute and outlawed Jew. His concern was that all persons commit themselves to the pilgrim life of following Jesus and that no social impediment prevented this. He also imbued the Jesuits with his understanding of mission and re-evangelization. In the Order's *Constitutions*, Ignatius wrote:

> The end of this Society is to devote itself with God's grace not only to the salvation and perfection of the member's own souls, but also with that same grace to labour strenuously in giving aid toward the salvation and perfection of the souls of their neighbours.[44]

In other words, the goal of the Jesuits was to love their neighbour on the path of salvation in the same way that they cared for themselves. Wherever the Jesuits were sent by the Pope, they continued their ministries with beggars, orphans, outcasts, and abused women.

The creation of the Jesuit religious order also aided the revitalization of the Roman Catholic Church at a time when it was being challenged by Lutheranism.[45] At the time of Ignatius's death in 1514, Jesuit houses were

---

42. Philip Caraman, *Ignatius of Loyola: A Biography of the Founder of the Jesuits* (New York: Harper & Row, 1990), 129–34.

43. Coupeau, "Five Personae," 37–39.

44. Ignatius, *Constitutions of the Society of Jesus*, 284.

45. Janet Ruffing considers that the creation of the Jesuit community was a social transformative work within the schema of the Roman Catholic Church. Ruffing, "Ignatian Mysticism of Service," in Ruffing, *Mysticism and Social Transformation*, 106–109.

located throughout Europe and in many parts of the New World; Jesuits numbered just over one thousand members, attesting to the efficaciousness of *The Exercises* and their "other means" of reaching the neighbour.

Ignatius's mission from God was simply to "help persons." For Ignatius, there was no division between a person's body and soul, so his missional ministry focused on doing everything necessary to enable persons to live intimately with God and serve God in accordance with God's will. This meant Ignatius removed any barriers, social or otherwise, that prevented them from living this life, and helped them to connect and communicate with God through participation in *The Exercises*. Ignatius's missional ministry towards others was clearly wholistic. My focus now turns to look at Ignatius's relationship with God to understand how he was driven and sustained in his personal mission.

Ignatius's Spiritual Theological Foundations

Ignatius's approach to the Christian life naturally stressed following Christ, but beyond that it was Trinitarian on the one hand, and experiential on the other. He understood God as a self-revealing loving God who engages Christian followers.

Trinitarian

God as Trinity is a significant theme throughout Ignatius's texts. This is evident in his vision at Manresa, recorded in *The Autobiography*, where he clearly saw God as Father, Son and Holy Spirit;[46] in his meditation on the Three and how they proceed from one another and how each is in the other; and, in his description of this in his *Spiritual Diary*:[47]

> I was knowing, or experiencing, or contemplating – the Lord knows –that to speak to the Father was to recognize that he was one Person of that Holy Trinity. This brought me to love that Person's whole self; and that all the more because the other two Persons were by their very essence were present in that One.[48]

Ignatius understood that God was three persons and that he could address any person in prayer or receive a consolation from any one of them, while

46. Ignatius, *The Autobiography*, 79–80.
47. Ignatius, *The Spiritual Diary*, 246.
48. Ignatius, *The Spiritual Diary*, 247.

simultaneously each person of the Trinity included the other persons. This understanding is apparent in *The Exercises*, where all persons of the Trinity are addressed and at the end of every contemplative session, a colloquy to one or all the members of the Trinity is made. Harvey Egan opines that this revelation to Ignatius of the mutual indwelling of the Trinity is in keeping with the patristic understanding of the Triune God, which is termed *perichoresis*. This understanding of the Trinity highlights God's "participative" nature within its persons. While Ignatius does not use the term, in my view this insight is helpful in the forming of an integrated mission that echoes the participative nature of God.[49]

On Following Christ

In *The Exercises*, Ignatius portrayed Christ's call to follow him as one of a king asking for participants in his mission:

> My will is to conquer the whole world and all my enemies, and thus to enter into the glory of my Father. Therefore, whoever wishes to come with me must labor with me, so that through following me in the pain he or she may follow me also in the glory.[50]

This "Meditation on Two Standards" describes in metaphorical language familiar to Ignatius's era that Jesus wanted followers to commit themselves to him and follow his lead as an army under his banner. Throughout Ignatius's spiritual theology, mission is intrinsic to God; God initiates it and reveals the ways God wants it carried out. For Ignatius, God's mission was inherent within Jesus' life, death, and resurrection.

A dominant motif of the Ignatian Christian life is following and imitating Jesus. As a pilgrim in the world, Ignatius exhorted a Christian to follow in the footsteps of Jesus in the same manner as Jesus walked. The life, death and resurrection of Jesus is the focus of the meditations in *The Exercises*. In addition to the meditations, Ignatius also encouraged the exercitants to read the Gospels, Ludolph's *The Life of Christ*, and Thomas à Kempis's *The Imitation of Christ*.[51] As

---

49. Egan, *Ignatius of Loyola*, 71.

50. Ignatius, *The Exercises*, 147.

51. Ignatius, *The Exercises*, 148. Ludolph's *Life of Christ* was also pivotal in Ignatius's commitment to Christ. See Ignatius, *The Autobiography*, 70. Ganss, in his "Introduction," *Ignatius of Loyola*, 15–26, considers the contents of *The Life of Christ* and how it influenced Ignatius's thought. Lu-Ann Homza also notes how *The Life of Christ* merged the four gospels into one chronological life of Jesus and that it corresponded to the biblical text, in a manner similar to *The Exercises*. It also included quotations from the early Latin Fathers. She also highlights popular

exercitants became satiated in Jesus, Ignatius invited those who chose to follow God to pray that they might "imitate" Jesus.[52] Again, when teaching about the virtue of humility, Ignatius noted that there is a progression from obedience to God, to indifference to a manner of living, to that of "imitating Christ" in the manner in which he lived. For Ignatius, a committed follower of Jesus will ask for grace from God to live as Jesus did. Thus, in speaking to probationary Jesuits, Ignatius stated: "For he [Jesus] gave us an example that in all things possible to us we might seek, through the aid of his grace, to imitate and follow him, since he is the way which leads people to life."[53] This christological foundation is fundamental to all of Ignatius's missional spirituality.

Intimacy with God and Christian Service

Ignatius's spiritual theology underscored that Christian service is the fruit of an intimate loving relationship with God. In *The Exercises*, one of the later specified contemplations is "one to attain love" (of God). Ignatius noted that:

> Love consists in a mutual communication between the two persons. That is the one that loves gives and communicates to the beloved what he or she has, or a part of what one has or can have; and the beloved in return does the same to the lover.[54]

In other words, God's love for a human and a person's love for God are expressed in a relationship of communication and mutual sharing; it is an intimate relationship. In Ignatius's teaching, following Jesus is not a mental assent to doctrines made about God but rather a conscious relationship of love that develops and grows, enabling a Christian to know God's will. Moreover, for Ignatius, such love "ought to manifest itself more by deeds than by words."[55] So for him, a Christian expresses their love for God through Christian service.[56]

---

spiritual, mystical, and Christian literature of the time published by Cardinal Francisco Jimenez de Cisneros, and comments that these were available to Ignatius to read. Lu-Ann Homza, "The Religious Milieu of the Young Ignatius," 17–19.

52. Ignatius, *The Exercises*, 147.

53. Ignatius, *The Constitutions*, 286.

54. Ignatius, *The Exercises*, 176–177.

55. Ignatius, *The Exercises*, 176.

56. Roman Catholic theologians who promote Ignatian mysticism argue that his mystical revelations are not the usual form of mysticism, that is, its goal is more than "union" with God; rather, Ignatian mysticism is a "service" mysticism, that is, union leads to service. Joseph de Guibert states that the infused gifts affect "both the spiritual and bodily faculties, thereby including such powers as the memory and imagination which serve for execution. Thus, these

The Spiritual *Exercises*

Ignatius used his *Exercises* in his call to "help souls" progress in a relationship with God and find their role in God's service. *The Exercises* achieve their aim by means of structured prayer and meditation, setting the exercitant on a four-week retreat from the world to embark on a reasoned, sensory, and imaginative journey through self-knowledge and the life of Christ. This is not a solitary exercise; Ignatius created it as a relational pilgrimage both with the spiritual director and, most importantly, with God as Trinity:

> It is more appropriate and far better that the Creator and Lord himself should communicate himself to the devout soul, embracing it with love, inciting it to praise of himself, and disposing it for the way which will most enable the soul to serve him in the future . . . to allow the Creator to deal immediately with the creature and the creature with its Creator and Lord.[57]

The four weeks are divided into different areas of focus: the first is sin, including one's own, and learning to examine one's conscience; the second is Christ's birth and life; the third is Christ's passion; and the last week, Christ's resurrection. Each day is divided into five times of prayer and meditation, each to take at least an hour. There is usually one meditation for each day, and these are specific, based on the biblical stories of Christ's life. Therefore, *The Exercises* are focused on Christ.

What is interesting about these meditations is Ignatius's methodology. Ignatius instructed exercitants to enter the meditation as though they are present in the story, they are to actively engage their minds and senses: seeing, listening, smelling, tasting, and touching. They are directed to the place or the road (if a journey is undertaken) in the scene; for example, when meditating on the Nativity, the exercitant is directed to imagine the road to Bethlehem, "consider its length and breadth, whether it is level, or winds through valleys and hills."[58] In this way, they are guided to enter the story of Christ's life, not just read it. Exercitants are to imaginatively "follow" Jesus within the text and, thereby, come to know God.

---

infused gifts themselves impel the mystic both toward union with God and toward service." Joseph de Guibert, *The Jesuits, Their Spiritual Doctrine and Practice: A Historical Study*, trans. William Young, (St Louis: The Institute of Jesuit Sources, 1986), 55. Harvey Egan also argues that while Ignatius attained union with the Trinity, the "distinctive characteristic of his mysticism" was its orientation towards apostolic service. *Ignatius of Loyola*, 119.

57. Ignatius, *The Exercises*, 125.

58. Ignatius, *The Exercises*, 150.

The exercitants on this meditational pilgrimage are also given prescribed prayers for each day. Some of them request God's help to understand something specified or to grant them a prescribed desire. For example, during the second week the exercitant is directed in this prayer: "I wish and desire . . . to imitate you [Jesus] in bearing all injuries and affronts, and any poverty, actual as well as spiritual, if your Most Holy Majesty desires to elect and receive me into such life and state."[59] Each session also ends with a colloquy to one or all the members of the Trinity and (sometimes) Mary, the mother of Jesus. As an example, in the first week, *The Exercises* set out the following colloquy for the exercitant: to ask Mary, Jesus, and the Father for mercy to "have an interior knowledge and abhorrence of my sin; to understand the disorder of my actions so I can detest them; knowledge of the world so that I may detest all that is worldly and vain."[60]

In this way, *The Exercises* are a structured, repetitive, lengthy, and prescribed process involving the whole person with God. They encompass the mind, senses, and emotions; attention to any movement within them is encouraged. *The Exercises* challenge exercitants to examine themselves in terms of sin, the people they are following, and the way they are living their lives. They also ask: are they praising, worshipping, and serving God in the way and manner God asks? Simultaneously, *The Exercises* teach a way of contemplating God so that such questions are posed to God and answers expected from God. During the second week, the exercitant is introduced to the idea that such a process requires a choice. This election is not whether the exercitant will serve God but, as a Christian, how and where they will serve. Like *The Exercises*, the election is a choice of both the mind and the affections; it requires a process involving rationality and emotional attentiveness. Ignatius ensures that exercitants are sensitive to all that is occurring to them during this time, so that the election is the will of God.

For Ignatius, discernment of the source of emotions and feelings, which he describes as "spiritual consolation" or "spiritual desolation," is important; for him, this is one of the ways that God communicates with persons. Ignatius describes a "spiritual consolation" as:

> When some interior motion is caused within the soul through which it becomes inflamed with love of its Creator and Lord. As a result it can love no created on the face of the earth in itself, but only in the Creator of them all.

---

59. Ignatius, *The Exercises*, 147.

60. Ignatius, *The Exercises*, 140.

Similarly, consolation is experienced when the soul sheds tears which move it to love for its Lord . . . (also) I include every increase in hope, faith, and charity, and every interior joy which calls and attracts one toward heavenly things and to the salvation of one's soul, by bringing it tranquillity and peace in its Creator and Lord.[61]

A spiritual desolation is defined as:

Everything which is the contrary of the Third Rule [spiritual consolation]; for example, darkness of soul, turmoil within it, an impulsive motion toward low and earthly things or disquiet from various agitations and temptations. These move one toward lack of faith and leave one without hope and love. One is completely listless, tepid, and unhappy, and feels separated from our Creator and Lord.[62]

In addition to consolation and desolation, Ignatius described in his *Spiritual Diary* other forms of encounter with God that he personally experienced: visions, infused tears, warmth, bright light, and devotions.[63] He also delineated other "motions" felt within. These take various forms. They can be acts of: the intellect, thoughts, lines of reasoning, or imaginings; the will, love, hate, desire, or fear; affective feelings including impulses, inclinations or urges, peace, warmth, coldness, consolation, or desolation. He noted that the source of these motions is either ourselves, God, or the devil, and *The Exercises* teach how to determine the source of a motion.[64] The goal is to understand those motions in which God is communicating with persons, so that they are able to discern God's will for themselves.[65] Overall, Ignatius understood that consolations from God will lead to greater faith, hope, and love for God.

---

61. Ignatius, *The Exercises*, 202.

62. Ignatius, *The Exercises*, 202.

63. Ganss notes that, by "devotion," Ignatius meant "an affection for God that is prompt, compliant, and warmly loving." Ignatius uses this term in connection with his ease at: finding God; showing respect for God; consolations that include union, discreet charity, and finding God in all things. *Ignatius of Loyola*, 437.

64. Ganss, "Notes on the Spiritual Exercises," *Ignatius of Loyola*, 424.

65. Harvey Egan, quoting Karl Rahner, notes how the *Spiritual Exercises* and particularly *The Rules for the Discernment of Spirits* provide for the practice of a systematic method of discerning God's will, and are the only detailed method for this purpose available to date. *Ignatius of Loyola*, 149.

Encountering the presence of God was a common experience of Ignatius's life, yet he did not disregard reason.[66] His *Deliberation on the Issue of Poverty* provides a good example of how he used *The Exercises'* election process and employed both reason and the experience of God's presence to discern God's will. *The Deliberation* is a part of the *Spiritual Diary* and speaks to a time when Ignatius was formulating *The Constitutions* and desired direction from God as to whether the Jesuits should receive money from the Sacristies they were given to supervise. Many such churches had fixed annual incomes from various sources, and the Jesuits were entitled to take monies for their needs from such resources. However, Ignatius felt that to do so was incongruent with their vow of poverty so he took the issue to God.[67]

Ignatius spent 2 February to 12 March 1544 to complete this consideration. In accordance with his methodology, he made a list of the advantages and disadvantages of the fixed income for the community. Based on rational thinking, he was inclined from the beginning to deny the Jesuits the income, however he continued to pursue God's affirmation on the matter. Ignatius was persistent, and even though he thought he had received assurance within himself from God that this decision was right, he refrained from making the election until he received confirmation of this view from the persons of the Trinity. Once he received this, his election not to take the income was made. Ignatius writes:

> When I was experiencing visitations or visions from the Divine Persons and the mediators, I felt complete firmness and confirmation of the matter. This perception was accompanied by a spiritual relish. It was as if tears were coming to my eyes amid much security of soul.[68]

Ignatius expected the process of election to involve mutual communication between God and the exercitant, and from his own experience, he knew that this will involve thoughts and feelings that require discernment. Therefore, for the aid of the spiritual director *The Exercises* contain a whole series of

---

66. These encounters mark Ignatius's Christian life; the only time Ignatius notes their absence is during his educational years. However, they resume after his ordination and become prevalent towards the end of his life. *The Autobiography* notes that in his later years Ignatius was able at "any hour, that he wished to find God." 111.

67. Ignatius, *The Deliberation on Poverty*, 225–28. *The Spiritual Diary* is Ignatius's record of his prayer life with God during this elective process. Ignatius, *The Spiritual Diary*, 235–70.

68. Ignatius, *The Spiritual Diary*, 259.

rules describing "motions" that an exercitant might experience and how to determine their source.[69]

Ignatius himself had to learn to discern experiences that led him towards God as opposed to those that led him away. For him, this ability was only discovered through his life experiences. For example, early in his life, *The Autobiography* records his repetitive vision of a gem-encrusted lizard. He felt that this was from God only to find later that its source was evil and his attraction towards it ill-placed.[70] He realized therefore that experiential encounters have their challenges and help is needed in navigating, rather than ignoring, them.[71]

The Exercises lead Christians into a way of knowing, loving and communicating with God, guiding them through the following: imaginative meditation on Scriptural passages on the Trinity and creation, and the life, death and resurrection of Christ; prayer; and a focus on inner motions and responses to a place of discerning God's voice and God's will for that person in their life. For Ignatius, a way of expressing one's love for God is serving God, and in the context of his life with the Jesuits, this meant missional service.

Concluding Remarks

After his "conversion" to a committed "following" of Jesus, Ignatius's life was mission oriented, both in the way the term is used today and in what is called re-evangelization. This mission was integrated in that it involved all activities that helped persons on their respective journeys with God. Fundamental to living such a life was Ignatius's loving relationship with the Triune God. Ignatius helped persons to discover this intimate life for themselves, so that they might know God and live out God's purposes for them.

---

69. Simon Chan notes that Ignatius's rules on discernment are considered one of the classic documents on the subject. Chan, *Spiritual Theology*, 204.

70. Ignatius, *The Autobiography*, 81.

71. Karl Rahner, a Jesuit himself, considered that Ignatius's spirituality affirmed that Christians could receive an "immediate and direct experience of God" and that this was available to all Christians, not just the "religious." *Ignatius Speaks*, trans. Annemarie S. Kidder, (Bend: Augustine Press, 2013). In *Karl Rahner and Ignatian Spirituality* (Oxford: Oxford University Press, 2001), chapters 2 and 3, Philip Endean links these thoughts of Rahner to Rahner's early work on Gregory of Nyssa, Evagrius, and Bonaventure. He also correlates Rahner's understanding of the experience of God in Ignatius to Rahner's theology on the experience of the reality of grace. For Rahner, the issue is not whether such experiences occur but how the Church discerns the source of these phenomena. In *Visions and Prophecies*, trans. Charles Henkey and Richard Strahan (Freiburg: Herder, 1963), Rahner argues that genuine visions and prophecies from God must be allowed but sets out criteria against which the source of such can be determined.

In his more personal texts, Ignatius's own loving and experiential relationship with God is revealed as one of visions and other mystical encounters. While receiving much from God through such experiences, he affirmed that this was God's choosing; it was God's way of communicating with him. This does not mean that he disregarded other forms of learning about God via reading Scripture and theological education; in fact, he emphasized them. However, he viewed these intimate encounters as another way of "knowing" and being in relationship with God. He chose to accept them and found a path of wisdom and discernment in order to understand God's way and follow it. He did this within a methodical practice of the Christian life: choosing poverty and dependency on God; practising prayer, Bible reading, and the sacraments; undertaking this life with friends who became the Jesuit Order; and remaining within and committed to the Roman Catholic Church.

His foundation was the Triune God, referring often to the Person and work of Christ, with whom he sought a loving relationship of mutual sharing, a relationship in which God communicated his will to Christian followers. It was this way of life that enabled God to use Ignatius to live missionally, reviving the Roman Catholic Church by helping beggars, orphans, prostitutes, and wealthy personages of his time to find Christ and discover a way of following Jesus.

Roman Catholic scholars have determined that Ignatius was "a mystic." Many Protestant evangelicals have difficulty with this term as it lends itself to "experiential" ways of knowing that are unquantifiable and open to misuse. However, the Pentecostal evangelical spiritual theologian, Simon Chan, affirms that God may use "urges, impulses and feelings" within Christians to lead and guide them. Therefore, he also argues that the role of discernment in the Christian life is important.[72] In particular, he considers Ignatius's rules on discernment are helpful along with practical wisdom and the counsel of others. Chan argues that "knowing God's will . . . is not just a matter of grasping a piece of information. It has to do with our whole attitude towards God and ourselves, with an ongoing relationship with God and loving him."[73]

For Ignatius, knowing God's will required both more rational and experiential ways, with the former often leading to the latter; traditional Christian practices often lead to an experiential encounter with God.

Further, Ignatius understood that finding God's will cannot be done alone. While recent scholars argue that Ignatius's ways champion the modern

---

72. Chan, *Spiritual Theology*, 200.
73. Chan, *Spiritual Theology*, 201.

individualistic Christian way,[74] I suggest that such arguments go too far. One cannot take Ignatius out of his context: *The Exercises'* purpose was ultimately to determine who God was calling into the Society of Jesus, that is, they were a call to community, whether ordinary practice within church life or within the Jesuits. In other words, *The Spiritual Exercises* were not aimed at the individual Christian per se, rather their goal was the building of community. Ignatius himself understood the Christian life as one lived with and for others.

In terms of this book, how can pilgrim Ignatius speak to Lausanne missioners today? I suggest that Ignatius underscored what Lausanne's members know but do not engage adequately, that Christian mission or service cannot be separated from one's life with Christ. It is God's mission and Christians must seek to know their role within it from attending to the Trinity; there must be a sense of wholeness between one's life with God and what one does. Lausanne in *The Commitment* identifies its tendency towards dualism in its approach towards God and the world. I suggest that ensuring Lausanne overcomes this dualism requires it (like Ignatius) to underscore the centrality of a relationship with the Triune God for mission by placing methods and practices within its guidelines for the discernment of God's will in the world.

For Ignatius, the priority was seeking an intimate life with God as he knew this led to following Jesus in a life of service and in community. Furthermore, Ignatius highlighted the Trinitarian nature of this life with God. As I have mentioned, Ignatius's description of the participative nature of the Trinity echoed the perichoretic understanding of the church fathers. I consider this is important in seeking to join an understanding of the practical *missio Dei* with the spiritual participative role of the missioner with the Trinity. While Ignatius did not give an example of how this participative nature works in the practice of mission, he did reveal that a participative understanding in spiritual practices enabled him to perceive God in the world. Therefore, I submit that Ignatius's way proffers to Lausanne an early example of how spiritual practices can benefit missioners: in their intimate relationship with God, finding God's will for them in a context, and an overall understanding of the nature of participation with the Trinity.

---

74. Moshe Sluhovsky in "Loyola's Spiritual Exercises and the Modern Self" argues that Karl Rahner's failure to interpret the traditional and non-individualistic aspects of *The Exercises* is too one dimensional and simplistic. *A Companion to Ignatius of Loyola: Life, Writings, Spirituality, Influence* (Leiden: Brill, 2014), 219.

6

Third Movement – Contemporary Theology Part 1

Orlando Costas's Radical Evangelical Missiology

The third movement of this book's method explores contemporary missiology and mission spirituality. In particular, I am bringing to the fore two voices from the majority Christian world who were bold enough to respond to their contexts in what I consider to be fruitful ways. Their writings span 1970s–early 1990s and both wrote for or from Latin America. This chapter focuses on the writings of the missiologist, Orlando Costas, who identified himself as a Hispanic, radical, evangelical Christian interested in the area of integral mission.[1] In his writings, he sought to form a contextual evangelical missiology that promotes missional practice for evangelical Latin American Christians residing in either Latin America or the United States.

As in the historical movement, I intend to explore the nature of Costas's writings to consider to what extent his texts espoused integrated mission and is therefore helpful to Lausanne now. I will argue that Costas's missiology, grounded in biblical interpretation and kingdom of God theology, supports an integral, contextual, and prophetic missional practice that incorporates evangelism and social responsibility equally. Furthermore, in terms of this book, Costas's approach is particularly relevant as his missiology was also founded in the spiritual concept of "following Jesus" to the periphery of society. Moreover, as his thought progressed, he began to incorporate spirituality into

---

1. See my reference to the use of "integral mission" by radical evangelicals in chapter 1, page 9.

his missiology. In his last published work, *Liberating News*, this was clearly evident as he linked spiritual practices with missional activity. From my perspective, Costas as an evangelical was amenable to change based on what he deemed appropriate biblical interpretation; he exemplified the small but growing number of evangelical theologians who are catching the importance of the Spirit for a missional life.

An Overview of Costas's Life and Contextual Influences

Costas only lived for forty-five years yet he left a valuable legacy in terms of his missiology to the evangelical church, both in Latin America and the USA.[2] Fellow radical evangelical missiologist, Samuel Escobar, in an article speaking of Costas's life, recalled Costas writing about his three conversionary experiences and how these had shaped his life and calling. First was his decision to follow Jesus Christ; second was his awakening to his Hispanic heritage; and third was his conversion to the reality of the world. Escobar notes: "He [Costas] did not view these conversions as accomplished facts; rather he sought to grow in-depth in each one of them, incorporating his new experiences and reflections into a deeper understanding of his vocation."[3]

I assert that Costas's perspective on Christianity and mission were significantly shaped by his life journey in such a way as to make him a prophetic voice in Latin American and US evangelical missiology. Therefore, in the next section, I will attend to those events and environments that significantly influenced him.

Costas's Childhood and Early Education

Costas was born in Puerto Rico in 1942 to parents who were committed Methodists. The family moved to Bridgeport, Connecticut, in 1954 when he was twelve. During this period the family attended the Hispanic Evangelical

---

2. He was diagnosed with cancer and died very shortly thereafter in late 1987. This early death leaves his work unfinished to a certain extent. He was always progressing in his thought; one is left wondering how it would have developed.

3. Samuel Escobar, "The Legacy of Orlando Costas," *International Bulletin of Missionary Research* 25, no. 2 (April 2001): 50. Costas wrote about these three conversionary experiences in "Conversion as a Complex Experience," in *Down to Earth: Studies in Christianity and Culture*, eds. John R. W. Stott and Robert T. Coote (Grand Rapids: Eerdmans, 1980), 173–91.

Mission.[4] The congregation was interdenominational and Costas notes that this was the beginning of his long ecumenical journey.[5]

His personal conversion to follow Christ took place in New York in 1957 while attending a Billy Graham Crusade. He described what happened as follows: "That night something strange occurred in my life which I can only describe as the beginning of a long spiritual pilgrimage."[6] Following this experience, Costas's parents sent him to board at the Bob Jones Academy, a fundamentalist Protestant educational centre, to complete his high school education. During this time, Costas became a "fundamentalist and a devout anti-ecumenical Christian."[7] While he later changed from having this theological perspective, he gives credit to the Academy for his interest and passion for evangelism and preaching.[8]

From the time of his re-location to the US, Costas experienced racial bias. While at the Academy, he experienced Protestant Caucasian prejudice at its worst. In this context, Costas became aware of his Latin American heritage and realized that he was different. He notes: "Later on I concluded that I not only did not belong to that world, but that I did not want to, even if allowed."[9] This marked the beginning of a journey back to his Latin American heritage and culture.

Costas's Early Working Life as a Pastor, Missionary, and Student

During the 1960s, Costas undertook theological and pastoral training and always supported himself by ministering in local churches. His first educational experience was at Nyack Missionary College in Brooklyn where he became a student pastor at the Evangelical Free Church. Here he met his wife, Rose, also a Puerto Rican. After this training, he and his wife decided to return to Puerto Rico, and he accepted a pastorate at the Baptist Church in Yauco.

---

4. Costas considered himself a Latin American and was supportive of Puerto Rico's political quest for independence from the USA. He made it clear that Puerto Rico is not a US state, is still a colony of the USA, and its culture is Latin American. See Orlando E. Costas, "Prologue," in *Christ Outside the Gate: Mission Beyond Christendom* (Maryknoll: Orbis Books, 1982), footnotes xii–xvi.

5. Orlando E. Costas, "Ecumenical Experiences of a Hispanic Baptist," *Journal of Ecumenical Studies* 17, no. 2 (Spring 1980): 118.

6. Costas, "Conversion as a Complex Experience," 176.

7. Costas, "Ecumenical Experiences," 119.

8. Costas, "Conversion," 178–79.

9. Costas, "Conversion," 178.

Simultaneously, Costas commenced undergraduate studies in Latin American history and politics at the Inter-American University.[10] For Costas, both his studies and pastorate were important learning experiences. He commented that his university studies enabled him to rediscover his Puerto Rican identity and culture. They also made him begin to question the US political hegemony in Latin America and "to *consciously* break with its culture."[11] In Costas's pastorate, he became aware of the church as an institution with its systems of belief, traditions, values, and ways of communicating the gospel. He decided to fully enter the Baptist tradition and became an American Baptist minister.[12] Ecumenically, he also broadened his horizons not only working with other Protestant denominations, but also Roman Catholics.[13] Costas, commenting on this time, noted:

> My pastorate (in Yauco), studies and travels enabled me to develop a deep Latin American identity, which in turn influenced my spouse's own self-understanding. When we returned to the mainland . . . we were a different family. We had found our roots.[14]

Costas attended Trinity Evangelical Divinity School and, later, Garrett Theological Seminary in the US for his graduate studies. He also became the Baptist minister of an inner city Mexican American and Puerto Rican congregation on the south side of Milwaukee.[15] It was during this ministry that Costas became involved politically with the reality of his world. Not long after he started his ministry, he realized that the Latin American minority was marginalized in the neighbourhood from the programmes and social benefits available. Consequently, Costas became involved in the community and helped organize the Latin American Union for Civil Rights.[16] Of this period, he notes that his political praxis was never segregated from his Christian life and ministry. It led him to reflect theologically on what this work meant for his ministry and mission, and it exposed him to the world of the poor and disenfranchised. He comments: "It made me realize that the Christian

---

10. Costas, "Conversion," 179–80.

11. Costas, "Conversion," 180. (Emphasis is Costas's). He noted his views did not make him hostile to Americans as persons.

12. Costas, "Conversion," 180.

13. Costas, "Ecumenical Experiences," 119.

14. Costas, *Christ Outside*, xii.

15. Costas, "Conversion," 180.

16. Costas, "Conversion," 180–81.

mission had not only personal, spiritual and cultural dimensions, but also social, economic and political ones."[17]

During the seventies, Costas and his family became missionaries in Costa Rica, and Costas also undertook doctoral studies with missiologist Johannes Verkuyl, in Amsterdam. During Costas's term as a missionary with the Latin American Mission (LAM), he was involved with the evangelism in-depth team and the *Seminario Biblico Latino Americano*.[18] LAM was in a process of Latinization, involving Costas in the creation of the Community of Latin American Evangelical Ministries (CLADE).[19] Costas, with other Latin American theologians, began to explore how to further a contextual Latin American theology. As he became involved with this, he became very vocal, but he found himself frequently being misquoted in North America; this led to him writing and publishing in English as well as Spanish. Thus began his prolific academic writing career in the field of missiology.[20] Through his writing, Costas commented that he became known "within Protestant North American circles as an emerging Third World theologian (missiologist)."[21] During the early seventies, he worked at the Costa Rican seminary, became involved in the Latin American Theological Fraternity, and in 1973 helped found the Latin American Centre for Pastoral Studies (CELEP). Globally, he was engaged with the work of the Lausanne Movement and the WCC.

Costas's Role as an Educator and His Expanding Horizons

In 1980, Costas became Professor of Missions at the Eastern Baptist Theological Seminary in Pennsylvania. Until this time, he had resisted returning to the USA. However, it was also becoming clear to him that "I had an important ministry to fulfil as a minority, Hispanic missiologist. I came to realize that there was a need in the United States for the interpretation of the Christian mission from the periphery."[22] He notes: "I came back, however, not to be one more professional in the growing American 'missiological market' but, rather, to continue to do missiology from the periphery this time, the periphery of the

---

17. Costas, "Conversion," 181.
18. Costas, *Christ Outside*, xii.
19. Costas, *Christ Outside*, xii.
20. Costas, *Christ Outside*, xiii.
21. Costas, "Ecumenical Experiences," 121.
22. Costas, *Christ Outside*, xiii.

American metropolis."[23] At Eastern, he developed relationships with Hispanic communities in the area and helped develop a department of Hispanic ministries. He also designed theology courses for laypersons from minorities.[24] In 1984, Costas moved to the Andover Newton Theological Seminary in Massachusetts to take up the Adoniram Judson Chair of Missiology. He remained in this position until his death in 1987.

Costas as a Radical Evangelical

Before I turn to consider Costas's missiological view, I consider it is also important to look at Costas's identification with the Christian radical evangelical movement. Costas described himself as a radical evangelical in order to distinguish himself from traditional evangelicalism. The group, now known as "radical evangelicals," evolved as an alliance primarily in response to the Lausanne Covenant. Despite Lausanne affirming social activity in the form of social responsibility, which represented a dramatic change in evangelical thinking at the time, members of the radical evangelical group were of the opinion that it did not go far enough.

Radical evangelicalism is primarily located in the Majority World and argues for a synthesis of evangelism and social activity so that there is no distinction between them in the work of mission.[25] They use the term "integral mission" or "integral evangelization" to indicate this understanding of mission. Prominent among the Latin American radical evangelicals were Costas, C. René Padilla, and Samuel Escobar,[26] all of whom participated at Lausanne. In 1970, they established the Latin American Theological Fraternity (LTF) in Bolivia.[27] It was their context of extreme poverty and political oppression

---

23. Costas, *Christ Outside*, xiv.

24. Escobar, "The Legacy," 53.

25. There are a few radicals in the global North and global West. Ross Langmead notes among others: Jim Wallis, Donald Kraybill, Athol Gill, Dorothy Harris, Viv Grigg, Colin Marchant, and David Sheppard. For the full list see: *The Word Made Flesh: Towards an Incarnational Missiology* (Dallas: University Press of America, 2004), 94.

26. Samuel Escobar was a member of the drafting committee of the Lausanne Covenant.

27. The Fraternity was renamed the Latin American Theological Fellowship in 2006. The organization was concerned that the word "fraternity" in North American English tended to define a group of men rather than both men and women. Ruth Padilla Deborst, "Who Sets the Table for Whom? Latin (CLADE) 1969–2012: A Revision with Eyes Toward a New Celebration," *Journal of Latin American Theology* 5, no. 2 (2010): 107–24.

that led them to collaborate in re-examining their biblical and theological understandings of mission, taking such situational circumstances into account.[28]

Ruth Padilla DeBorst describes Latin America at the time of the Lausanne Congress:

> Throughout the continent, deaths for political motives added up to at least 200,000 during the 1970s, and some 100,000 people "disappeared." Unavoidable even to conservative Christians was the need to respond to the social, economic, and political concerns of a land that was bleeding to death with civil wars, dirty wars, revolutions and repressions, contras, and invasions, growing poverty, and the decreasing hope of viable solutions.[29]

For such Latin American radicals coming to the first Lausanne Congress, there was evident need to give equal emphasis to Christian work for social, economic, and political transformation as evangelism. At the Lausanne Congress, the radicals came together as an ad hoc group to advocate for their theological position. They responded to *The Covenant* by creating their own statement entitled "Theology and Implications of Radical Discipleship."[30] This document argued that the gospel was broader and more communitarian than espoused by *The Covenant*. God through the Holy Spirit had created a new humanity, leading to the formation of a community that was to exhibit God's shalom to the world. For them, there was no dichotomy between God's spoken word and the word made visible in the lives of Christians. Therefore, God's people were called to proclaim the gospel, embody it in their lives as a new society, reveal it in their sacrificial service to others through their prophetic denunciation of anything that denied God's lordship, in their pursuit of God's justice, and in their care for creation.[31]

---

28. Sharon E. Heaney submits that the LTF became "the voice of evangelical theology on the continent." *Contextual Theology for Latin America*, 60.

29. Padilla Deborst, "Who Sets the Table for Whom?," 117.

30. Al Tizon, *Transformation after Lausanne*, appendix 1, 239–42. Another copy of the statement is also available in J. D. Douglas, ed., *Let the Earth Hear His Voice: International Congress on World Evangelization, Lausanne, Switzerland* (Minneapolis: World Wide Publications, 1975). The statement was presented to Lausanne by John Stott. The statement was accepted by the Congress, although it did not have the authority of *The Covenant*. However, at the time, the statement and its acceptance kept the radicals within the umbrella of Lausanne. Tizon, *Transformation after Lausanne*, 41.

31. Tizon, *Transformation after Lausanne*, 240.

After the first Congress, the radicals continued to work with Lausanne but also began to formalize themselves both organizationally and theologically.[32] Within Lausanne, many of the radicals participated in sub-committees and critiqued Lausanne when it acted aversely to their views. For example, when Lausanne, at its sub-committee on World Evangelization, affirmed evangelism as the most important work in mission, Costas, with fellow colleagues Ron Sider and Vinay Samuel, objected in the form of a Statement of Concerns. The statement argued that as well as unreached people groups, Lausanne ought also to think about unreached social, economic, and political institutions.[33] However, by 1982 and despite the radicals' efforts to remain included within Lausanne, they still felt on the fringes of international evangelicals. Thereafter, they concentrated on contextualizing theology in their own regions.[34]

Costas always aligned himself with the radicals, and his contextual theologizing is consistent with their views. Costas, in distinguishing radical evangelicalism from traditional evangelicalism underscored that the radicals were not so concerned with the Bible from a theoretical perspective; rather, their interest lay "with its content and implications for life . . . Thus radical evangelicals approach Scripture as a rule of practical faith – that is, a faith that becomes flesh, that is spiritually energizing and, therefore historically transformative."[35] It is essentially a practically focused evangelicalism.

---

32. Radical evangelicalism expanded organizationally and globally from 1970 to 1990. As well as the formation of the LTF, the African Theological Fraternity and the Asian Theological Fraternity were also created. In 1987, two more prominent radicals, Vinay Samuel and Chris Sugden (whose interests lie predominantly in Asia) established the International Fraternity of Evangelical Mission Theologians (INFEMT). This organization seeks to be a central agency for the various fraternities. It brings theologians from these various regions together at congresses and aids their theological process. INFEMT also created its own publishing house, Regnum Books; theological journal, *Transformation*; and educational institution, namely, the Oxford Centre for Mission Studies located in Oxford, England.

33. Tizon, *Transformation after Lausanne*, 47.

34. Tizon, *Transformation after Lausanne*, 49.

35. Orlando E. Costas, *Liberating New: A Theology of Contextual Evangelization* (Grand Rapids: Eerdmans Publishing, 1989), 11. Costas argued that radical evangelicalism has a long history. He submitted that it has roots in such "world formative" movements as the Wesleyan Movement in Great Britain, the early Baptist mission of William Carey in India, the Moravian missions in the eighteenth century, the anti-slavery movement in Great Britain and the USA, the early feminist and Social Gospel movements in nineteenth-century North America, and more recently, the Civil Rights movement and the Witness for Peace movement. Padilla Deborst has recently described this method of biblical interpretation as reading and being read "by the Word of God in light of our contextual realities, which ask questions of the Word and are in turn questioned by the Word. It is a coming and going between person, context, and Word, a hermeneutical flow that permits neither independent propositional abstraction nor non-reflective pragmatic action." Ruth Padilla Deborst, "From Lausanne III to CLADE V," *Journal of Latin American Theology* 6, no. 1 (January 2011): 11.

As I have highlighted above, the constant threads through Costas's life were his commitment to radical evangelicalism and mission; his renewed identity as a Hispanic; his pastoral ministry combined with his education; his ecumenical pilgrimage; and his involvement with the world, "especially the world of the forgotten and exploited."[36] I submit that these threads are all apparent in his missiology. I also consider that Costas's ability to make his context relevant to his missiology is also significant and was a product of his constant theological reflection upon his ministerial practice. This praxis influenced Costas's view of the world and how he thought God wanted Christians to interact with it. With this in mind, I will now turn to his views on this subject.

Costas's Radical Evangelical Missiology
Evangelization, Sin, Salvation, and the Kingdom

Costas defined evangelization[37] as:

> *Bearing witness* to the God who saves us from the misery of the human condition. It is an intensely personal and extensively social witness that requires immersion in a particular socio-historic context and participation in the struggles of humanity.[38]

For him, evangelization was both contextual and integral. Reflecting upon the historical religious momentum and social events in Latin America during his lifetime, he opined that an authentic spiritual awakening had taken place, one that had re-shown Protestants the social dimension of the gospel and God's concern for socio-political issues such as injustice.[39] Costas affirmed this rediscovery and sought to encompass such social activity within an understanding of evangelization. His goal was to ensure that within the practice of evangelical witness, the work for social justice was given the same emphasis as personal evangelism. Costas opined that to attempt such a goal a critical and constructive reflection upon the content of the gospel in evangelical

---

36. Costas, "Conversion," 181.

37. Note Costas's use of the term "evangelization." This term includes both social activity and evangelism. The Roman Catholics in Latin America used the same term with a similar rubric.

38. Costas, *Liberating News*, 21. (Emphasis is mine.) As the idea of evangelization as "bearing witness" runs throughout Costas's work, I consider it as the key phrase in his definition.

39. Costas, *Liberating News*, 13. He also noted that Roman Catholics who previously related to God through culture were also rediscovering the call to personal faith and a re-evangelization of the culture.

Christianity was required.[40] Therefore, Costas's writings reflected upon his biblical understandings of sin, salvation, and the kingdom of God and go on to reveal how these biblical concepts have a broader scope than those professed by the majority of evangelicals. In my view, Costas made a biblically informed and persuasive theological argument for this position on these biblical concepts in his writings.

With regard to sin, he wrote that the Bible represents it as "a destructive force that thwarts and deforms human life."[41] He considered sin to have three attributes, namely: disobedience to the lordship of God,[42] injustice and alienation,[43] and unbelief and idolatry.[44] He noted that all of these characteristics are personal actions and ones that humans choose to make. However, he argued further that sin is not only personal, but it has communal aspects.[45] It has a structural identity observable in societies and institutions that detrimentally affects people.[46] In the context of Latin America, he submitted that an example of such structural sin was the exploitative behaviour of the European invaders when they conquered the nations of South America. Such behaviour had damaging consequences for rural peasants, workers, marginalized peoples, children, women, and young people.[47] By identifying such structural sin, Costas underscored that it is not an abstract concept, but a concrete reality – one that has devastating effects.[48]

For Costas, the biblical concept of salvation is an antidote to sin. Salvation is based in the good news of the kingdom inaugurated in the life, death, and resurrection of Jesus Christ, and it reconfirms God's redemptive purpose for

40. Costas, *Liberating News*, 18.

41. Costas, *Christ Outside*, 21.

42. Costas quoted various biblical verses from both the Old and New Testaments to support this claim. He defined disobedience as "the open rejection of the Word of God." Such persons become deaf, have closed minds, and refuse to dialogue with God. Consequently, they become subject to the wrath of God. Costas, *Christ Outside*, 22.

43. Costas described injustice as hatred or repudiation of the neighbour. Costas submitted such acts not only harm others but also alienate people from others and themselves. He quoted the sin of Adam and Eve in the biblical book of Genesis to support this view. Costas, *Christ Outside*, 22–23.

44. Costas, *Christ Outside*, 22–24.

45. Costas, *Christ Outside*, 25. Costas pointed to the actions of Achan and the communal consequences of such action in chapter 7 of the book of Joshua.

46. Costas, *Christ Outside*, 26.

47. Costas, *Christ Outside*, 33–35.

48. Costas, *Christ Outside*, 21. Costas continually emphasized that sin is real, not an abstract concept. In so doing, he underscored that God is concerned with actual life issues.

the whole of the world, not just human beings.[49] Costas identified the following characteristics of salvation, with all of them being correctives to his stated characteristics of sin, namely: obedience to the kingdom of God,[50] justification and liberation from sin,[51] and reconciliation and communion.[52] As Costas's understanding of sin incorporated the concept of social and structural sin, so his interpretation of salvation also has social and structural aspects. He argued salvation cannot only have a personal dimension, it must also include the redemption of social sin; otherwise the latter would remain intact.[53] Thus he stated: "Every movement that dignifies human life, that promotes equitable economic relations, and that encourages solidarity among individuals and peoples can be said to be, therefore, a manifestation (though partial) of the saving power of the gospel."[54] For Costas, the Bible reveals God's concern for the whole world, humans as individuals, societies, structures within those societies, and things.[55] He emphasized that institutions and structural frameworks do not necessarily operate upon godly values or in God-intended ways, and so Christian social missional activity is required in these domains. Costas argued that such work is redemptive and bears witness to God.[56]

Costas indicated that scholars of his generation were in agreement that the focal content of Jesus's message, both in word and deed, was the coming

---

49. Costas, *Christ Outside*, 27,

50. Costas, *Christ Outside*, 27–29. Costas noted that to those who accept God's mercy the Holy Spirit gives such obedience as a gift.

51. Costas, *Christ Outside*, 29–30. For Costas, this is redemptive justice available because of the crucifixion and resurrection of Jesus Christ. It is granted to those who place their faith in Jesus, thus liberating them from sin and giving them freedom to pursue such justice in the world.

52. Costas, *Christ Outside*, 30–31.

53. Costas, *Christ Outside*, 26.

54. Costas, *Christ Outside*, 30. His notation of such redemption being only partial was because he held the opinion that, until God's reign is fully present eschatologically, the complete salvation of systems and societies is not possible.

55. Costas, *Christ Outside*, 163.

56. This is a good example of Costas's biblical interpretation differing from that of traditional evangelicals. John Stott, head of the Lausanne drafting committee, argued that while God intended to redeem all things in the eschaton, at this time redemption is only available to humanity: "For the salvation offered in the gospel of Christ concerns persons rather than structures." Stott had no concept of structural sin. He noted further: "Please do not misunderstand me. Material poverty, physical blindness and unjust imprisonment are all conditions that in different degrees dehumanize human beings. They should provoke our Christian concern and stimulate us to action . . . My point, however, is that deliverance from these things is not the salvation that Christ died and rose to secure for us." Stott and Wright, *Christian Mission in the Modern World*, 150, 153.

and nature of the kingdom of God.[57] Costas described this kingdom as the inbreaking of a "new order of life" inaugurated through the ministry, death and resurrection of Jesus.[58] It has both historical and eschatological dimensions. Relying on Mark 1:15 in which Jesus proclaimed that the kingdom was at hand, Costas argues that the kingdom is available to all in history, although not to its full extent, as it is also a future hope; its full presence is awaited when Jesus returns to complete his rule. Thus, this new order of life is both "now" and "not yet."[59] However, Costas underscored the historical nature of this new order and submitted that it is the context for God's mission: "To participate in the mission of God is to announce the good news of the Kingdom."[60] Again, for Costas, this new order was not an abstract concept but one that Christians should live out, empowered by the Holy Spirit, in the daily reality of their lives.

On a personal level, Costas underscored that this new order requires Christians to undergo a radical change in their values and attitudes. It requires reorienting one's relationships from self to God and others, "from an individualistic and egocentric consciousness to one communally and fraternally oriented."[61] He also emphasized that this new order affects all areas of life; it embraces history and the universe. Thus Christians, predominantly through the church, are called to be in the world to help transform its systems, structures, and institutions towards acting out of the principles of God's order, namely, love, justice, freedom, and messianic peace.[62] For Costas, this means that Christians must grow in their ability to both theologically reflect on the content of the Bible and the world in which they live. Evangelization on a social level requires sensitivity to the issues of one's day, together with appropriate recognition of those aspects of the new order that are relevant to the situation faced. At times, this broader understanding of evangelization will mean Christians will affirm and work with structures that are furthering the new order and promoting the common good. In other situations, where structural sin is present, Christians are called to "unmask and resist" those

---

57. Costas, *Liberating News*, 54. Scholars also refer to the kingdom of God as the reign of God.

58. Costas, *Christ Outside*, 90.

59. The kingdom of God is a central tenet of liberation theology. Liberation theologians are more optimistic about the extent that God's reign available now than many evangelical theologians.

60. Costas, *Christ Outside*, 91.

61. Costas, *Christ Outside*, 92. Costas identified the biblical story of Zacchaeus as a good example of this (Luke 19:8–9).

62. Costas, *Christ Outside*, 91, 92–95.

institutions that employ methods of injustice.[63] Costas then cemented his views by demonstrating how "kingdom priorities" might challenge the Americas of his era.

To do this, Costas employed socio-historical analysis.[64] He suggested that Christians should affirm life and denounce institutionalized violence. In the Americas, he suggested that Christians should defend the rights of the poor,[65] denounce methods of torture and support fair legal procedure,[66] defend human freedoms (such as the right to vote), and condemn the arms race. To do this, he opined that human solidarity is required. For Christians this means supporting endeavours that work to overcome divisions among races, genders, economic classes, etc. He included in this challenge the division among Christian groups, promoting an ecumenical stance. He called for the church to commit itself to integral evangelization and healthy church growth so that this work is accomplished.[67]

Costas's biblical understanding of sin, salvation and the new order of life that God was inaugurating through Jesus involved the whole world. It was not merely concerned with the individual person and her personal world; rather, God's attention included social structures and ways of life. Therefore, in defining evangelization, it was incumbent upon the church to give the same emphasis to the transformation of social structures and society as it did to personal evangelism. In this manner, Costas's writings underscored that evangelization is integral and liberating.[68]

---

63. Costas, *Christ Outside*, 93.

64. Costas, *Christ Outside*, 94–98.

65. Costas, *Christ Outside*, 95. Costas was critical of President Carter's US administration that gave attention to human rights in general but failed to emphasize the human rights of the poor. He also decried the US administration's pressure on the International Monetary Fund on two counts: first, in forcing Peru and Jamaica to employ excessively austere financial programmes and second, its support of a loan for the repressive government of Argentina.

66. While Costas was critical of all regimes that employ torture, he specifically indicated that the Pentagon's perpetuation of the ideology of "national security" aided such repressive policies. Costas, *Christ Outside*, 95.

67. Costas, *Christ Outside*, 96–98. By church growth, Costas was speaking of integral growth, not just numerical growth. About the latter, he was critical of the church growth movement of his era. See Costas's book, *The Integrity of Mission: The Inner Life and Outreach of the Church* (New York: Harper & Row, 1979).

68. Therefore, in my view, it makes sense that Costas's last book is entitled *Liberating News*. Costas affirmed the use of the word "liberation," noting that, in both the Old and New Testaments, a key focus of God was providing freedom out of captivity.

Evangelization as a Task of Discipleship

At the outset, I consider it important to emphasize that Costas, in his work, did not equate the task of evangelization with spirituality. He subscribed to the Christian view that segregates mission in the world from tasks such as prayer and contemplation. He did express quite clearly that a Christian's spiritual life is important for the work of mission. However, I will deal with how he linked his understanding of those elements of a Christian life to the work of evangelization later in this chapter. In this section, I will solely consider Costas's work on evangelization as a practice of discipleship.

Costas's writings opined that the Christian practice of evangelization is for all Christians, not just those who consider themselves called to the work.[69] In other words, it is inherent to Christian discipleship. He described the characteristics of authentic discipleship and faithful Christian mission as "following, participating, and obeying" Jesus.[70] For Costas, the call to *follow* is not a mere intellectual assent to Christian doctrine; rather, it is a *continual process* of Christians following Jesus themselves through an effective relationship with God and leading other persons to follow likewise.[71] Following also includes living as a servant of the kingdom and *participating* in God's mission.[72] Costas argued that it is the Holy Spirit that transforms God's people into channels of God's grace; in other words, transformation is received as a gift rather than achieved through self-discipline. He submitted that evidence of the Spirit's presence in a Christian's life is a changed lifestyle that emanates "freedom, service, justice, and peace."[73] It is this transformation that enables a Christian and a Christian community to participate in evangelization as he defined it.[74] Finally, Costas argued that discovering where a Christian and a Christian community will be effective in God's mission requires "obedience." He noted this latter term has a different meaning in the Bible than its use in modern day English. He viewed scriptural obedience as "neither blind acceptance of inflexible laws nor conformity to rigid ideology. To obey, in the

---

69. Costas was critical of mission societies and agencies. He maintained that their historical tie to Western colonialism, entrepreneurialism and capitalism deformed their effectiveness "as channels of wholeness and liberation." Costas, *Christ Outside*, 59; also see chapter 4.

70. Costas, *The Integrity of Mission*, 24.

71. Costas, *The Integrity of Mission*, 16. (Emphasis is mine.)

72. (Emphasis is mine.)

73. Costas, *The Integrity of Mission*, 10. Costas, *Liberating News*, 30.

74. Costas argued further that if such a life change is not evident in a Christian or Christian community, then that person or church is unable to evangelize others. Costas, *Liberating News*, 30.

biblical tradition, means to incline one's ear, to listen in faith, and respond by faith to God's word."[75] It is both hearing and doing.[76]

Costas indicated throughout his work that Christianity does not operate in a "vacuum"; rather, it is lived out in a socio-historical reality. Therefore, in Costas's view, for Christians to undertake contextually relevant evangelization, they must both attend to God's biblical word and understand their socio-historical contexts.[77] He affirmed that the Holy Spirit aids Christians with this contextual process of relating biblical understanding into concrete life practices.[78] He also placed responsibility on the ministers of churches to aid their congregations in this. Thus, Costas conceived discipleship as a continual process of personal transformation, focused on moving outward to proclaim the values of the kingdom after having attended to God's biblical word and the demands of one's reality.

Furthermore, Costas indicated that while evangelization is a task of discipleship, it is not primarily an individual pursuit. For him, this work is entrusted to the community of God and therefore the base for this work is the congregation.[79] However, he realized that for a congregation to understand that evangelization is their work and not that of missionaries, a mental transformation has to take place at an individual and group level.[80] Costas opined that it is the role of church ministers to "inform" the congregation of this broader view by way of teaching and preaching God's word and carrying out the necessary work to understand the social reality in which they were situated.[81] After this work is done, Costas underscored the importance of theological reflection in the process of contextualization. For him, theology was not the work of the professional per se; it is committed reflection by the community of God, relating faith to the context of their lives.[82] In this

---

75. Costas, *The Integrity of Mission*, 22.

76. It is interesting to compare his methodology of "hearing and doing" with the methodology of liberation theologians, which is "see, hear, and do." For liberation theologians, understanding one's environment or issue comes before connecting to the biblical word.

77. Costas, *The Integrity of Mission*, 24.

78. Costas, *The Integrity of Mission*, 23.

79. Costas, *Liberating News*, 133–36. Costas traced from the Old Testament through the New Testament to post-Testament times to show how evangelization is the task of the people of God in community.

80. Costas, *The Integrity of Mission*, 27.

81. Costas particularly encouraged a congregation to learn the biblical, historical, and theological facts about the life, ministry, death and resurrection of Jesus in this regard. Costas, *The Integrity of Mission*, 48–49.

82. Costas, *The Integrity of Mission*, 50.

way, a community is formed that is able to move outward to transform its neighbourhood for the kingdom of God, enabled by the Holy Spirit in a socio-historical relevant manner.[83] In this process of individual and communal change, Costas placed responsibility upon ministers to mobilize, educate and organize their congregations and underscored the authority of the Bible as the primary theological source for this change, enabled by the work of the Holy Spirit.[84]

Costas stressed that evangelization is a work of communal discipleship. In his proposed missiology, churches are transformed into communities that live out in word and deed the new order of life inaugurated in the life, death, and resurrection of Jesus. These congregations turn outward to their world to practise ways of love, justice, freedom, and peace among their neighbours, social structures, and institutions. While Costas underscored that transformational change is required in followers of Christ and congregations, he did not deal with how this change might occur other than to state it is a task of the Holy Spirit aided by the role of Christian ministers. Instead, his writings focused on connecting biblical paradigms to missiological concepts. His practical emphasis was on the socio-historical foundations of life in Latin and North America. He stated his view of the history of injustice, inequality, and poverty in these regions and suggested ways that churches might involve themselves in social transformative activity that would be more in line with God's new order. His methodology was very much a "top-down" approach. Although he wanted communities to reflect theologically together in connecting biblical understanding to daily life, I aver he placed great weight on the role of ministers in teaching, advising, and guiding Christian communities in their local methods of evangelization.

Evangelization as a Prophetic and Contextual Task

Costas's missiology emphasized that evangelization is a prophetic and contextual work. This was central to his understanding of mission.[85] He argued

---

83. Costas, *Liberating News*, 144.

84. See chapters 3 and 4 of Costas, *The Integrity of Mission*.

85. Costas did not define prophetic evangelization. He proffered biblical models to describe its nature, for example, Isaiah 40–45 where the Persian King Cyrus ends the Israelite exile. It is interesting to note that Costas highlighted that historical and political change instigated by a non-Christian can bring in kingdom values. Costas considered that God's Spirit could work in the world/history apart from the church, although he emphasized that God primarily works through the community of God's people. The evangelical, Carl Henry, criticized Costas for

that prophetic evangelization takes place when there is a proclamation of God's reign, salvation is experienced, and shalom is achieved. Costas developed his prophetic missiological methodology based on Jesus's ministry as narrated in Mark's gospel and a text in Hebrews. From his biblical understanding, inherent within Jesus's ministry was the concept of mission based in the periphery and this provides a paradigm for contextual evangelization.[86] It also affirms the biblical/theological concept of the preferential option for the poor.

Costas noted that most of Jesus's work was focused in the area called Galilee, found on the edges of the Palestinian/Jewish world. He defines such an area as "the periphery" and includes in this definition the twelve disciples and the other followers of Jesus. The first disciples represent the minority of Jews who accepted Christ; other disciples were non-Jews who chose to follow Jesus. In other words, they were outcasts and outsiders.[87]

Costas highlighted that Galilee was a multi-cultural area and that Galilean Jews tended to be a little unorthodox, were frowned upon by the "pure" Jews of the south, and Roman authorities despised them. Therefore, Galilean Jews were generally scorned and, yet, as Costas indicates, Jesus chose to identify with them. Furthermore, Costas commented on how the gospels mention Galilee as the main area of Jesus's ministry. The Gospel of Mark highlights that Galilee was the place where Jesus publicly proclaimed the kingdom of God and carried out his ministry.[88] Costas submitted that: "Galilee is the place where Jesus established his messianic credentials, built the base of his messianic community, and began to experience his messianic sufferings for the world."[89]

Costas noted that it was from Galilee that Jesus moved towards Jerusalem to confront the authorities and powers and suffer death; in other words, Jesus moved from the periphery to challenge the centres of power and not vice versa.[90]

---

this position. Henry believed that God only worked through the church, his people. Costas responded to Henry in *Christ Outside*, 40–42n10. Costas also considered that Esther is a model of prophetic practice, particularly for minorities. He indicated that, despite her rise to the centre of power as queen, Esther remembered that she was a Jew and that ultimately, she belonged to God. Costas applied this model of prophetic practice to those minorities who find themselves in centres of influence. For example, Costas challenged American Hispanics not to forget the plight of illegal aliens from Mexico, Central America, and the Caribbean; successful Black Americans to work for urban Blacks caught up in difficult situations; and White feminists to promote females of other minorities to places of significance. Costas, *Liberating News*, 42.

86. Costas, *Liberating News*, 49.

87. Costas, *Liberating News*, 50.

88. Costas, *Liberating News*, 51–55.

89. Costas, *Liberating News*, 55.

90. Costas, *Liberating News*, 55–59.

In Mark's gospel, after his resurrection Jesus returned to Galilee ahead of the disciples who followed him there, where they were reconciled with him and called to go and make disciples.[91] From Costas's theological reflection on Mark, he averred that Galilee is theologically significant and a symbol that should inform all contexts of evangelization.

Grounded in his reflection on Mark's gospel, Costas considered its implications for evangelization. Firstly, evangelization has a socio-historical base in the periphery. Costas defined base as "a fundamental association rooted in the lowest level, or most marginal spaces, of society."[92] He advocated that evangelization is best carried out from the "bottom up" by forming "faith communities among the despised and rejected" of society.[93] Secondly, the message of the kingdom is a public message for proclaiming among the multitudes. Costas argued that what qualifies people as a multitude theologically is "their social and spiritual condition – their bearing the brunt of injustice, powerlessness, oppression and poverty on this planet."[94] Thus Costas submitted that multitudes are everywhere, citing the barrios and ghettos of urban USA as examples.[95] He also indicated that the fruit of this model was observable in the Latin America of his day. He pointed to the poor and oppressed who had embraced the gospel and adopted the principles of the kingdom into their lives.[96] He stated definitively: "Evangelization can be prophetic and therefore liberating only if it has a committed witnessing base in the trenches of history."[97] Thirdly, the periphery is the base for global evangelization. He argued that the church ought to retain a global perspective and not become completely parochial in its outreach. However, wherever evangelization is undertaken, it should follow this pattern of starting with the multitudes on the periphery of society rather than centres of power.[98] In one of his last published articles, Costas, employing these concepts, suggested that Hispanic and other minority churches found on the periphery of North American society were in prime positions to be catalysts for evangelization in that nation.[99]

---

91. Costas, *Liberating News*, 59–61.

92. Costas, *Liberating News*, 61.

93. Costas, *Liberating News*, 62–63.

94. Costas, *Liberating News*, 64.

95. Costas, *Liberating News*, 64.

96. Costas, *Liberating News*, 66.

97. Costas, *Liberating News*, 66.

98. Costas, *Liberating News*, 66–70.

99. Orlando Costas, "Hispanic Theology in North America," in *Struggles for Solidarity*, eds. Lorine M. Getz and Ruy D'Costa (Minneapolis: Fortress, 1992).

Costas further supported this theory of prophetic missiology from the periphery by theologically reflecting on the locus of Jesus's crucifixion. Quoting Hebrews 13:12–13 Costas noted, "So Jesus also suffered outside the gate in order to sanctify the people through his own blood" and argued that, by dying outside the centre of Jerusalem, Jesus changed the place of salvation.[100] Up to that time in Israel, Costas informed his reader, the place of God's salvation was the temple within the city and salvation was for Israel alone. Therefore, Jews considered salvation a benefit of being God's chosen people and consequently perceived themselves as the goal of God's mission.[101] Costas stated that Jesus dying outside of Jerusalem changed this and had the following implications for God's people.

First, Jesus shifted the focus of salvation from mere benefit to service and commitment. The writer to the Hebrews commented that Jesus's death sanctified persons for ministry. The writer identified such service as sharing one's material benefits with the poor and acting for their well-being.[102] Second, the place of salvation was no longer the temple but outside on the periphery of society among the multitudes, the despised and rejected. He noted that the writer to the Hebrews called Jews to follow Jesus to the place outside the gate; Costas determined this to mean that the church is called out among the multitudes to know Jesus amid outcasts and rejects.[103] In other words, to identify with Jesus, the church is called to "encounter Christ in the world" and to suffer with others on the margins of society.[104] Costas made it clear that he did not mean by this movement, that the church should create another ecclesial compound there as a fixed place for salvation. He averred that the church is called out to the wilderness as "sojourning communities" that serve the outsiders there and, through its life, the church shares the good news of the kingdom. [105] Finally, Costas identified that the purpose of God's mission

---

100. Costas, *Christ Outside*, 189. Mission from the periphery (based upon Hebrews 13:12) was the theme of the mission session at the Melbourne WCC meeting in 1980. This was two years prior to the first publication of *Christ Outside the Gate* in 1982. See Section IV, "Power in the Context of Mission," of the "Melbourne Conference Section Reports," *International Review of Mission*, 69 no. 276–277, 431–434, https://doi.org/10.1111/j.1758-6631.1980.tb01362.x.

101. Costas, *Christ Outside*, 188, 191, 193.

102. Costas, *Christ Outside*, 189.

103. Costas, *Christ Outside*, 192.

104. Costas, *Christ Outside*, 192. I have highlighted Costas's words here because I consider that behind them is the idea in Matthew 25 that God can be encountered when a Christian serves a person in need. This is a theme that I intend to identify and discuss in a later chapter; therefore, I think quoting Costas's actual words is important.

105. Costas, *Christ Outside*, 192–93.

is the eschatological kingdom. The church and its service are fruits of this mission, not ends in themselves. Thus, he exhorted the church not to engage in what he described as "cheap social activism," that is, activism for personal gratification;[106] rather, "let us be prophets of hope in a world of disillusionment and false dreams, pressing forward to the city of God – the world of true justice and peace, of unfeigned love and authentic freedom."[107]

Costas affirmed that evangelization is prophetic work for the communal people of God. They are called to "follow Jesus" in the manner of his missional practice by becoming sojourning communities, particularly among the poor, oppressed and rejected on the peripheries of society. Here the community is called to move outward among the multitudes. In courageous obedience and enabled by the Holy Spirit, it is to live the values of the kingdom and work to challenge and redeem unjust systems and institutions into structures that are life-giving. By living in this way, the church/Christian community becomes a prophetic, contextual, and positive herald of the good news of the kingdom; it becomes light and salt to the nations and a signpost of the eschatological kingdom that is yet to come.[108]

Evangelization as a Spiritual Task

Costas was a missiologist, not a spiritual theologian, and therefore his writings did not deal directly with the subject of spirituality. However, his writings are not without hints in this area and how they may relate to a practice of mission. I also opine that there are changes in Costas's thoughts on the area of spirituality as one progresses chronologically through his writings. Therefore, in this section, I will highlight both those areas where Costas's early writings suggest a spiritual dimension and also his views as they appear in his final words.

For me, one of the most overt statements Costas made on the issue of spirituality is this: "Mission without spirituality cannot survive any more than combustion without oxygen."[109] This quotation clearly shows that he

---

106. Costas, *Christ Outside*, 193–94.

107. Costas, *Christ Outside*, 194.

108. Samuel Escobar argues that this concept of Costas's of "working in the periphery" is relevant for today's context. He submits that in the first two decades of the twenty-first century, the Church has increasingly found itself outside the established order and in the periphery of society, therefore "The idea of a missiology that comes from the periphery of the modern world is relevant when we explore the future." *In Search of Christ in Latin America: From Colonial Image to Liberating Savior* (Downers Grove: InterVarsity Press, 2019), 315–17.

109. Costas, *Christ Outside*, 172.

considered a spiritual life is necessary for an evangelical practice of mission. However, if one surveys Costas's early comments about prayer and Christian conversion, it becomes apparent that his early view of spirituality was that it related to a Christian's inner life and personal relationship with God. For Costas, spirituality at this stage in the development of his thought was the domain of Christian conversion and prayer, not mission. He also described both prayer and conversion as personal spiritual experiences that involve an encounter with Christ. This dualistic thinking segregating the spiritual and the active in the Christian life was not unusual for Christians in Costas's era.

As a method, separating life into outward and interior dimensions provides a way of conceptualizing aspects of a Christian's life so that they are easy to study or discuss in a bounded way. This means that, for Costas, the practice of evangelization was not part of a Christian's spirituality per se, although, ironically, he made it clear that a Christian's entire life is guided and enabled by the Holy Spirit. Academically, segregating such topics also allowed Costas to focus on the practical side of missiology without having to discuss missional spirituality. Thus, one does not find in Costas's work any lengthy discussion of subjects such as prayer. His writing was primarily missiological in terms of activity. However, in my opinion, Costas's early comments do highlight that he was realizing that the two subjects were connected in some way.

First, Costas perceived that spirituality is an essential and motivating source for evangelization. He submitted that an encounter with Christ gives Christians a conviction of the truthfulness of God and inspires them to evangelize. He also opined that an initial conversion to follow Christ is required before a person can evangelize because a Christian is bearing witness to what she has experienced.[110] This idea is reinforced in Costas's understanding of mission as a dialectical relationship. He argued that there is both centrifugal and centripetal movement by Christians involved in mission to and from the world. The first movement is outward towards the world but there is also a movement inward for the purposes of renewal and re-evangelization, if necessary. Again, outward service requires a return to the centre for refreshment, support, and inspiration.

Second, Costas noted that his dialogue with Roman Catholic and Orthodox friends made him consider the relationship between liturgy and evangelism or worship and witness. In *The Integrity of Mission*, he opined that for him the church in its evangelistic witness was a sacrament pointing to God and God's

---

110. Costas, *Christ Outside*, 184.

new order of life, thereby encouraging others to worship God.[111] He was also of the opinion that worship was a celebration of what God has done and is continuing to do in transforming the world. Therefore, mission and worship are linked in that one is a celebration of the other.[112] It is clear from these comments that Costas was beginning to think about the interconnectedness between these realms.

It is in *Liberating News*, however, that Costas appeared to have adopted a more comprehensive approach. His chapter on conversion focused on the role of the Holy Spirit, who Costas defined as "the giver of new life in terms of God's power in creation and redemption."[113] He then described "the converted existence or the new life in the Spirit" as a "creative and liberating journey." He stated, "spirituality is the practical expression of the journey, the praxis – or reflective engagement – of the faith."[114] He defines praxis as "hearing and doing God's word, reflecting on God's path and following it."[115] Costas averred that it has three dimensions: discipleship, dialogue, and discernment.[116] Therefore, in one of his final statements, he redefined his understanding of spirituality to include the activity of Christians and thus mission. Then, in his final chapter of *Liberating News*, he discussed the practices of the church that he described as the "basic evangelising community."[117] Here he stated that everything the church is sent to do should have an "evangelistic cutting edge" and he expanded his thoughts on worship to include the Eucharist. He submitted that the practice of Holy Communion is not for the church alone; it is also a communal witness to the elements of forgiveness, solidarity, and unity of God's order of life.[118] Here we begin to see further connections between what might be described as a personal/communal spiritual practice and a prophetic proclamation related to missional activity.

I also consider that there are other areas in Costas's work that link spiritual and evangelistic practice. One strong element of Costas's missiology

---

111. Costas, *The Integrity of Mission*, 59–60. He defined sacrament as a sign that points to a reality beyond itself.

112. Costas, *The Integrity of Mission*, 90–91.

113. Costas, *Liberating News*, 121.

114. Costas, *Liberating News*, 125.

115. Costas, *Liberating News*, 7.

116. See Costas, *Liberating News*, 125–30.

117. I would argue that the name and the practices of this community make it difficult not to see the liberation movement's base ecclesial communities as a model of this church. See Costas, *Liberating News*, chapter 8, 131–49.

118. Costas, *Liberating News*, 139.

is obedience. As noted before, he defined it to reflect his biblical understanding of the word, namely, "to incline one's ear, to listen in faith and to respond by faith to God's word."[119] In my view, this concept of listening prescribes attentive silence before the "other" who is attempting to vocalize something. It reminds one of monastic practices of attentive silence. However, Costas did not express any further ideas of how listening and doing come together, nor did he describe the nature of this listening until *Liberating News,* when he commented on how dialogue is a dimension of a Christian's praxis, particularly in terms of inter-religious communication. Costas described dialogue as committed sharing and listening: "Dialogue is, therefore, an exercise in two-way witness. From the Christian perspective, *it begins in silence*, with a willingness to listen to others and the Great Other, who often speaks through our neighbour."[120] Thus, I submit there is a suggestion that Costas might have had in view such monastic practices linked with an evangelistic task.

In Costas's overall concept of mission from the periphery, he also made a link between service with, and for, the poor and encountering Christ. Costas indicated that Jesus, during his lifetime, ministry, and death, identified with the poor and oppressed. He was often among them and had an especial care for them. In several places throughout his writings, Costas focused on the biblical parable told by Jesus and recorded in Matthew 25 where Jesus identified with prisoners, the hungry, the naked and destitute. In *The Integrity of Mission*, Costas argues that, in this parable, Jesus exhorts Christians to show their love for God by serving the poor, because in service they will grow in their experiential knowledge of him and because he promised to be present in the midst of those in need.[121] Similarly, in *Christ Outside the Gate*, he argued that for a Christian to witness about Jesus, she must truly know him experientially; this means she must go to those with whom Jesus identified, namely, the poor and oppressed. Costas writes: "Wherever there is oppression, there is the Spirit of Christ incarnated in the *experience* of the oppressed; there is God contextualized in the present history of the nonpersons of society."[122] In an article entitled "The Mission of Ministry" Costas, writing about mission priorities, noted that the Holy Spirit's mission is the same as that of Jesus. He argued that it is the "pneumatic" Christ that hides behind the "poor and meek" today and so the church, to fully identify with Jesus, "will need to be a

---

119. Costas, *The Integrity of Mission*, 22.

120. Costas, *Liberating News*, 127. (Emphasis is Costas's.)

121. Costas, *The Integrity of Mission*, 52.

122. Costas, *Christ Outside*, 13. (Emphasis is Costas's.)

humble and poor community, living in passionate solidarity with them (the poor and meek) as the historical Jesus made their cause his own and died as their representative par excellence."[123]

For Costas, the pattern of Jesus's mission was incarnational in that it involved a downward movement in order to raise others up. He submitted that the church is called in its mission to do likewise. Therefore, the move to the periphery to be with those in need is biblical and characteristic of Christ. This is the place that Jesus promises to be present and provides an opportunity of renewal and liberation to serve. In *Liberating News,* Costas wrote that after a trip to Sri Lanka he reconfirmed his conviction, based on the evangelistic praxis of Jesus, that:

> an authentic contextual evangelisation should start from the periphery with an immersion in the pain and agony of the people who live on the fringes and the bottom of society. In such an immersion experience, one encounters the risen Lord, enlarging and deepening one's limited vision of human reality, challenging one's presuppositions, renewing one's mind, and liberating and empowering one's life for service as a channel of grace in the "Galilees of the nations."[124]

Here, Costas was describing both a missional journey of service and spirituality. Unfortunately, he died before these words were published, but in my view, this text reveals that he was moving in his thoughts towards considering how personal and communal experience together with evangelization are interconnected and are best integrated.

Concluding Remarks

Costas, as an evangelical Hispanic pastor and missionary, was confronted with the reality of the injustices imposed upon his own peoples, both in Latin America and the USA. As a missiologist in the trenches of society, he returned to the Bible to reflect upon injustice and was able to propose, through a focus on God's kingdom, a way of integral mission that encapsulated Christian work for social justice. For Costas, evangelization that speaks to the values and attributes of God's kingdom is prophetic and enables Christians to participate and further God's mission – the goal of which is the transformation of the world.

---

123. Orlando Costas, "The Mission of Ministry," *Missiology* 14, no. 4 (1986): 469.
124. Costas, *Liberating News,* 69.

For the purposes of this book, I consider that Costas as a radical evangelical is a good example of an evangelical who is willing to challenge his own biblical understanding when confronted with the realities of a situation. His re-reading of the gospel together with social scientific research provides a way of "following Jesus" that missiologically made sense in his context. Therefore, in my view as Lausanne changes its biblical grounding for mission to "loving God and neighbour" and broadens its perspective of the world, Costas's work and theological methods remain relevant. Moreover, his paradigm of "following Jesus in the peripheries of society" is one that Lausanne could reconsider missiologically today. This is particularly so as minority world churches find themselves in the peripheral areas of society and also as missioners seek to discern where God's locus for loving one's neighbour is preferred; as Costas's retelling of his experience reveals, it is in the margins that God promises God's presence.

Furthermore, Costas identified that mission required a "spirituality." During most of his life, he did not link it directly with his proposed active way of mission, however, this began to significantly change towards the end of his life. His last text dispelled the dichotomy between spiritual and secular life, viewing all a Christian's life as spiritual. He proposed connections between personal spiritual practices and mission; the Eucharist and liturgy for him both have evangelising elements. He also described how Christian service in the margins can lead to experiences of God that benefit the missioner. He affirmed that the praxis of the Christian journey including missional practice was a "spiritual path."

For me, Costas's missiology of following Jesus is a spiritual missiology as it combines the spirituality of following Jesus with mission. Therefore, this missiology together with his links between spiritual practice and mission continue as a relevant resource for Lausanne should it attempt to combine its missional practice with spiritual and experiential practices. In my view, Costas's work as a contemporary evangelical voice supports my call for a practice of integrated mission.

7

Third Movement – Contemporary Theology Part 2

Segundo Galilea's Spirituality

In this chapter, I am continuing to explore contemporary theology through attending to the spiritual theology of the late Father Segundo Galilea. Galilea sought in his work to guide Roman Catholics, particularly those involved in social action in Latin America between the 1960s and 1990s, towards renewing their understanding of spirituality and living what he termed a "spirituality of liberation." For him, this spirituality (the practice of living the Christian faith or discipleship) is about appropriately "following Jesus" in one's historical, cultural, economic, and political situation. Therefore, for him, a Christian spirituality in Latin America was a contextual response to the world in which Latin Americans lived: one of violence, oppression, and a disregard of the poor.

In this chapter I will suggest that Galilea's spiritual theology guides Christians to practice the elements of the Christian faith in ways that both engage their contexts and encounter God. In so doing, Galilea advocated for a spirituality in which there is no division between what is sacred and what is secular, and he linked Christian missional activity with Christian spiritual practices so that a Christian engages in a contextual integrated mission. Christians are called to live rooted and nourished in a relationship with God and to work for biblically-inspired missional activity as a contemplative experiential practice.

As Galilea's spirituality is contextual, I consider it is helpful to understand his particular environs. First, I will briefly establish Galilea's contextual influences before exploring the contents of Galilea's written texts.

Contextual Influences
Personal

Little is written about Galilea's life; what is known is reducible to biographical details and vocational titles. He was born on 3 April 1928 in Santiago, Chile. He graduated from the Catholic University of Chile in Santiago in 1955 and was ordained as a Roman Catholic priest in 1956. He spent the first five years in ministry as a part-time pastor of a church in a working-class parish of Santiago, as a spiritual adviser at a major seminary, and as editor of the Chilean Journal, *Pastoral*. In 1963, he joined the teaching staff at the Centre for Intercultural Formation in Cuernavaca, Mexico. From 1968–1976, he was the Director of the Latin American Pastoral Institute in Quito, Ecuador; when the Institute later moved to Medellín, Colombia, he became a professor there. From the late 1970s onwards details of his life are sparse, but he is known to have travelled extensively throughout the world, giving retreats and speaking on the subjects he wrote about – the re-evangelization of those worshipping within the Roman Catholic Church and the revitalization of their spirituality, particularly within the context of Latin America. He spent some of his later years in Cuba trying to understand how Christianity could thrive within a communist-ruled political system. Sometime after that he returned to Santiago, Chile, where he died in May 2010.

Galilea's working life as a Roman Catholic priest was set in a historical context of increasing secularity, urbanization, poverty, and economic and political oppression. Roman Catholicism was undergoing change through the event and documents of the Second Vatican Council (1962–1965). The Latin American bishops sought to locally contextualize the changes proposed by the Second Council in their meetings at Medellín in 1968 and Puebla in 1972. Also, within predominantly Latin American Roman Catholicism, there was the development of the religious base ecclesial communities among the poor, out of which arose political and social action and, subsequently, liberation theology.

Urbanization and Oppression

During the period in question, most of the governments in Latin America were either dictatorships or oppressive in their policies; they were also economically reliant on the West. Their policies were accelerating the divide between rich and poor, resulting in increasing poverty. Urbanization was also occurring as poor peasants moved to the cities to find work to support their families. As a result, major cities were developing shantytowns and the poor of Latin America were becoming visible.

In Galilea's country of birth, the economy was heavily dependent on the USA for exports and was growing erratically. Rural and urban poverty was extensive and there was a visible gap between the rich and poor. In the 1960s, Santiago was Chile's fastest growing city; it experienced a housing shortage as a consequence of its booming population. The housing shortage led to the development of shantytowns to the north, east, and south of the city. These living areas were deprived of electricity, running water, and sewage facilities until the 1990s. In 1992, Santiago's population exceeded five million – over thirty-nine percent of Chile's total population.[1] Politically, Chile was ruled by the repressive military dictatorship of General Pinochet from 1973 until 1990.[2]

Journalist John Gunther, writing in 1965 about South America, commented on the sudden phenomenon of the shantytown: "The precipitousness of this evolution is almost beyond belief, and the number of persons involved enormous."[3] He noted that a third of the population of Lima, Peru, were forced to live in shantytowns. In Rio de Janeiro, Brazil, twenty percent of the population lived in *favelas*.[4] Gunther described these places as:

> sub-human squalor . . . miserable huts (built) out of tin cans, hunks of stone and cardboard on the sharpest slopes . . . there are no amenities whatever, not even water or a postal service. Filth and flies are everywhere. Dogs howl and children drip with slime. I have seen nothing worse even in Johannesburg or prewar China.[5]

For many living in these circumstances, the division between rich and poor was totally unacceptable. Thus, from the grassroots populace developed

---

1. Rex A. Hudson, *Chile: A Country Study* (Washington, DC: Federal Research Division, Library of Congress, 1994), 10.

2. In a *Washington Post* obituary of Pinochet based on a Chilean government document that had taken the testimony of 30,000 people, journalists reported the Pinochet government killed at least 3,197 people and tortured approximately 29,000. Two-thirds of these reported atrocities took place in 1973. Monte Reel and J. Y. Smith, "A Chilean Dictator's Dark Legacy," *Washington Post*, December 11, 2006, https://www.washingtonpost.com/archive/politics/2006/12/11/a-chilean-dictators-dark-legacy/596e14a3-d86c-496f-8568-05f81c199a81/.

3. John Gunther, *Inside South America* (New York: Harper & Row, 1966), 72.

4. Brazilian term for shantytown.

5. Gunther, *Inside South America*, 72.

an outcry against the political and social systems that were supporting such disparities, and demands were made for social justice and new systems. The response, however, from many government forces was one of further oppression, violence and death. Many involved in this grassroots work were Roman Catholics; many of whom went missing or lost their lives for these causes, including the influential leader, Archbishop Oscar Romero.[6]

In my view, Galilea's early ministry in Chile among the poor, and his continued work in Mexico, Ecuador, and Columbia, gave him a broad experience of the import of these policies throughout Latin America.

The Roman Catholic Church

During the 1960's and 1970's, the Roman Catholic Church in Latin America was also experiencing transformation. The Church's social landscape was challenged in terms of its structure; the Church's political stance was questioned. Furthermore, the content and practice of its faith was also undergoing change.

The Second Vatican Council (Vatican II) (1962–1965) brought many changes to the Roman Catholic Church. One of these was an alteration of the Church's self-understanding; it was to perceive itself as a pilgrim people of God with, among other things, a focus on mission and evangelization.[7] This new identity was interpreted at Medellín (a meeting of the Latin American bishops in 1968 that attempted to contextualize Vatican II into a Latin American setting) as one that turned the church's focus towards the poor in Latin America.[8] Ten years later, at the Puebla meeting, the bishops also affirmed the theological concept of God's biblical preferential option for the poor, as highlighted in the work of liberation theology.[9] This change in approach was significant for the

---

6. Gustavo Gutiérrez, when describing Archbishop Romero's martyrdom, stated: that "it was undoubtedly a milestone in the life of the Latin American Church." *A Theology of Liberation* (Maryknoll: Orbis Books, 1988), xliii.

7. *Decree Ad Gentes: On the Mission and Activity of the Church*, Chapter 1:2, https://www.vatican.va/archive/hist_councils/ii_vatican_council/documents/vat-ii_decree_19651207_ad-gentes_en.html from Vatican II states: "The pilgrim church is missionary by her very nature, since it is from the mission of the Son and the mission of the Holy Spirit that she draws her origin."

8. Gustavo Gutiérrez stated that the Latin American Church came of age at Medellín and took the "reins of its own destiny." *A Theology of Liberation*, 73.

9. The liberation movement did not have as much influence at Puebla (1979) as they did at Medellín (1968). The Secretary General of the Latin American bishops in 1979 was Lopez Trujillo; he was a conservative and critical of the movement. However, the bishops could not ignore the increasing numbers of poor in Latin America and so they identified and named the theological concept of the "Preferential Option for the Poor." Deane William Ferm, *Third World Liberation Theologies: An Introductory Survey* (Maryknoll: Orbis Books, 1986), 54. This

Church, as in the past it had supported the stance of the various governments in power. Galilea strongly advocated for these changes and the work of the Latin American bishops generally.[10]

The structure of the Roman Catholic Church at parish level was also undergoing change. Small parish group meetings known as the Communidade de Bases (CEBs) evolved due to a shortage of Roman Catholic priests in Latin America.[11] Permitted by the institutional Church, these groups were led by trained members of the laity and were encouraged to meet twice a week. Their numbers expanded quickly; the form of the Roman Catholic Church was reshaped into parish institutional churches with many CEBs connected to them.[12] Participants within the CEBs were encouraged to pray and, for the first time, read the biblical text themselves.[13] This led to participants working together to promote a better life for themselves by becoming politically and socially involved.[14]

---

theological idea states that God has a special concern for the poor and marginalized as evidenced throughout Scripture. It does not state that such persons obtain salvation because of their socio-economic status.

10. See Segundo Galilea, "Between Medellín and Puebla," *CrossCurrents* 28, no. 1 (Spring 1978): 71–78.

11. Leonardo Boff, in his work *Ecclesiogenesis*, trans. Robert R. Barr (Maryknoll: Orbis Books, 1986) traces the history and nature of these communities, as well as dealing with questions related to their biblical and theological status within the Roman Catholic Church. See also *Church: Charism and Power: Liberation Theology and the Institutional Church*, trans. John W. Dierksmeier (Eugene: Wifp and Stock, 2012).

12. There were approximately 80,000 such groups in Brazil at the end of the 1970's. Ferm, *Third World Liberation Theologies*, 12. The CEBs were formally recognized at Puebla.

13. See the work of Carlos Mesters, who researched the way the Bible was read by the CEBs in *Defenseless Flower: A New Reading of the Bible*, trans. Frances McDonagh (Maryknoll: Orbis Books, 1989). Mesters notes that participants read in a particular way: they took their difficult, everyday circumstances, including their poverty, to the Bible and discovered within its pages a God who heard the cry of the poor and who supported their stand against injustice. While valuing the benefits of local contextual reading in the CEBs, Mesters also notes its challenges, recognizing there is no easy means for creating balance between these. Per Frostin in his article, "The Hermeneutics of the Poor: The Epistemological Break in Third World Theologies," *Studia Theologica* 39 (1985): 127–50, notes how such Third World theologies have highlighted other ways of "knowing" than those propounded in Western theology. They are grounded in an arena of commitment, where praxis and spirituality are not divorced from theology and take into account context and a solidarity with the poor.

14. Gerard West, commenting on this way of reading, noted that in First World countries the major interlocuter of the biblical text is the educated non–believer while in the context of the "Third World" like Latin America and South Africa, the interlocutor is the poor and oppressed. He argued that it is the difference in the interlocutor that resulted in the new approach to examining the text and its understanding. "The Bible and the Poor," in *The Cambridge Companion to Liberation* Theology, ed. Christopher Rowland (Cambridge: Cambridge University Press, 1999), 129–31.

As a consequence of the growth of the CEBs, many priests moved to live in the shantytowns in an expression of their solidarity with those living in poverty. They began to work with and for the poor. This shift towards the poor was not welcomed by governments and led to resistance and violence by those in power. Despite Galilea's professional interest in spirituality and pastoral work within Roman Catholicism, I have no evidence that he was involved with the CEBs directly; however, as a person involved in directing pastoral work, he could not have been ignorant of their significance.

It was out of the political and social activities of these CEBs, together with the involvement of Roman Catholic priests with the poor, that Latin American liberation theology developed. The liberation movement was a response to its context, and many priests and theological academics, such as Gustavo Gutiérrez,[15] Leonardo Boff, Clodovis Boff,[16] and Jon Sobrino,[17] wrote about these events in a theological manner. Gutiérrez was one of the first to encapsulate the movement as a whole into a theology in his ground-breaking work, *A Theology of Liberation*, published in 1973.

Liberation Theology

Liberation theology, which predominantly arose in the Roman Catholic Church, affected many Roman Catholics in Latin America.[18] It changed how they thought about their faith and how they lived their lives. Galilea supported the work of the liberation movement and its theology to the extent that it did not counter the theology of the Roman Catholic Church. I consider

---

15. Gutiérrez is a Peruvian Dominican priest and theologian who has spent most of his life living with and caring for his poor parishioners in Rímac in Lima. He is also a Professor at the Pontifical University of Peru. He is known as "the father" of liberation theology. He has also written in the arena of spirituality, see for example, *We Drink from Our Own Wells*.

16. Clodovis Boff and Leonardo Boff are brothers and wrote together *Introducing Liberation Theology*, trans. Paul Burns (Maryknoll: Orbis Books, 1987). Clodovis has also written on liberation hermeneutics. See *Theology and Praxis: Epistemological Foundations* (Maryknoll: Orbis Books, 1987). Leonardo Boff is known for his work on the Trinity, See *Trinity and Society* (Maryknoll: Orbis Books, 1988). He also was removed from the priesthood because of his critical stance towards the institutional Roman Catholic Church.

17. Jon Sobrino is a Spanish-born Jesuit priest who is known for his liberation work in El Salvador. He has written in the fields of liberation spirituality and Christology. See for example: *Christ the Liberator* (Maryknoll: Orbis Books, 1978); *Christology at the Crossroads: A Latin American Approach*, trans. John Drury (Maryknoll: Orbis Books, 1978); and *Spirituality of Liberation: Toward Political Holiness*, trans. Robert. R. Barr (Maryknoll: Orbis Books, 1988).

18. It was not solely a Roman Catholic theology; there were Protestant theologians involved in the movement, for example, Rubem Alves (a Presbyterian) and José Miguez Bonino (a Methodist clergyman).

that the following key elements of the liberation movement are evident in Galilea's spirituality.

The liberation movement adopted the use of the hermeneutical circle for its own purposes. The hermeneutical circle method commences in context, rather than in the biblical text. A thorough understanding of one's context is explored by considering contemporary social scientific research. This leads to the formation of contextual questions that have import for Christian practice. These questions are then taken to the sources of the Christian faith to which Galilea as a Roman Catholic would subscribe namely, the Bible, Conciliar Documents, and traditions of the Roman Catholic Church for answers; the to and fro between questions and texts lead to plausible solutions for practice.[19] It is my view that Galilea adopted such a methodology in his work, particularly in his guidance upon how to read the Bible.

Second, theologically, liberation theology raises awareness that God has a preferential option for the poor and that all Christians are called to work to alleviate poverty. It encourages solidarity with the poor as a way of working with them to improve their lives. It also underscores that sin is not only personal but also structural. It advocates that those structures within society that maintain inequality, injustice, and oppression are sinful. God's redemptive plan includes the restoration of such structures, therefore, political and social work that seeks transformation based on the values of God's reign is also evangelistic and redemptive. For liberation theologians, God's ultimate goal is the redemption and restoration of all of God's creation; thus, evangelism involves both public and personal transformational work. Galilea was supportive of such work in his writings, but his concern was that such activity was centred in a relationship with God, to provide nourishment and direction for the participant.

Finally, drawing on biblical theology, liberation theologians conclude and underscore that God works in, and through, historical events and continues to do so today.[20] They affirm that God is both immanent and transcendent, but they particularly uphold divine immanence. Liberation theologians remind Christians that God cares about people and the world in which they live and

---

19. Clodovis Boff defines these stages as: (i) socio/analytical mediation, (ii) hermeneutic mediation, and (iii) practical mediation. "Epistemology and Method of the Theology of Liberation," in *Mysterium Liberationis, Fundamental Concepts in Liberation Theology*, eds. Ignacio Ellacuría, S.J. and Jon Sobrino, S.J. (Maryknoll: Orbis Books, 1993), 83.

20. See J. Severino Croatto, *Exodus: A Hermeneutics of Freedom*, trans. Salvator Attanasio (Maryknoll: Orbis Books, 1981).

seeks justice for all in history.[21] Galilea supported this entire view of God, and his spirituality emphasized the immanence of God.

There is no doubt that Galilea embraced the liberation movement generally within his writings. However, Galilea is not a major liberation theologian such as those mentioned previously. Nonetheless, as Deane Ferm underscores, he is an individual "whose writings are not only influential but representative of the rich diversity of Latin American liberation theology."[22]

I regard Galilea as a significant liberation theologian in terms of liberation spirituality. He was not a radical and did not advocate violent activity; his work promoted synthesis rather than rupture. He emphasized drawing together traditional understandings of the Christian faith with contemporary insight to reveal contextually appropriate ways of living a Christian life in local circumstances. Fundamentally, Galilea was not a revolutionary but a priest of the Roman Catholic faith with a missionary and pastoral focus. He was an intellectual and academic within the Roman Catholic Church who supported missional activity and sought to express his views through his publications. In my view, while theologians like Gutiérrez have written in the arena of liberation and spirituality, Galilea's total focus on spirituality, particularly in placing the Christian practice of integral mission[23] within a contemplative lifestyle, makes his texts an important resource with invaluable insight for this book.[24]

Popular Catholicism

Living within his Latin American context, Galilea saw an inherent tension in the spirituality of Roman Catholic Christians. As well as his concern for those involved in political and public activity, his concern for all Roman Catholics was their lack of a healthy spirituality, and he felt that many persons were in crisis.[25] For Galilea, one of the issues was the practice of popular Catholicism; he called it a "religious *mestizaje*". At the time, eighty percent of Roman

---

21. Liberation theology has broadened into other arenas as a consequence of such beliefs, for example, Black and Feminist theologies.

22. Ferm, *Third World Liberation Theologies*, 47.

23. My use of integral mission here has the same meaning as that of the radical evangelicals.

24. Even though Galilea's texts primarily speak to the Latin American context, other spiritual writers advocate for their global appeal. Henri Nouwen, in his "Forward" to Galilea's *The Way of Living Faith*, trans. John W. Diercksmeier (San Francisco: Harper and Row, 1988), argues that Galilea's spirituality of liberation is also significant for those in North America. vii–x.

25. Galilea, "Liberation as Encounter with Politics and Contemplation," in *The Mystical and Political Dimension of the Christian Faith*, ed. Claude Geffré and Gustavo Guitérrez, Concilium 6, no. 10; Theology of Liberation (New York: Herder & Herder, 1974),: 19–33, 20.

Catholics in Latin America were involved in it. Popular Catholicism was based on the practise developed by Amer-Indians, whereby they had adopted Roman Catholic practices into their own cultural ways, leading to a mixed faith that was characterized by devotion, ritual and symbol. In Galilea's opinion, such elements were deformed in that they were not in keeping with biblical understandings of such symbols and rituals and were not based in a deep commitment and encounter with Jesus Christ. Galilea's view was that this type of spirituality was inadequate to support the challenges Roman Catholics faced in their society. However, his approach to such ritualistic religion was not to castigate it; rather, he held the view that the distorted beliefs, rituals, and symbols were best re-evangelized from within, that is, given a contemporary relevant meaning in keeping with those espoused by the Bible and Roman Catholic traditions.[26] In short, Galilea sought to create a contextual, biblical, Roman Catholic spirituality to meet the varying needs of the Latin American population, one that embraced liberation practices and undergirded its work.

Galilea's Understanding of Mission
Mission Is Evangelization

Galilea understood the missional work of the Roman Catholic Church as evangelization. In defining this term, he brought together Pope Paul VI's papal document *Evangelii Nuntiandi*[27] with the Second Vatican Council's changes, as adopted by the Latin American bishops in their document from the meeting at Puebla in 1973. In doing this, Galilea affirmed Pope Paul VI's view that evangelization was the Roman Catholic Church's reason for being,[28] the Second Council's emphasis that the Church was not primarily an institution but rather a "pilgrim people of God," and that one of its primary concerns was mission and evangelistic practice. Galilea submitted that "evangelization" must fulfil the following:

1. It must preach and share Jesus Christ as the God who saves and leads human beings to his allegiance and following.

2. It must be evangelization "incarnate." That is, it must bring about transformation of the human beings actually alive in Latin

26. See, Segundo Galilea, *The Challenge of Popular Religiosity* (Quezon City: Claretian Publications, 1988).

27. Pope Paul VI, *Evangelli Nuntiandi*, December 1975, https://www.vatican.va/content/paul-vi/en/apost_exhortations/documents/hf_p-vi_exh_19751208_evangelii-nuntiandi.html

28. Galilea, "Between Medellín and Puebla," 71.

America today, with their history, cultures, aspirations and social organization – their whole reality.

3. It must be integrally liberating. It must transform selfish, unjust, and sinful persons, groups, families, and societies into a just community of sisters and brothers, a community that will qualify for incorporation into the Kingdom of God.

4. It must be missionary. It must be directed primarily to those persons and groups most in need, most de-Christianized, and most acutely marginalized.

5. It must find its inspiration in the discipleship of Jesus the Evangeliser, true source of all missionary spirituality. [29]

This definition, together with the documents upon which it is based, make it clear that in Galilea's perspective the Latin American Roman Catholic Church espouses evangelization as an incarnational and integral task involving the transformation of individuals, communities and societies and it is grounded in a missional spirituality of "following" Jesus.

Evangelization Includes the Work for Social Justice

Like all Christian theologians, liberation theologians affirmed that Jesus's life, death, and resurrection inaugurated the "reign of God."[30] For them, this reign involves attitudes and values exemplified in the life of Jesus and in the prophetic statements of the Old Testament prophets. One of these important values was social justice. Oppression, violence, abuse of power, corruption, and an imbalance in the distribution of wealth were therefore systemic social sins often endemic in social structures. Therefore, the church's work as the pilgrim people of God towards transforming such structures was as evangelistic as leading a person to faith in Christianity. Thus, liberation theologians advocated that the salvation and redemption Jesus had brought into the world through his death and resurrection were wholistic; God was redeeming and restoring all of creation, both social structures and persons. The Latin American bishops' meeting at Medellín had endorsed such a theological view by declaring that both development and human liberation were a foretaste of the kingdom of

---

29. Segundo Galilea, *The Beatitudes: To Evangelize as Jesus Did*, trans. Robert R. Barr (Quezon City: Claretian, 1984), 2.

30. This reign is only partially present. They, like other Christians, realize that it will not be fully present until Jesus's promised return.

God.[31] Galilea's writing assumed this view, namely, that working for social change in keeping with God's perspective was an evangelistic task. Therefore, Galilea affirmed that "Christian liberation is therefore a global task: it is interior and personal, and at the same time socio-political, economic and cultural."[32] Galilea affirmed that evangelization included both personal and social transformation in keeping with the values and attributes of God's reign.

Galilea biblically supported this view by arguing that Jesus's life confronted unjust powers in his role as a "religious" leader. For Galilea, evangelization was about contextually "following Jesus." He was aware that, in his context, Jesus had become overly transcendent in popular Catholicism, while in some radical liberation theologies he was portrayed as a political revolutionary.[33] For Galilea, both extremes were unbiblical. Therefore, he advocated that Latin American Roman Catholic Christians needed to come to "know"[34] the historical human Jesus to counter their overly transcendent or policiticized views, in order to follow him.[35]

Galilea opined that Jesus is the model to emulate.[36] Moreover, he was of the view that, while not a revolutionary, Jesus's life disclosed socio-political concern. He argued that to disincarnate Jesus from his historical, political, and social context was to create a Christology that leads to a view of the church and its mission extricated from its social and political context.[37] Like other theologians of his era, he submitted that Jesus was a Jew living in Palestine, in a particular historical, political, and social era. His life was subject to the ideas, hopes, and conflicts of that time and his teaching touched on political concerns. Further, his ministry led to conflict with the religious powers; he

---

31. Segundo Galilea, "The Theology of Liberation: A General Survey," vol. 1 of *Liberation Theology and the Vatican Document*, trans. Olga Prendergast and Alberto Rossa (Quezon City: Claretian, 1985), 31.

32. Galilea, "The Theology of Liberation: A General Survey," 25.

33. Galilea was aware that there were liberation theologies, rather than a singular theology. He considers that those Christian liberationists who relied on ideology rather than the Bible for their activity were not truly liberation theologians, even though they called themselves such. See Galilea, "Liberation Theology and New Tasks Facing Christians," in *Frontiers of Theology in Latin America*, ed. Rosino Gibellini, trans. John Drury (Maryknoll: Orbis Books, 1979), 169–71.

34. Knowledge for Galilea was not factual knowledge but wisdom that is learnt through encountering Jesus in faith and love. Segundo Galilea, *Following Jesus*, trans. H. Phillips (Maryknoll: Orbis Books, 1981), 13.

35. Galilea, *Following Jesus*, 13.

36. This is an example of Galilea seeking to re-evangelize the deformed Christology within popular Catholicism.

37. Galilea, *Following Jesus*, 100.

underwent a political trial and was convicted and crucified as a subversive. [38] Therefore, Galilea advocated that the Bible portrays Jesus with a socio-political dimension to his ministry.

At the same time, Galilea also indicated that there is no biblical justification to argue that Jesus was a political strategist or a social leader. Rather, in his humanity, Jesus was a religious leader who announced the inbreaking of God's reign as a "religious-pastoral" message.[39] Jesus communicated through word and deed God's values for society and those that follow him. Galilea submitted:

> The kingdom of God as a promise that even now is present among us implants in society values that will allow for the criticism of all forms of social and structural sin, including all forms of exploitation and domination. Thus, the preaching of the kingdom is not properly speaking a political discourse, but it can give rise to authentic liberation movements among human beings: insofar as it makes them conscious of various sinful situations and insofar as it inspires them to transform society because of a Gospel of the kingdom in which they have believed.[40]

For Galilea, Jesus throughout his life proclaimed a prophetic rather than a political message – one that sought reconciliation between God and God's creation, and one that clearly set out the values and attitudes of God's reign. For him, Jesus's modus operandi was to create a liberative movement through fraternity.[41] Thus, for Galilea, followers of Jesus are called to contextual social action for social change through the creation of a society based on a brotherhood and sisterhood, in line with reign values. For Galilea, such work is a prophetic rather than a political task.[42]

---

38. Galilea, *Following Jesus*, 102.

39. Galilea, *Following Jesus*, 102.

40. Galilea, *Following Jesus*, 103.

41. Galilea, *Following Jesus*, 10.

42. Galilea, "The Theology of Liberation, A General Survey," 46–47. Galilea did not discount that some Christians are called to work specifically in the political arena. He affirmed such calls and proffered Moses as a good model for such vocations. However, for him, this was not the call of all Christians; theirs was the religious-prophetic work of Jesus himself. Galilea, "Liberation as an Encounter," 31.

Evangelization Is Prophetic

Galilea argued that Jesus's work in the realm of social justice is prophetic of the attributes and values of God's reign. In the context of Latin America, liberation theology is known for having helped revive a prophetic role for the Roman Catholic Church. Gustavo Gutiérrez defined the prophetic role as one that denounces and announces in ways that engender hope.[43] Therefore, those who work for social change within the liberation movement simultaneously criticize those governments whose policies lead to major social disparities and offer hope to those who suffer under them, with whom they work in solidarity. Thus, according to Gutiérrez's definition, their work in underscoring and seeking change in keeping with the values of God's reign, both present and anticipated, is prophetic.

Galilea defined the term "prophet" as "a person who discerns the signs of the times in order to undertake the attitude and the response which the Spirit wills."[44] This definition, unlike Gutiérrez's, emphasizes the role of the prophet as one who is attentive to both her context and the Holy Spirit – and acts accordingly. In describing this role, Galilea highlighted the ministries of Elijah, Moses, John the Baptist, and the historical Jesus as prophetic.[45] Specifically, he described Elijah's stand against the power systems of the day, oppression, and King Ahab as prophetic; he opined that, in the New Testament, John the Baptist was prophetic in the same way.[46] He considered that Moses was a "politician" and his work was "political prophecy," as he stood with the oppressed Israelites against Pharoah and led them out of Egypt through the Exodus.[47] These prophets sought social change through publicly criticizing unjust systems and declaring a message of liberty and hope – as did Jesus. They reminded those around them of the values and attributes of God. Furthermore, Jesus proclaimed that God's reign was being inaugurated through him and he pointed to the nature of complete liberation yet to come.[48] Thus, although the wording of Galilea's definition differed from that of Gutiérrez, by relying on the biblical prophets as paradigms of the role, he effectively described a prophet's role as encompassing the same goals. Furthermore, by pointing to the social

---

43. Taken from Ruffing, "Introduction" in *Mysticism and Social Transformation*, ed. Ruffing, 11.

44. Segundo Galilea, *The Future of Our Past: The Spanish Mystics Speak to Contemporary Spirituality* (Notre Dame: Ave Maria Press, 1985), 65.

45. Galilea, "Liberation as an Encounter," 29.

46. Galilea, "Liberation as an Encounter," 30.

47. Galilea, "Liberation as an Encounter," 30.

48. Galilea, "Liberation Theology, A General Survey," 40.

nature of the biblical prophets' work, Galilea affirmed that such work carried out by the Church in Latin America is biblical, prophetic, and evangelistic.

Another important aspect of Galilea's definition and examples is that all the prophets mentioned, including the historical Jesus, had real experiences of God in their formative years that continued through their entire lives. Thus, Galilea represented the biblical prophet as one who connected with God and underscored this spiritual and prophetic dynamic for the Christian life.[49] This synthesis of the spiritual, prophetic, and missional aspects of Christianity was fundamental to his work.

Galilea also underscored that the prophetic task is a communal one. He referred in his texts to the Church as either the Roman Catholic Church as an institution or the CEBs.[50] Galilea submitted that the institutional Church in Latin America is responsible for speaking out and creating a prophetic consciousness among its people. In an oppressed context, Galilea argued that it is not enough for the Roman Catholic Church to denounce ideologies, rather it ought to:

> denounce the mechanisms of wealth and power which generate these conditions as well as the various forms of materialism, the cult of power and wealth, totalitarianism and the exclusive emphasis on economics. The Church must criticize the ideals of a society which focuses on producing wealth for the few and thereby accumulates power in their hands.[51]

Galilea also acknowledged that the grassroots communities as "church" were already embodying such prophetic work through their public work for social justice within their neighbourhoods.

For Galilea, evangelization involved social and personal transformation with a religio-prophetic edge. Social structures that demean the values of God's reign are to be criticized by the institutional Church and change is built through the building of fraternal communities who "follow" the historical Jesus in their contexts. For Galilea, one's attentiveness and relationship with God is key to this social and personal transformation.

---

49. Galilea, "Liberation as an Encounter," 21.
50. Galilea, "Between Medellín and Puebla," 74–75.
51. Galilea, "Between Medellín and Puebla," 74.

Galilea's Spirituality

Galilea rejected what he perceived as false dichotomies; he preferred to create a synthesis where possible. For him, the modern approach of finding understanding through a method of division and dissection meant that comprehension of the whole was often lost. Therefore, through his work, he attempted to reunite concepts that had undergone this artificial division. One of these was the secular/public and sacred/spiritual divide in the life of a Christian. For him, there is no such segregation; all of a Christian's life is a matter of Christian practice or discipleship and therefore all of a Christian's life is spiritual. In my view, Galilea's understanding of discipleship was synonymous with his description of spirituality.

Galilea described Christian spirituality as follows: first, there is a foundational form that is true for all Christians in any historical period or environment. Second, there is the flexible living out of that life in response to the challenges in one's culture and social context.[52] For Galilea, the core identity of the spiritual life is a journey "following Jesus," aided by the Holy Spirit, in response to God's initiative towards humankind; this is the life the Christian is called to follow and embody. He takes this paradigm from his reading of the gospels and his focus on the beatitudes.[53]

There are many Christian historic traditions that have focused on discipleship as "imitating the way of Jesus." Within this book, I have noted that both Wesley and Ignatius of Loyola were influenced by the work of Thomas à Kempis and his underscoring of discipleship as the "imitation of Christ."[54] For Galilea, there was more to the spiritual life than mere imitation; for him, it had to be a contextualized following, and this is why he preferred the latter term rather than "imitation."[55] It is how Christians live out these values and attitudes of Jesus in their social, political, economic, and cultural contexts that creates a contemporary spirituality.

Galilea also disliked the idea of spirituality being divided between an internal and external journey in which one is vertical (moving towards God)

---

52. Segundo Galilea, *Way of Living Faith*, 3–5. He argued that attempting to define the term "Christian spirituality" is almost impossible. He was of the opinion that such a term is so rich and complex that any definition will only partly encompass the true meaning. For him, Christian spirituality ought to be contextual and therefore any definition will also be affected by the context of its practice.

53. Galilea, *Way of Living Faith*, 48–49; Galilea, *The Beatitudes*, 9.

54. Thomas à Kempis, *The Imitation of Jesus*, ed. Harold C. Gardiner (New York: Doubleday, 1955).

55. Galilea, *Way of Living Faith*, 30.

and the other is horizontal (moving towards neighbour). In this respect, he was critical of Platonic and oriental thought; he considered these had infiltrated Christian spiritual thinking, moving it away from genuine biblical spirituality. I contend that, to address this, he adopted liberation theology's emphasis upon God's action in history and argued that horizontal activity can also lead one towards God.[56]

Therefore, I argue that Galilea saw his task as conceiving a wholistic, indigenous spirituality for Latin American Roman Catholic Christians that supported, nourished, and encompassed a prophetic practice of evangelization. In order to achieve this, he undertook a reflective contemplative process in which he posed questions that arose from the lack of a contemporary spirituality to the gospels and other traditional practices of the Christian faith. In so doing, he discovered ways of re-situating traditional spiritual practices in a contemporary setting in a manner that created renewal and a relevant spirituality for Latin America.[57] The following are his proposals of how to live a spirituality of liberation and they reveal how spiritual practices can be linked to the work of evangelization.

Galilea's Contemplative Practice

Galilea often used the term "contemplative" in his writings. He described Christian contemplation "as a profound, loving and hidden intimacy (through faith) with the living God." It means to "experience God really, even though obscurely, in every phase of human life."[58] He spoke of the contemplative experience as part of a Christian's pilgrimage, a way of life that fosters a heightened awareness or encounter of God's presence in all of life. In other words, contemplative practice cultivates a posture of attentiveness to, and a relationship with, God in everyday life. In this way, Christians come to "know" God as a person knows another person and learns God's values, attributes, and desires.

One of Galilea's main concerns was that those involved with the evangelistic work for social justice root and nourish their efforts in an experiential relationship with God founded in biblical and traditional Christian practices. Galilea's texts do not provide examples or descriptions of such experiential encounters with God; rather, they provide an interpretative framework to the

---

56. Galilea, *Following Jesus*, 55.

57. Galilea, *Way of Living Faith*, 16–17.

58. Galilea, *Way of Living Faith*, 100.

traditional practices of the Christian faith, to show how such practices could lead Christians into God encounters. For him, the purpose of these encounters was to help Christians source, contextualize and nurture their evangelization in and with God. In this manner, he re-evangelized those practices, giving new life to them.

Prayer

As one might expect, Galilea strongly encouraged the practice of prayer. He stated that prayer is the "eminent and irreplaceable form of the experience of God";[59] "it is a loving response to the God who loves us."[60] He encouraged both its personal and communal practice as means for encountering Jesus.

Reading the Bible

Galilea promoted reading of the Bible meditatively and spiritually in a manner that focused on attentiveness and listening.[61] For Galilea, a reader was to read contemplatively, expecting to encounter a consciousness of God from the text, rather than exegetically or theologically as a student or detective. He particularly encouraged Christians to read the gospels "because the words and attitudes of God are recorded there."[62] He also emphasized reading the beatitudes because, for him, these were the spiritual values of God's kingdom that Jesus himself incarnated and inaugurated. They were the "great prophecy of the gospel, precisely because they propose an ideal that is completely unattainable on earth but at the same time into which we might grow."[63] For me, this emphasis on meditating on the gospels and beatitudes was to encourage politically and socially active Christians to encounter and experience Jesus as portrayed in the biblical text, as a challenge and counter to their overly transcendent view of him. In suggesting this methodology, Galilea was encouraging these readers to know and experience this Jesus as the foundation for their evangelization.

In this reading, Galilea also promoted a contextual hermeneutic approach. He suggested that readers focus their reading by taking a question from their context that requires a solution to the text. He did not directly explain this approach in his work but illustrated it using examples. One example is

---

59. Galilea, *Way of Living Faith*, 101.

60. Galilea, *Way of Living Faith*, 102.

61. Galilea underscored the importance of the Bible both for the church and the individual Christian. He encouraged Christians to have a copy of it by their bedside, and to listen and read it as often as they could. *Way of Living Faith*, 48.

62. Galilea, *Way of Living Faith*, 100.

63. Galilea, *Way of Living Faith*, 49.

Galilea's interpretation of the parable of the good Samaritan. First, as a reader, he posed a question from his context relevant to the passage: "Who are our neighbours in the concrete circumstances of our personal history? Are they our friends? Christians? Our fellow citizens? Or are they also the inhabitants of other countries?"[64] Galilea then proceeded to give his analysis of the chosen biblical passage, noting that it is by way of "meditation on this parable" that "a discovery of who is my neighbour according to Jesus's criteria will come to light."[65] Second, Galilea attended to the question that the doctor of the law poses to Jesus and then analyzed Jesus's response. Galilea emphasized that this "is a counsel given not only to the doctor of the law but *also to us*."[66] Third, Galilea examined the victim as the one in need and then considers those in need in his situation, namely, the poor: "the campesinos, the Indians, the sub-proletariat."[67] Fourth, he focused attention on the Samaritan, the one who showed compassion, who set aside his own immediate interests and entered the world of the "other" and, in so doing, became a brother to the victim. He noted: "My neighbour is not the one who shares my religion, my country, my family or my ideas. My neighbour is that one to whom I am committed. We become brothers and sisters when we commit ourselves to those who need us."[68]

In this to and fro between the contextual question, text, and contemporary situation, Galilea used the hermeneutical circle interpretive model, employed widely by liberation theologians. In so doing, he revealed to a reader a way of encountering Jesus himself together with God's teaching in a manner relevant to her own present context. Furthermore, Galilea encouraged both personal and communal reading of the Bible, the latter both in the context of the "community" and the institutional church.[69] Therefore, he was promoting both a private and communal "meditative" reading of the text. He also affirmed that reading biblical texts in this manner could help Christians with their missional work.

Practising the Sacraments

At the time of Galilea's writing in Latin America, there were diverse views within the Roman Catholic Church regarding the sacraments. Within the

---

64. Galilea, *Following Jesus*, 25.

65. Galilea, *Following Jesus*, 26.

66. Galilea, *Following Jesus*, 25. (Emphasis is mine.)

67. Galilea, *Following Jesus*, 26–27.

68. Galilea, *Following Jesus*, 28–29.

69. Galilea, *Way of Living Faith*, 47–48.

increasingly secularized "Catholic" society, the sacraments and the "mystery" attached to them was downplayed and, as a consequence, their general practice devalued.[70] The overly "spiritual" approach of popular Catholicism was also viewed with suspicion.[71] Further, few liberation theologians emphasized their practice as they were not considered significant for the work of liberation. In contrast, Galilea encouraged practising the sacraments, advocating that their practice is fundamental to a Christian's spirituality.

Galilea argued for balance between overly "spiritualized" practice and their disregard, so that their true value is re-discovered.[72] He underscored the practice of the sacraments as another place of encounter with Christ "in the biblical sense – that is, an experience of faith, of love, of imitation, and sharing in his transforming life."[73] They are a place where God's mercy and grace are experienced and where Christians can acknowledge that God is the source of their activity, choices, and commitments.[74] Thus, he encouraged regular participation in the Eucharist and Penance/Reconciliation as personal and communal sources of encountering Christ.

As well as being a source of contemplative practice, Galilea also considered that practising the sacraments is a prophetic missional activity. He suggested that the traditional sacraments of the church are structures of grace instituted by God to publicly stand against the structures of sin in the world; in other words, they are prophetic symbols. He noted: "The sacraments are the nemesis of social and structural sin."[75]

Galilea submitted that love and fraternity are offered in the sacraments to counter structures of hatred and division; forgiveness and reconciliation are offered to counter sectarianism and cruelty; kingdom values are offered to counter exploitation and injustice; love and mercy to counter evil; liberation to counter slavery; and life to counter death.[76] Furthermore, he suggested that as "money" represents "the goods of this earth and the work of human hands," "wine and bread" in the Eucharist represent "the fruit of this earth and the work of human hands." Participation in the Eucharist, where the bread and wine are distributed to all equally, both rich and poor, reveals God's ability to bring

---

70. Galilea, *Way of Living Faith*, 52, 62.

71. Galilea, *Way of Living Faith*, 52.

72. Galilea, *Way of Living Faith*, 53.

73. Galilea, *Way of Living Faith*, 57.

74. Galilea, *Way of Living Faith*, 64.

75. Galilea, *Way of Living Faith*, 67.

76. Galilea, *Way of Living Faith*, 71.

justice and reconciliation.[77] For Galilea, participation in the sacraments is both a means of encountering God's love and mercy and a communal, prophetic public proclamation of the values of God's reign. They are both contemplative and missional.

Service with and for the Poor as a Sacramental Evangelistic Practice

Latin American urbanization led to the visibility of the urban poor. Liberation theologians drew attention to them in order to underscore God's preferential option for them. The Roman Catholic Church also adopted and affirmed this biblical concept at the meeting of the Latin American bishops at Puebla in 1979.[78] Therefore, Roman Catholic Christians understood that they were called to especially care for the poor as both a prophetic act – as it bears witness to the attributes and values of God's reign – and evangelization. For Galilea, service or action with and for the poor is therefore missionally prophetic; he also considered it a sacramental practice where one can encounter Jesus.

Galilea described the collective poor as a sacrament of Christ.[79] He founded his argument on the parable of the last judgement in Matthew 25. He contended that in this text Jesus identified himself with the poor: he therefore also suggested that those who serve the poor can encounter God in the persons they serve. By so arguing, Galilea opined that both social service and action with and among the poor is a spiritual practice, like that of a sacrament. Thus, working with the poor for transformation is more than a biblical missional practice ordained by God; it is also a place of contemplative action where Jesus is encountered and experienced.

> As often as you did it for one of my least brothers, you did it for me (Matthew 25:40). Such service is a real encounter with the Lord, hence a wellspring of spiritual experience and contemplative prayer. Christ's identification with the poor is not simply a juridical one, so that when we serve the poor it is "as if" we were serving

---

77. Galilea, *Following Jesus*, 39.

78. Galilea summarizes this history in *Way of Living Faith*, 125–28.

79. The proposal that "the poor" are a sacramental way of experiencing Christ based on Christ's identification with those who are hungry, thirsty, and without clothes in Matthew 25: 31–46 was proffered by liberation theologians. Gustavo Gutiérrez speaks of the "sacrament of the neighbour" in *A Theology of Liberation*, 115. While I am not arguing for the sacramental nature of the poor as a socio-economic group, I do suggest based on this gospel passage that God is present in an especial way where service to such persons happens.

him. In some mysterious way the identification is true and real, as the experience of the church's saints make clear.[80]

Referring to Jesus's identification with the poor in the same Matthean parable in *The Way of Living Faith,* Galilea also stated: "[F]aith reveals the poor person to us as the sacrament of Christ, mysteriously identified with him."[81] Thus for Galilea, service with and for the poor is a "religious experience" in a manner similar to other spiritual practices.[82]

Galilea argued further that there is a dialectical relationship between serving and acting with and for the poor and practising traditional religious practices, such as prayer. He argued that for Christians to recognize and experience Jesus in the poor, they must first encounter Christ through a traditional practice. Galilea argued that as Christians carry out their sacramental activity with and for the poor, they will be propelled back to seek a fuller revelation of God in prayer, the sacraments, and biblical reading that will then lead them back to service. For Galilea, the core of the missional Christian life is in this "to and fro" of seeking and loving God and seeking and loving one's neighbour, particularly the poor, all of which, in his view, is seeking and loving God. Galilea perceived that this inter-related rhythm of Christian practice explains the link between the two greatest commandments of Jesus recorded in the gospel of Matthew 22:37–40, that is, to love God and neighbour, one leading to the other and vice versa.[83]

Galilea, by way of such arguments, revealed how service especially to the poor is both a sacramental practice and a missional activity. In other words, he synthesized mission and contemplation within one act and shows how each aspect of the activity requires the other. While this thinking was not new, its revival in a particular context re-evangelized both missional activity and traditional contemplative practice with the effect of revitalizing involved missioners.[84]

---

80. Galilea, "Liberation Theology," 179.

81. Galilea, *Way of Living Faith,* 130.

82. Galilea, *Way of Living Faith,* 134.

83. Galilea, *Following Jesus,* 58–60 and "Liberation Theology," 180.

84. Leonardo Boff made a similar argument in his article, "The Need for Political Saints, From a Spirituality of Liberation to the Practice of Liberation," trans. Linde Rivera and Leon King, *CrossCurrents,* Vol. 30, no. 4 (Winter 1980–1981), 369–76.

Concluding Remarks

Post Vatican II, "Catholics" were called to participate in evangelization; this was the Church's raison d'etre. For Galilea, mission in Latin America had its challenges, particularly as, in his view, Christians had an insufficient spirituality to undergird it. For him, spirituality was about "following Jesus," but he knew that the "transcendent Christ" of popular Catholicism would not support working in the trenches of poverty. He therefore sought to connect Catholics with the historical Jesus and show how all Christian practices, including missional activity with and for the poor, had the potential to be both an encounter with God and a source of direction and strength through the Holy Spirit.

I consider that Galilea's work is important because he underscored that a missioner's spirituality is essential for missional practice. In his context, he wanted to ensure that liberational practice was rooted in and animated by God, not a secular philosophy. His work reveals that through a contemplative reflective process traditional Christian practices both spiritual and missional can be re-evaluated so that they become the framework for evangelization. From my perspective, his work underscores the importance of integrated mission.

Furthermore, Galilea's work reveals to Lausanne how such a framework can evolve. He encouraged Christians to embark on a journey of prayer and a meditational, contextual reading of the Bible. He highlighted how traditional participation in the sacraments is not only contemplative but also missionally prophetic of God's reign. Similarly, in arguing that social action and service among the poor are sacramental, he shows how such evangelization is also contemplative – leading missioners to the poor where God's presence is available for blessing. Furthermore, by underscoring that all practices of devotion and service are interdependent, he showed how all these Christian practices root a person and a community in God for the benefit of mission and the missioner.

I consider that Galilea's contextual framework for a spiritual life encompassing social commitments with and for the poor is well thought out. He navigates the reader into a life that is constantly and dialectically turning and returning to God and neighbour. It is not ethereal but grounded in the Christian practices of the church and daily life. In this way, Galilea provided a spirituality of contemporary reflective praxis so that those engaged in liberative ministry discover the nourishment and discernment they require as they grow in their relationship with God. This approach brings to mind the work of another liberation theologian, Clodovis Boff, who encourages Christians to develop a "hermeneutical habitus," i.e. a way of life that is continually interpretive both of life and the biblical text.[85] I submit that this is what Galilea was doing in his suggested spirituality; he showed a Christian how to obtain a contextual hermeneutical habitus. Such a life is grounded through living a dialectical relationship with God through the sources of the Christian faith and in serving God in the poor. This life is inherently missional and spiritual and provides a basis for an integrated missional practice. Galilea declared:

> Authentic contemplation, through the encounter with the Absolute God, leads to the absolute of one's neighbour. It is the meeting place of this difficult symbiosis which is so necessary and creative for Latin American Christians committed to the liberation of the poor.[86]

While Galilea's work addressed a particular situation, I consider that his creation of a contextual missional spirituality is a useful resource for dialoguing with Lausanne. Although Lausanne's mission is not entirely focused on the urban poor, Galilea's aim to ground evangelization efforts so that they are biblical, relevant to a particular context, based in a real relationship with God, and nourishing for the missioner is a helpful framework for Lausanne's consideration.

---

85. Boff, *Theology and Praxis*, 152.
86. Galilea, "Liberation as an Encounter," 28.

8

Strategic Practical Theology Part 1

A Round Table Discussion on Mission and Spirituality

This chapter is in the form of a roundtable critical discussion. It brings together my interpretations of the selected theologians' texts and Lausanne's documents to analyse their respective ideas on the relationship between mission and spirituality. There is within this method an element of repetition, as many of the subject matters have been highlighted in previous chapters. However, I intend through bringing the various opinions of the respective theologians together, via placing various questions to their respective texts, to highlight areas of similarity in their ideas. This emphasis on looking for "similarities in difference" engages the ideas of David Tracy. He considers that, where there is diversity, it is the similarities that are significant.[1] I consider that the round table process confronts the differing horizons of my chosen

---

1. Challenged by the interpretative work of Mircea Eliade, David Tracy notes that "the paradigmatic in the real" can be discovered in the ahistorical and atemporal repetition of archaic myths, rituals, symbols, and images. See "The Challenge of the Archaic Other: The Hermeneutics of Mircea Eliade," in *Dialogue with the Other: The Inter-Religious Dialogue* (Grand Rapids: Eerdmans, 1990), 66. I interpret this to mean that looking for what is similar and repeated over time and space provides insight into what may prove to be an important paradigm. It is this search for "similarities in difference" that I am employing so that the outlines of an integrated mission emerge. Tracy does emphasize that this process of analogy will only work well if the differences between the parties are real. I opine that the theologians in this book differ sufficiently to make the analogical process useful.

theological participants and links them in meaningful, creative, and fruitful ways towards an understanding of integrated mission. In the next chapter, I intend to use these outcomes to suggest practical ideas that would enable Lausanne to adopt a fully integrated mission approach.

The Round Table Questions and Discussion
What is Mission?

David Bosch, in his insightful *Transforming Mission*, argues that "mission remains undefinable."[2] Having reviewed the various paradigms of mission from New Testament times to the twentieth century, he opines that: "The definition of mission is in a continual process of sifting, testing, reformulating. Transforming mission means both that mission is to be understood as an activity that transforms reality and that there is a constant need for mission itself to be transformed."[3] Thus, for Bosch, there is a continual movement in mission as it develops in a context. Similarly, Wrogemann notes that there are varying dimensions to mission: "[It] is constantly being experienced and perceived in surprisingly different ways."[4] In the same vein, Schroeder and Bevans argue that: "Christian mission is both anchored in fidelity to the past and challenged to fidelity in the present. It must preserve, defend and proclaim the *constants* of the Church's traditions; at the same time it must respond creatively and boldly to the *contexts* in which it finds itself."[5]

For all these missiologists, mission is rooted in the biblical understandings and traditions of Christianity and, simultaneously, is a movement that is often unexpectedly innovative, as it evolves within its circumstances. Since mission is always on the move, there is opportunity to reframe Lausanne's evangelical mission by retrieving the elements of spirituality that it has forgotten, overlooked, or rejected.

---

2. Bosch, *Transforming Mission*, 9.

3. Bosch, *Transforming Mission*, 511. Bosch suggests that mission is a multi-dimensional task that should proclaim and integrate in various ways six identifiable events in the New Testament: the incarnation of Christ, his death on the cross, his resurrection, his ascension, the outpouring of the Holy Spirit, and the Parousia. *Transforming Mission*, 512. He submits: "It is the good news of God's love, incarnated in the witness of the community, for the sake of the world." *Transforming Mission*, 519. Interestingly, he does not include the proclamation of God's kingdom in word and deed. All round table conversationalists have elements of the six events in their understanding, with Costas and Galilea also including God's kingdom.

4. Wrogemann, *Theologies of Mission*, 1.

5. Bevans and Schroeder, *Constants in Context*, 1. (Emphasis original.).

The theological participants in this round table come from differing historical eras, geographical areas, and social and religious climates. Consequently, their respective texts contain both constants and variations within their approaches to mission.

Galilea, as a Roman Catholic, developed a view of contemporary evangelization by melding Pope Paul VI's understanding of mission in *Evangelli Nuntiandi* and the Latin American bishops' statements from Puebla.[6] In so doing, he took the new ideas on social or structural sin into account in his mission. Therefore, Galilea's concept of evangelization included the following: preaching and sharing Jesus as the one who saves, seeking commitment to Jesus from individuals, enabling such persons to transform their lives in keeping with the values of God, and helping them to establish themselves within communities of brothers and sisters. In a social setting, it also includes working against social sin found in economic, political, and cultural arenas and helping transform them into areas that operate with the attributes and values of God's kingdom. For Galilea, mission is an integral task: it is work with individuals, communities, and societies to bring wholeness. Simultaneously, he also simply stated: "Evangelization is the following of Christ the Evangelizer and cooperation with him in his evangelising praxis or it is nothing."[7] Ultimately for him, mission is grounded in a spiritual relationship with God, following the pattern of Christ; it is a participatory endeavour.

Ignatius had a missional outlook from the beginning of his committed Christian life. As Bosch indicates, Ignatius was the first Christian to use the term "mission" as going overseas to convert the "heathen" to Christianity.[8] However, I aver that a reading of his life reveals that he had a far more integral view of mission than just this idea. His personal call from God was to "help souls."[9] He interpreted helping souls to mean aiding persons to become pilgrims of Jesus[10] through coming to know the Triune God, in a mutual relationship of love,[11] so that they could find and live God's purpose for them. This interpretation led to Ignatius participating in a wide array of work, from becoming a spiritual director to those taking his *Exercises*, to ministering among the poor and

---

6. Galilea, *The Beatitudes*, 2–3. Pope Paul VI, *Evangelii Nuntiandi* (December 1975).

7. Galilea, *The Beatitudes*, 4.

8. Bosch, *Transforming Mission*, 228.

9. Ignatius, *The Autobiography*, 87, 89, 99.

10. Ignatius, *The Autobiography*, 107.

11. Ignatius, "Contemplation to Attain Love," *The Exercises*, 176.

marginalized, including Muslims, Jews, beggars, orphans, and prostitutes.[12] He also helped form, and became the Superior General of, the Jesuit Order, a group of persons called by God to serve God in the world.[13] Like Galilea, however, Ignatius's life was founded in the biblical concept of "following" Jesus. Ignatius self-identified as a Christian pilgrim following his leader, Christ, and it is this life that he shared with others.[14]

Wesley, likewise, as a field preacher in the evangelical revival was an evangelist who founded his missional life on the biblical command to love God and neighbour. For Wesley, loving one's neighbour was not solely about encouraging other persons to find justification in Christ; it was also about enabling such persons to continue on their respective journeys in the Christian life and transform their lives through God's grace into Christ's likeness. For Wesley, sanctification was intimately tied to loving one's neighbour. Therefore, his preaching was diverse; his sermons covered a variety of matters from "On the Scripture Way of Salvation"[15] to "The Use of Money,"[16] so that a Christian might live appropriately. He formed and organized the Methodist societies so that persons seeking new life in Christ or those who were newly committed Christians could come together to be encouraged through prayer and Bible study in living out the Christian life in society.[17]

Like Ignatius, Wesley had a broad view of mission. He perceived it as helping men and women to find God and live their lives loving God and loving their neighbours. For Wesley himself, loving his neighbour involved him in various arenas from evangelism to ministries with the poor and marginalized. Methodists likewise created schools for the poor, orphanages, and changed systems in hospitals and prisons so that the care for patients and prisoners was

---

12. Caraman, *Ignatius Loyola: A Biography*, 129–34.

13. The first paragraph of the initial document regarding the possible establishment of a new Order (drafted by Ignatius and presented to the Pope for consideration) reads: "Whoever desires to serve as a soldier of God beneath the banner of the cross in our Society, which we desire to be designated by the name of Jesus, and in it to serve the Lord alone and his vicar on earth . . ." Quoted by Ganss, *Ignatius of Loyola*, 45. The full title of the Jesuit Order is the Society or Companions of Jesus; they perceived themselves as a group who served and followed their leader, Jesus. They served according to Jesus's will and with and for him.

14. Ignatius, in the second week of his *Exercises*, issued a call as if the words are from Jesus. He wrote, "Therefore, whoever wishes to come with me [Jesus] must labour with me, so that through following me in the pain he or she may follow me also in the glory." *Exercises*, 147.

15. Wesley, *Works*, 2:156.

16. Wesley, *John Wesley*, 238.

17. For the Rules of the Societies and Bands written by Wesley, see Wesley, *John Wesley*, 177, 181.

improved.[18] Wesley himself took an interest in medicine, economics, and the abolition of slavery. Wesley, like Ignatius, treated persons as whole persons. However, he was ultimately committed to "following Jesus" and enabling others to do likewise through Jesus's commands to love God and neighbour.

Costas's view of mission was more aligned with that of Galilea; for him, mission is also evangelization. This is not just evangelism through preaching, testimony and sharing one's faith, but also social action and participation in human struggles. He described evangelization as "bearing witness" to the God who saves us: "It is an intensely personal and extensively social witness that requires immersion in a particular socio-historical context and participation in the struggles of humanity."[19] For Costas, God's kingdom, or as he termed it, "God's inbreaking new order," is pivotal to the Christian message – to participate in evangelization is to announce this new order of justice, freedom, peace, and love.[20] For him, Jesus died to redeem all things, including persons and systemic evil. Therefore, through word and deed Christians are to bear witness in all areas of life to this new order and Jesus's reconciliation of creation with God. Like Galilea, Costas (as a radical evangelical) argued for integral mission – giving equal attention to individual and social transformation.

Costas as a missiologist kept his work to that of missiology, however he still argued that it was biblically appropriate to "follow Christ" in the manner of his mission. Through his exegesis of the Gospel of Mark, he suggested that there was a biblical paradigm at work that revealed Jesus did not operate from centres of power; rather, he chose life with the marginalized on the periphery of society.[21] It was from here that Jesus sought to confront the powers of his day. Costas then applied this paradigm to areas of local mission arguing that to follow Jesus's pattern of mission involves churches sojourning in the peripheral areas of life.[22]

Lausanne's approach to mission has traditionally defined mission as evangelism and social responsibility, separating and giving priority to human conversion over social duty.[23] However, I consider that there is some change in Lausanne's approach evident in *The Commitment*; Lausanne is both

---

18. See Jeffrey, "Introduction," 21–24. Also, Hindmarsh, *The Spirit of Early Evangelicalism*, 205–14.

19. Costas, *Liberating News*, 21.

20. Costas, *Christ Outside*, 90–91.

21. Costas, *Liberating News*, 49.

22. Costas, *Liberating News*, 64, 66.

23. *The Covenant*, covenants four, five and six, *Making Christ Known*, 20, 24, 28.

broadening its areas of social mission and seeking to synthesise social mission with evangelism to create a more comprehensive view of God's missional goals.[24] In *The Commitment,* like Wesley, Lausanne seeks to set its mission within the biblical command "to love God and neighbour."[25] While Lausanne's emphasis remains on mission practice, I aver that there is implicit within *The Commitment* spiritual concepts such as these: God's love is the source of mission;[26] Christians in mission are "called to live as Christ lived and to love as Christ loved";[27] and mission following Christ is incarnational.[28] These spiritual themes reflect a spirituality of "following Jesus."

Overall, I consider there are significant similarities in each of these respective theological participants' views on mission. First, the term "mission" itself is not emphasised in their respective works. Wesley and Ignatius both preferred different terms like "loving your neighbour" or simply "helping persons." Both Costas and Galilea spoke of evangelization while Lausanne speaks of evangelism and social responsibility. I think this is helpful as the term "mission" is linked with the colonial misdeeds and sins of the past.

Second, none of these theological participants, except Lausanne, distinguished between evangelism and social mission; they viewed persons wholistically, that is, they dealt with the person and their social circumstances together. Further, in light of recent changes in the knowledge of how social structures operate, both Costas and Galilea expanded their understanding of sin to account for this. They recognized that sin is both personal and structural, and therefore included in God's redemption. Thus, Wesley, Ignatius, Costas, and Galilea all took a comprehensive approach to the practice of mission, not separating or prioritizing particular areas as having greater importance. In my view, while Lausanne has a history of prioritizing evangelism over social duty, its current approach of seeking more synthesis in mission practice should be encouraged using precedents from the four theologians in this book. All the theological participants, in their own particular way, are agreed that mission practice involves both leading persons to faith in Christ and transforming the social circumstances in which they live, all in accordance with the values of God's kingdom.

---

24. *The Commitment,* "Preamble," 14–15.
25. *The Commitment,* part I, 1, A, 17.
26. *The Commitment* "Preamble" and part I, 1, 17–19.
27. *The Commitment,* part 1, 4, B, 25.
28. *The Manifesto,* section A, 4, *Making Christ Known,* 37.

Third, all the theological participants in varying ways make reference to grounding missional practice within a spirituality and all make reference to the pattern of "following Jesus" as a model for living the Christian life and ministry. For Lausanne, it is in the form of declaratory statements. For Costas, it is in his statement that "[m]ission without spirituality cannot survive any more than combustion without oxygen,"[29] his biblical paradigm of Mark's gospel, and some connections between spiritual practices and mission; however, for Wesley, Ignatius, and Galilea, it is the foundation of their missional lives. Spirituality in the form of an intimate relationship with God the Creator, Jesus the Son, and the Holy Spirit is key to missional service of all kinds. For them, loving God and knowing God experientially and biblically leads to participation with God in God's mission, in the mode of following Christ in service to the world.

Responding to the social issues of their respective times and locations, all the participants varied in their mission efforts: Wesley participated in the abolitionist movement of the slave trade in England; Ignatius was involved with prostitution in Rome; Costas and Galilea concerned themselves with the oppression and poverty in Latin America; Costas associated with and aided the poor Latino minorities within the United States; and Lausanne encourages endeavours with HIV, racial and cultural bias, and poverty. Yet, they all operated within the constants of the biblical narrative: loving God and neighbour; becoming more Christlike; bearing witness to God's kingdom; living out the values and attributes of the beatitudes; and helping those to whom Jesus showed especial care; and all sought to introduce persons to God and encourage them to "follow Jesus" through the Holy Spirit as they did themselves. Mission for all of them was different and yet similar, and all either explicitly or implicitly refer to a form of spirituality that is the life blood and the animating force for mission.

If Mission Practice Is Grounded in a Spirituality (Either Explicitly or Implicitly), Why Not Keep the Current Distinction between Mission Practice and Spirituality Rather than Integrating Them?

This is an interesting question as it supports Lausanne's and Costas's more missiological and practice oriented approaches. However, I consider that when this question is asked of the theological participants' texts, some disclose that a division means the full dynamic of missional practice is lost.

---

29. Costas, *Christ Outside*, 172.

The texts of Wesley and Galilea reveal, and Costas's work supports, an understanding of service, particularly among the poor and marginalized, as either sanctifying and/or sacramental – service is an act where the presence of God as Holy Spirit is experienced to bless and nurture. In these circumstances, service is not merely a God ordained duty; it is a place where the Holy Spirit is present and able to encounter missioners directly. The Holy Spirit is a beneficial presence for the missioners, both for themselves and their tasks. In this way, an act of missional service becomes a real participation with God in an event of "loving one's neighbour"; it is simultaneously also a sanctifying event and a contribution to spiritual formation.

In Wesley's sermon "On Visiting the Sick" which is grounded in Matthew 25:36, he argued that there is a relationship of interconnectivity between the person performing an act of loving one's neighbour and the Holy Spirit:

> Whenever, therefore, you are about to enter upon the work, seek his help by earnest prayer. Cry to him for the whole spirit of humility, lest if pride steal into your heart, if you ascribe anything to yourself, while you strive to save others you destroy your own soul. Before and through the work, from the beginning to the end, let your heart wait upon him [God] for a continual supply of meekness and gentleness, of patience and long suffering, that you may never be angry or discouraged at whatever treatment, rough or smooth, kind or unkind, you may meet with.[30]

Wesley suggested that Christians visiting sick people or attending to any of the tasks mentioned from Matthew 25:35 onwards – that is, works of mercy – should pray to God, both before and through the performance of the task, so that they become aware of God's presence through the Holy Spirit who is able to give them the gifts of the Spirit to accomplish it.[31] Thus, Wesley opined that the "place of service" is where the Holy Spirit encounters the Christian in order to bestow sanctifying grace. For Wesley such an act is a "means of grace"[32] and

---

30. Wesley, "On Visiting the Sick," *Works*, 3:390

31. Wesley, "On Visiting the Sick," *Works*, 3:385–97. Wesley in this sermon encouraged persons to carry out "works of mercy," in this case, visiting the sick, and, by extension, missional tasks that comprise loving one's neighbour.

32. Wesley described the "means of grace" as: "outward signs, words, or actions, ordained of God, and appointed for this end, to be the ordinary channels whereby he might convey to men, preventing, justifying or sanctifying grace." "The Means of Grace," *Works*, 1:381

therefore part of a Christian's spiritual formation in the likeness of Christ.[33] Wesley did indicate a condition to this encounter, namely, for Christians to experience the Holy Spirit, they need to open themselves through an act of piety. Whenever he referred to either works of piety or mercy in his sermons, Wesley always kept the two categories together; in so doing, he emphasised that they are interrelated means of grace, and both sanctify.[34]

Galilea made a similar argument, although he described "the poor" as a "sacrament of Christ"[35] with service to them and the marginalized a "religious experience"[36] with sanctifying effects. Galilea opined that those involved in social activity within the liberation movement, working for justice and peace among the poor, should understand their acts within God's narrative. By so doing and via the performance of such tasks, they could encounter Christ through the Holy Spirit.

Galilea suggested that the official sacraments of the Roman Church (word and rites) "are *not* the only experience of Christ and his grace. We know that our neighbour, the poor, and the community are also presences and experiences of Christ and his liberating grace."[37] Thus while Galilea described the poor as a sacrament, he in effect said that the experience of serving such persons is a spiritual practice that provides an opportunity to encounter Christ and, therefore, such service has a sacramental quality.[38] In this way, service to the neighbour provides access to a source of God's grace in Christ, and through the Holy Spirit that is sanctifying, liberating and a gift. These sanctifying gifts enable persons not only to follow but also to live like Jesus. Galilea affirmed:

---

33. Wesley argues that both works of piety and works of mercy are means of grace: "Are there no other means than these, whereby God is pleased, frequently, yea, ordinarily, to convey his grace to them that either love or fear him. Surely there are works of mercy, as well as works of piety, which are real means of grace." "On Visiting the Sick," Works, 3:385

34. Randy Maddox also notes that in three of Wesley's major sermons, "The Character of a Methodist" (1742), "The Scripture Way of Salvation" (1765), and "On Working Out Our Own Salvation" (1785), Wesley linked love of God and love of neighbour respectively with works of mercy and piety in a reciprocal relationship and noted both are required for sanctification. "Visit the Poor: Wesley's Precedent for Wholistic Mission," 41.

35. Referring to Christ's identification with the poor in Matthew 25:40, Galilea states, "The meaning of the poor that appears intuitive to Christianity has its ultimate evangelical root here: faith reveals the poor person to us as the sacrament of Christ, mysteriously identified with him." *Way of Living Faith*, 130 (see also 138).

36. Galilea, *The Way*, 134.

37. Galilea, *The Way*, 54. (Emphasis is mine.) See also "Liberation Theology," 179.

38. Galilea did not argue anywhere in his work for an extension of the official sacraments of the Roman Church to include the sacrament of the poor. Therefore, I interpret his meaning of service to the poor as being like a sacrament, which is in keeping with this quote.

The Word of God and the sacraments are, in Christian life, an encounter with the sanctifying and liberating Jesus, through the Holy Spirit who nourishes and gives life to them . . . In a very profound way, life according to the Spirit makes available to us the norms, wisdom, and spiritual sensitivity with which Jesus lived and acted . . . Sharing in the mentality and the customs of Jesus infused by the Holy Spirit enables us to discern and act evangelically. A good part of spirituality consists in discerning and carrying out the realizations and paths with which God calls us and makes himself present in our lives.[39]

Like Wesley, Galilea understood that loving one's neighbour is a spiritual experience in which God is available to bless and sanctify the missioner. It is simultaneously a place of Christian formation and an act of mission. He stated: "In this way the Christian experience of commitment to one's neighbour, particularly the poor, begins to form part of the very experience of God, and becomes *sanctifying* – it evangelizes us." It transforms the Christian "[t]o see human realities, society, and history with the eyes and standards of Jesus. These standards are different from worldly criteria."[40]

Like Wesley, Galilea also argued that for this encounter to occur, the Christian has first to encounter Christ through a traditional Christian practice, such as prayer. For Galilea, "prayer communicates to us the experience of Jesus"; an ability to participate with Jesus in God's mission; an opportunity to dialogue and communicate with God; and an ability to discover God in those persons Christians are called to serve.[41] He submitted that prayer is not a retreat from the world to be with God; rather, it is an opportunity to encounter Jesus every day, so that Christians develop a unity with God and are able to see things, to judge, to act, and to love in accordance with the values and attributes of God.[42] Galilea argued that it is through this prayer relationship that Christians are directed in their commitment to the world and led to a complementary encounter with God in their neighbour. This second encounter "incarnates the first and gives an historical dimension to the encounter with God."[43]

Galilea biblically based his view on Matthew 25:35–40 where Jesus identifies with the hungry, thirsty, strangers, the naked, the sick, and the

---

39. Galilea, *The Way*, 37–38.
40. Galilea, *The Way*, 139. (Emphasis is mine.)
41. Galilea, *Following Jesus*, 48.
42. Galilea, *Following Jesus*, 49–50.
43. Galilea, *Following Jesus*, 59.

prisoner. He noted, "Here the encounter with the suffering and needy brothers and sisters (the 'little ones') and the resultant service is an experience of Christ – as contemplative, therefore as a personal encounter with the Lord."[44] Galilea then linked these two encounters with Jesus's command "to love God and neighbour." He considers the first encounter in prayer "reminds us of the first commandment, to love God above all things . . . The second recalls the commandment that is like the first, to love our neighbour as ourselves and the presence of Christ in this love."[45]

Wesley's view was also based on the same verses in Matthew. He did not reference Jesus's identification with the poor because, as his sermon "The Reward of the Righteous" (based on Matthew 25:34) explained, at the time the focus on grace had led persons to abandon good works[46] – tasks which Wesley was trying to encourage through emphasizing their sanctifying qualities.[47] However, to support this argument of sanctification, Wesley emphasized the presence of the Holy Spirit in such situations and linked works of piety and works of mercy to loving God and neighbour.

In my view, the similarities in Galilea's and Wesley's arguments are significant. First, despite their historical, contextual, and theological differences, they both argued that missional tasks are part of a Christian's spirituality. Galilea considered service to the poor provides an opportunity for the missioner to experience God in a sacramental way and also to receive sanctifying transformation. Wesley, likewise, also saw such service as a location where God the Holy Spirit is available to bless and sanctify the Christian in a manner that is important for the Christian's formation. For both, missional service, whether described as sacramental or sanctifying, is part of a Christian's

---

44. Galilea, *Following Jesus*, 59

45. Galilea, *Following Jesus*, 59.

46. Wesley, commenting on the social context of the sermon stated, "It is now above forty years since this grand scriptural doctrine, 'By grace ye are saved through faith,' began to be openly declared by a few clergymen of the Church of England. And not long after, some who heard, but did not understand, attempted to preach the same doctrine, but miserably mangled it . . . Some of these, in order to exalt the value of faith, have utterly deprecated good works. They speak of them as not only not necessary to salvation, but as greatly obstructive to it." "The Reward of Righteousness," *Works*, 3:403.

47. In "The Reward of Righteousness," Wesley argued: "Good works are so far from being hindrances of our salvation; they are so far from being insignificant, from being of no account in Christianity; that, supposing them to spring from a right principle, they are the perfection of religion . . . To those who attentively consider the thirteenth chapter of the First Epistle to the Corinthians, it will be undeniably plain that what St. Paul there describes as the highest of all Christian graces, is properly and directly the love of our neighbour. And to him who attentively considers the whole tenor both of the Old and New Testament, it will be equally plain, that works springing from this love are the highest part of the religion therein revealed," *Works*, 3:405.

transforming path in their relationship with God; it has a place in God's narrative for each Christian. In other words, such tasks are both endemically missional and spiritually formative.

Second, both indicate that this meeting with the Holy Spirit is experiential. The encounter is real with a missioner experiencing the presence of God and receiving the gifts required to perform the service. The encounter produces a knowledge of God that is not "book understanding"; it is empirical. Interestingly, Costas also supported this view, recognizing that a Christian's personal experience of God is important for such missional activity.[48]

In his commentary on Matthew 25:35–40, Costas noted Christ's identification with the "poor" and the presence of the Holy Spirit among such persons.[49] He submitted that it is through work with those on the margins of society that a Christian will experience:

> [A]n immersion in the pain and agony of the people who live on the fringes and bottom of society. In such an immersion experience, one encounters the risen Lord, enlarging and deepening one's limited vision of human reality, challenging one's presuppositions, renewing one's mind, and liberating and empowering one's life for service as a channel of grace.[50]

So, like Wesley and Galilea, Costas affirmed that living in the experience of the poor, and particularly while serving them, God is encountered in a way that leads to Christian formation.[51]

Third, Wesley and Galilea both argued that such service is related to prior spiritual practices. I understand this to mean that there is a relationship of interdependency in what Wesley would term "works of piety" and "works of mercy." Both Galilea and Wesley determined that to experience God in such missional service, a Christian must have a prior experience of God in a spiritual practice so that there is a continued recognition of God's presence

---

48. In *Christ Outside*, Costas stated: "Mission without spirituality cannot survive any more than combustion without oxygen,"172. Spirituality here means a personal relationship with God. He noted that Christians, to bear witness, must have such an experience. Costas, *Christ Outside the Gate*, 184.

49. Costas commented that a Christian will experience Christ in serving the "poor," "Wherever there is oppression, there is the Spirit of Christ incarnated in the experience of the oppressed; there is God contextualized in the present history of the nonpersons of society." Costas, *Christ Outside*, 13. Note he did not say that God is present in the poor. He prefers "in the midst" or "behind." See also Costas, *The Integrity of Mission*, 52.

50. Costas, *Liberating News*, 69.

51. Costas, *Liberating News*, 50–63.

in the place of service and spiritual formation and blessing may occur. This means that missional service is properly placed within an overarching explicit Christian spirituality. Thus, loving one's neighbour becomes both a practice of missional service and spiritual formation; its complete nature is revealed as an integrated practice.

This finding has implications for Lausanne. Its document, *The Commitment*, is encouraging, as it grounds missional practice in biblical statements about the source of its work, and implicitly references a spirituality. However, in my view, it could be improved by expressing Lausanne's spirituality more explicitly and linking its mission practices to those practices of spirituality that connect missioners to God. Lausanne presently perceives spirituality as a means of supporting the missional task. It does not embrace an understanding that God employs mission as a process whereby missioners are transformed. It fails to apprehend that missional service is sanctifying and/or sacramental; that when missioners undertake to "love their neighbour" God both evangelizes the neighbour and sanctifies the missioners in ways that enable the latter to grow in their abilities to live like Jesus. Therefore, for God, mission simultaneously involves spiritual transformation for both missioner and neighbour. Accordingly, by advancing an explicit integrated missional practice Lausanne could enrich its current understanding of mission and spirituality by recognizing and expressing the true transformative nature of mission to the encouragement and benefit of its missioners.

If Missional Practice Is Also a Practice of Spiritual Formation, What Are Other Elements of an Integrated Spirituality? In Particular, What Other Practices Do the Theological Participants Recommend for Experientially Connecting with God in Ways That Would Help in a Missional Context?

Among our theologians, there are various Christian practices that they aver link persons with God experientially, all of which are traditional spiritual practices: prayer, meditational Bible reading, and practising the sacraments, particularly partaking in the Eucharist.

Prayer
Both Wesley and Galilea considered that prayer was a spiritual practice that connected a Christian experientially to God. Moreover, Wesley in his sermon, "On the Means of Grace," affirmed that prayer is a means of grace, a channel by which God can bless the praying Christian and by which the Christian grows in knowledge and love of God. He argued from Scripture that Jesus

encourages such prayer. He also noted that prayer is only effective if the Holy Spirit is present. Prayer is communication between the person praying and the Holy Spirit and the vehicle that God has ordained to bless.[52] For Wesley, as is the case with engaging in service, a person who prays can experience the presence of God's Holy Spirit.

Ignatius's life and *Exercises* affirm prayer as a practice that provides an experiential knowledge of God's real presence. His *Exercises* are punctuated with prayer; each meditation begins and ends with prayer (the latter called colloquies). Ignatius directs the exercitant to the purpose of the prayer and to whom the prayer should be made (the particular member of the Trinity or Mary), but the prayer itself is extempore. Ignatius described the colloquy as: "[T]he way one friend speaks to another, or a servant to one in authority."[53] He portrayed such prayer as a personal and respectful conversation and, consequently, directs the exercitant to expect a response. Ignatius's *Spiritual Diary* affirmed that this approach to prayer was also his own.

Lausanne also encourages prayer although not in the manner of Galilea, Wesley or Ignatius. In a subcommittee meeting in 1982, its subsequent document, *The Grand Rapids Consultation on Evangelism and Social Responsibility,* acknowledged the need for prayer, stating:

> Only if they [congregants] are rooted in a vertical relationship to God in worship can the church's two ministries of *kerygma* (proclamation) and *diakonia* (service) be held in proper tension. Only in this way, too, can evangelism and social responsibility be kept from degenerating into merely human activity and even propaganda.[54]

In *The Commitment,* for the first time, Lausanne included a small prescriptive section on prayer that encourages intercessory prayer for the following: more missionaries, the "lost," God's glory to be revealed, and God's kingdom to come. It comments that: "In the midst of all these priorities, let us commit ourselves afresh to pray. Prayer is a call, a command, and a gift. Prayer is the indispensable foundation and resource for all elements of our mission."[55]

I aver that such movement by Lausanne towards directive prayer is laudable, but it is not the type of prayer described by the other theologians. Galilea's,

---

52. Wesley, "On the Means of Grace," *Works*, 1:384–86.

53. Ignatius, *The Exercises*, 138.

54. Stott, *Making Christ Known*, 174. (Emphasis original.)

55. *The Commitment*, section II, D, 6.,96

Ignatius's, and Wesley's respective texts suggest that within their prayers each searched for God's presence and help. In my view, Lausanne's guidelines fall short of this; its intercessory approach to prayer lacks the participative and experiential understanding of the others. Lausanne assumes that those who pray know God's will based on biblical injunctions and therefore its guidelines prescribe prayers for help and blessing only. It does not emphasise the relational aspect of prayer between God and those that pray. Despite this comment, the inclusion of intercessory prayer as a practice linking mission with God provides an important starting point in guiding to other forms of prayer that are more contemplative of God.

Meditational Bible Reading

For Galilea, an experiential knowledge of Jesus was an essential foundation for a missional life. His texts advocate that, in addition to prayer, meditational reading of the Bible and the "spiritual classics" provide a way for Christians to experience God. He distinguished this meditational reading from that of a Christian student who approaches a text with a scientific method to analyze and find rational meaning. He submitted that a reader who comes to the Bible as a follower of Jesus seeks a different kind of knowing, namely, an experiential knowledge of God.[56] Galilea described this type of reading as a private and personal reading of God's word and he particularly encouraged reading the gospels and the beatitudes. For him, these parts of the Bible are where Jesus's words are found; the beatitudes synthesize the Sermon on the Mount (and this sermon explains the spiritual values that are present in God's kingdom). Galilea described such reading as "a true sacrament of the presence of the Spirit of Jesus among us. To read the gospels with the attitude of a disciple is to encounter Jesus." For him, reading Scripture is one of the ways where the Christian receives an experiential "knowledge" of God.[57]

Galilea also directed how this type of reading is done. In so doing, he also showed how such reading can be contextual. By asking contemporary questions of texts, such as "Who is my neighbour today?" to the text of the "good Samaritan," he was able to show how to read in the campesino so that the text is relevant and revelatory in speaking to the reader's context.[58]

---

56. Galilea, *Following Jesus*, 13.

57. Galilea, *Way of Living Faith*, 48–49.

58. Galilea, *Following Jesus*, 26–29. Campesino is Spanish for peasant farmer. Galilea was often speaking to rural people, farmers who were part of the Liberation Movement in Latin America. Galilea was therefore trying to show these persons how to make the biblical text relevant to their context.

Wesley also encouraged meditational reading of the Bible and other classic Christian texts. He described this type of reading in his preface to *The Christian Pattern*:

> Be sure to read not cursorily or hastily, but leisurely, seriously, and with great attention; with proper pauses and intervals, and that you may allow time for the enlightenings of the divine grace. To this end, recollect every now and then what you have read, and consider how you may reduce it to practice . . . Labour to work yourself up into a temper correspondent with what you read; for that reading is useless which only enlightens the understanding without warming the affections.[59]

Wesley, as an early evangelical, encouraged reading that goes beyond rational understanding to that which affects the heart. It is reading that is experiential, motivating, and a means of grace. As with other means of grace, the reader is exhorted to pray prior and after such reading. For Wesley, reading, listening, and meditating on the Scriptures with the Holy Spirit present, as commanded by Jesus, provides God with an opportunity to grace the reader with gifts of wisdom.[60] Thus Wesley underscored reading as a means of drawing intimately into God's presence.

Similarly, Ignatius encouraged reading books about the lives of the saints and *The Imitation of Christ* by Thomas à Kempis.[61] Meditational reading was also central in his *Exercises* so that the exercitant was encountered by Jesus. The *Exercises* focus upon a contemplative reading of the gospel stories that becomes experiential of Christ's life. It is using one's imagination to be present in the situations of the text, to visualize, to use all one's senses, and to reflect.[62] Ignatius was aware that discerning God's voice in this manner of reading is not instantaneous. This is why his *Exercises* also provide instructions upon discernment. However, it is evident in both Ignatius's *Autobiography*

---

59. From part of the "Preface to Wesley's Abridgement of Thomas à Kempis' '*The Imitation of Christ*,'" *John and Charles Wesley*, 88.

60. Wesley, "On the Means of Grace," *Works*, 1:386–89.

61. Ignatius encouraged the exercitant to read these during *The Exercises*' second week. *The Exercises*, 148.

62. Ignatius advised how to read the biblical text contemplatively at the beginning of the second week when the exercitant begins contemplating the Incarnation. See Ignatius, *The Exercises*, 148–51.

and *Spiritual Diary* that "knowing" God through such meditational reading provided a real experience of God.[63] It was foundational to his life with God.

Costas does not speak to the issue of meditational Bible reading as it is not within his subject matter of missiology. However, in my view, his biblical definition of obedience has indirect implications for Bible reading and prayer. His definition of obedience involves both listening and doing – underscoring that biblical obedience is not merely doing what one is told, it also implies the act of listening. "To whom is a Christian called to listen?" one might ask. God? The Bible? This act of listening prior to doing takes away the presupposition that one knows what is being asked in a particular situation. Instead, it invokes the necessity of attentiveness to God through prayer or Bible reading for gaining specific direction in a particular context and time. In prayer, listening to God requires silence. In Bible reading, attentiveness to God requires becoming immersed in the text as in meditational reading. In my view, listening within obedience evokes a more contemplative stance in spiritual practices. Consequently, it is reasonable to assume that Costas suggests that to act obediently requires first contemplative prayer or meditational Bible reading.

Lausanne does not comment on the issue of meditational Bible reading as one would expect, as it is not part of its current understanding of missional practices.

Practice of the Sacraments

Galilea emphasised the practice of the sacraments, particularly the Eucharist and Penitence. He also considered that by participating in these practices Christians could experience God. He noted: "The sacraments are an encounter with the living Christ . . . that is, an experience of faith, of love, of imitation, and of sharing in his transforming life – they are in and of themselves liberating and sanctifying, showering upon us Christ's mercy."[64]

Wesley's understanding of the Lord's Supper was similar to Galilea's on the Eucharist. His doctrine on the sacraments to which he adhered was that of the Anglican Church of his era, namely, "an outward sign of an inward grace." Albert C. Outler notes that Wesley conceived of sacramental grace as God's

---

63. Ignatius set out lengthy and descriptive "Rules for the Discernment of Spirits" *in The Exercises*, 201–7.

64. Galilea, *Way of Living Faith*, 57.

love in action in the lives of faithful men at worship.[65] In his sermon, "On the Means of Grace," Wesley affirmed that the Lord's Supper is such a means.[66]

Further, in his sermon, "The Duty of Constant Communion," Wesley noted that partaking in the Lord's Supper is both the command of God and a mercy to Christians. In relation to the mercy bestowed, he stated:

> The grace of God herein confirms to us the pardon of our sins and enables us to leave them. As our bodies are strengthened by bread and wine, so are our souls by these tokens of the body and the blood of Christ. This is the food of our souls: this gives strength to perform duty and leads us on to perfection.[67]

Again, Wesley affirmed that, for him, God through the Holy Spirit is present in an experiential way at Holy Communion to provide grace to sanctify and strength to serve. For Wesley, taking the Lord's Supper is more than a symbolic act; it is another Christian practice where God is present to bestow grace and strength.

Ignatius also affirmed that the Eucharist was a special place where God met with him. Ignatius recorded in his *Spiritual Diary* that in the preparation or partaking of Mass he was frequently overcome with the experience of God; at such times he often received the gifts of *loquela* and devotion.[68] Through such descriptions, Ignatius clearly indicated that God met with him during the Eucharist in experiential ways that helped him to affirm his understanding of God's will and to grow in love for God.

Costas mentioned the practice of Holy Communion as a public demonstration of the gospel rather than an experiential encounter with God. His understanding of the place of the Eucharist within mission is explained in question four below. Also, as one might expect, Lausanne does not mention

---

65. Outler, *John Wesley*, 333.

66. Wesley, "The Means of Grace." *Works*, 1:389–390.

67. Wesley, "The Duty of Constant Communion," *John Wesley*, 335–36.

68. Ignatius, *The Spiritual Diary*, 267. *Loquela* is the gift of incontrollable tears. In his *Spiritual Diary*, after receiving confirmation from God on his question as to whether the Jesuits should take money from the sacristies, he describes a gift of *loquela* received during Mass: "they came so slowly, interiorly, gently, and without noise or great motions that they seemed to arise so entirely from within that I do not know how to explain the matter. Throughout the entire duration of the interior and the exterior *loquela* everything was moving me towards divine love and the divinely granted gift of the *loquela*. Along with itself, the interior *loquela* brought deep in my soul a harmony so great that I cannot express it."

the practice of the sacraments, as they are not in its view directly related to mission.[69]

For Galilea, Wesley, and Ignatius, God meets experientially with those who partake in the practices of prayer, meditational reading of Scripture, and the sacraments, bestowing mercy, blessing, and knowledge of God. Lausanne also indicates that God is available to Christians in prayer, but I consider that there is not the spiritual insight and understanding for the missioner that Wesley and Galilea portray. For they understood that it is through these practices that Christians are able to perceive and experience God's presence in the tasks of loving one's neighbour. Interestingly, Ignatius did not comment on God's presence in the practice of service or mission. He did note, however, that such experiential times with God enabled him to see God in the world. In other words, for Ignatius there was a connection between spiritual practices and the ability to see God in the everyday.[70] In my view, Galilea and Wesley, together with Ignatius, understood the importance of spiritual practice for experiencing God personally, and for perceiving God in the practices of loving one's neighbour and seeing God in the world. Therefore, these traditional spiritual practices are deemed by these three theologians to be essential for faithful and obedient practices of mission.

If Missional Practice Is Integrated with Christian Spiritual Practice, Do Other "Spiritual Practices" Have a Role Beyond the Personal?

I propose that the answer to this question is also in the affirmative. Galilea perceived the sacraments as possessing a missional role. Likewise, Costas expressed an expanded missional role for Christian worship and participation in the Eucharist.

Galilea suggested that the traditional sacraments of the church are not only a means of Christians encountering Jesus; they are also "structures of grace" instituted by God to publicly stand against the structures of sin in the world. He argued that: "Grace appears in the sacraments as the structure of hope and

---

69. Two recent evangelical publications promote the importance of the sacraments as participative events with God. See Gordon T. Smith, *Evangelical, Sacramental, and Pentecostal: Why the Church Should Be All Three* (Downers Grove: IVP Academic, 2017); and Hans Boersma, *Heavenly Participation: The Weaving of the Sacramental Tapestry* (Grand Rapids: Eerdmans, 2011). Smith and Boersma's views are referenced further in the final chapter herein.

70. For example, Ignatius's *Spiritual Diary*, 246, noted that after a time of prayer when God revealed to him the workings of the Trinity, Ignatius was able to see God's presence in the world. He wrote that whenever he saw three things, such as animals or rational creatures, "I saw them as images reminding me of the Holy Trinity."

liberating grace."[71] Therefore, as "structures of grace" the sacraments have a missional purpose. Galilea submitted that love and fraternity are offered in the sacraments to counter structures of hatred and division; forgiveness and reconciliation are offered to counter sectarianism and cruelty; kingdom values are offered to counter exploitation and injustice; love and mercy to counter evil; liberation to counter slavery; and life to counter death.[72] Focusing particularly on the Eucharist as a structure of grace, Galilea submitted that participation in this sacrament where the bread and wine are distributed to all equally, both rich and poor, reveals God's ability to bring justice and reconciliation.[73] In this way, the Eucharist and the sacraments more generally are a communal, prophetic and public proclamation of the values of God's reign.

Influenced by his discussions with Roman Catholic and Eastern Orthodox friends, Costas wrote about the liturgy and worship of the local church, including the Eucharist, in his last published work, *Liberating News*. He quoted and endorsed the following statement by the Eastern Orthodox Church.

> In order to become a really powerful expression of the church's mission in this world, worship must be meaningfully understood by its participants (1 Corinthians 14:6–15). It is through full participation in the liturgy that the people realize both the teaching and then the life, death and resurrection of Jesus Christ, which is the very reality of what we are trying to proclaim. In other words, the liturgy itself is the proclamation of the gospel in an existential and experiential manner.[74]

Costas thus argued that "singing, praying and confessing their faith in the language of the people enable congregations to have an outreach ministry even while they are praising and praying to God."[75]

Costas also considered that, in the practice of the Eucharist, the church is a sign of the promise and presence of the kingdom of God. This event is a proclamation of the new order that Jesus has inaugurated of love, justice, peace, and a new way of living. Furthermore, it reveals the "unity" between God as Trinitarian community and the community of God's people.[76]

---

71. Galilea, *Way of Living Faith*, 67.

72. Galilea, *Way of Living Faith*, 71.

73. Galilea, *Following Jesus*, 39.

74. Quote from *Go Forth in Peace: Orthodox Perspectives on Mission*, ed. Ion Bria (Geneva: WCC, 1986), 20, in Costas, *Liberating News*, 137–38.

75. Costas, *Liberating News*, 138.

76. Costas, *Liberating News*, 139.

Thus, Galilea and Costas, as the two contemporary theologians, speak into today's understanding of structural sin; they also reveal how practices such as worship and participation in the sacraments are not just personal means or signs of grace but are public, and prophetic demonstrations of God's grace and the values of God's kingdom. Such public worship, particularly the Eucharist, is also a prophetic and political statement; it stands against the evils of oppression, injustice, and discrimination by declaring that within God's reign all who come to the table are treated equally and given grace freely, without preference. Thus, integrated mission, by incorporating practices of loving God and neighbour together with celebration of the Eucharist, creates a renewed way of understanding such practices; they are celebrations and prophetic declarations of an alternate and just way of life that God inaugurated though Jesus Christ.

Do More Rational Ways of "Knowing" God (e.g. Intellectual and Cognitive Readings of the Bible) also Contribute to the Knowledge of God in a Spirituality?

For most evangelicals, the Bible is the supreme authority for godly issues. Lausanne clearly states both within *The Covenant* and also in *The Manifesto* that the Bible is their authority for God's character and an understanding of mission: "We affirm that in the Scriptures of the Old and New Testaments God has given us an authoritative disclosure of his character and will, his redemptive acts and their meaning, and his mandate for mission."[77] This means Lausanne's approach to understanding the mind of God in mission takes no account of experience or tradition, but seeks to rely instead on its interpretation of the biblical text.[78]

---

77. Stott, *Making Christ Known*, 231.

78. The Chicago Statement on Biblical Hermeneutics (1982) affirmed evangelical views of the Bible established during the reformation and identified the process of evangelical biblical hermeneutics. According to evangelical Iain Provan, this statement is the only quasi-official document written to date on evangelical hermeneutics. It contends that it provides a consensus of evangelical academic views on the subject. The principles from the reformation that it affirmed are: (1) sola scriptura, the Bible is God's inspired word and is the supreme and only authority for Christians; (2) the biblical text only has one single meaning, that is, the one that the author originally intended; (3) any interpretation of the biblical text must be in keeping with an understanding of the whole Bible. "How Can I Understand, Unless Someone Explains it to Me? (Acts 8:30–31): Evangelicals and Biblical Hermeneutics," *Bulletin for Biblical Research* 17, no. 1 (2007): 3.

I consider that Costas, as a radical evangelical, would uphold the general tenor of Lausanne's approach, that is, that the Bible is the paramount source for understanding God. However, he had a broader hermeneutic from that of traditional evangelicals in two main ways. First, he highlighted that, as a radical, he upheld the Bible as a rule of faith and practice, that is, he was more concerned with the content of the biblical text for the practice of life rather than the creation of a theoretical perspective. He submitted that "radical evangelicals approach Scripture as a rule of practical faith – that is, a faith that becomes flesh, which is spiritually energising and therefore, historically transformative."[79] Second, Costas also expanded his sources of interpretation to include both tradition and experience, as long as they do not contradict the explicit teaching of the Bible.[80]

Having read many of Costas's texts, I opine that he had a rational biblical approach to both biblical interpretation and hermeneutical application. When he interpreted a text, he first used exegesis to understand a biblical narrative, and then he theologically reflected upon it to establish a biblical paradigm within the text. Second, he read social scientific research on the issue to which he was seeking a biblical response. Third, with this knowledge he returned to the paradigm for further reflection, and then applied it to the situation. Using this correlational system, he was often able to apply the same biblical paradigm differently to particular contextual situations.

By using this methodology, Costas interpreted the Gospel of Mark to suggest that within the text there is a paradigm that reveals Jesus's pattern for his mission oriented ministry. It is one that especially cares for persons living on the periphery of society, those who are despised, poor and often outcast. Costas shows how starting in Galilee, Jesus chose to reside with such persons and spent much time with them before turning towards the powers in Jerusalem. From this pattern, Costas suggested there is biblical evidence for churches to have a sojourning presence among society's fringes. In particular, minority churches already present in the periphery of American society, have a missional call. Furthermore, he also suggested those who are oppressed in Latin America are especially cared for by God. Thus, in my view, his rational and paradigmatic interpretation of the Bible leads to a missiology that understands and invokes missional practice within the spiritual theme of "following Jesus."

Similarly, both Wesley and Ignatius used reason in their work. Wesley's sermons are fine examples of logical, rational, and well thought out pastoral

79. Costas, *Liberating News*, 11.
80. Costas, *Liberating News*, 3–6.

theology. Their respective content was always based on a biblical/theological approach that took account of society's views about issues at that time. Similarly, Ignatius in *The Exercises* encouraged the use of reason. In the first step of an election, an exercitant is called to make a list of advantages and disadvantages of the decision being made; if the godly choice is apparent, then the issue is complete. Only if it is unclear is the issue taken to God directly. Thus, Ignatius, while encouraging experiential awareness of God, did not subjugate reason.[81]

I aver that those evangelicals concerned about the place of experience in integrated mission do not have to reject such an approach as being based upon a lack of rational or biblical due process. I aver that to deny the role of reason and biblical missiology within a spirituality is at odds with an integrated way. However, to dismiss experiential ways of knowing God because it takes one into a realm of subjectivity is also imprudent. I consider there needs to be balance; structures are required to guard against heresy and ensure that one's spirituality remains within a biblical understanding. Karl Rahner, one of the twentieth century's eminent theologians, in his volume, *Visions and Prophecies,* wisely advocates that one cannot dismiss times of special revelation; rather, such revelations are best subjected to examination and evaluation from a set of established criteria in order to establish their veracity.[82]

One of the checks that is readily available and biblical is ensuring that an integrated mission is not only an individual pursuit but also a communal one. A further benefit of communal spiritual practices is that they counter the recent movement towards Christian individualistic spiritual practice. My next question will reveal that one of the significant similarities in the thought of the theological participants is their mutual understanding of Christian spiritual practice as both an individual and corporate process.

What Are the Participants' Views on the Individual and Corporate Dimensions of the Christian Spiritual Life?

Wesley, like virtually all leading theologians throughout church history, viewed Christianity as a strongly social religion. By this, he meant that Christianity is practised with others and for others. This corporate understanding was pivotal to how he lived his own life and to that of the Methodists. For Wesley,

---

81. Ignatius, "The First Method of Making a Good and Sound Election," *The Exercises*, 163–64.

82. Karl Rahner in *Visions and Prophecies* spoke of the nature of Christian visions and prophecies, and of establishing a set of criteria for evaluation.

sanctification or growth in loving God and neighbour was best carried out in the context of community.[83] His personal participation in the "Oxford Methodists" reveals how the practices of prayer, Bible reading, and missional service were all carried out with others.[84] This corporate understanding does not exempt an individual approach, rather it prioritizes the community aspect of the Christian life which best serves Christian formation.

Wesley expanded the idea of the original Oxford group into what was to become the United Societies of Methodists. The society meetings were places where persons gathered to worship, hear a sermon, and pray. They provided opportunities for people to encourage each other in practical holiness. Societies also gathered for what were termed "love feasts" where people shared their respective experiences of God. They also participated in public fast days and covenant renewal services, the latter being an opportunity for those participating within a society to corporately promise to serve God.[85]

As noted previously, societies were divided into classes and bands. The classes comprised smaller groups to encourage discipleship. Class leaders kept attendees accountable in terms of how they lived their lives and encouraged the practice of the means of grace. The classes were avenues for spiritual care and bearing one another's burdens as members learned how to love God and neighbour together.[86] The bands were for committed Christians and were small; each band had between five to seven persons. They were also divided on the basis of gender and marital status. These were groups focused on confession of sin and prayer as they sought to obey the commands of God. Wesley considered them pivotal to the Methodist way of life, although attendance was voluntary.[87] For Wesley, growth in grace was best achieved in the pursuit of Christian life together.

Similarly, Ignatius formed a group of friends who perceived themselves as best serving God communally; together they became the first Jesuits. They committed themselves to following Jesus in the form of a company of men – like the apostles did. They followed God's directions either through the Pope or as directed through their lives of attentiveness to God in their Christian

---

83. Kevin M. Watson, *Pursuing Social Holiness: The Band Meeting in Wesley's Thought and Popular Methodist Practice* (New York: Oxford University Press, 2014), 44, 45. DOI:101093/acprof:oso/9780199336364.001.0001.

84. Hindmarsh notes the discipline of the Oxford Methodists' piety. *The Spirit of Early Evangelicalism*, 15–16.

85. Watson, *Pursuing Social Holiness*, 52–56.

86. Watson, *Pursuing Social Holiness*, 57–62.

87. Watson, *Pursuing Social Holiness*, 63–71.

practices, including participation with God in *The Exercises*. For them, life was lived in common.[88]

Today, *The Exercises* are often interpreted as a means by which an individual can find God's personal direction for them. However, in their original context, Ignatius intended them to be a means by which people discerned into which state of life God was calling them. Were they being called to live as Jesuits (or not)?[89] In other words, Ignatius used them primarily to discern who was called to his communal pilgrim way. Ignatius's *Spiritual Diary* also confirms his use of *The Exercises* to direct the functioning of the Jesuit community itself. Therefore, Ignatius was not primarily creating an individualistic approach to spirituality; he valued community, especially in the form of the Jesuits. I consider that Ignatius understood the benefits of communal living for his missional spiritual way of life. To be clear, I am not denigrating the contemporary individualistic use of *The Exercises*; rather, I want to emphasize that their contextual communal origins are still relevant.

Galilea's proposed spirituality was set within the liberation movement and its CEBs. These communities are where the spiritual practices of prayer and Bible reading are carried out; many of these groups participate in the work against oppression, and for justice, in Latin America. Galilea's whole purpose was to instil a spiritual life that would enable social activists to see their tasks as part of a Christian spirituality – that their work promotes the characteristics of God's inbreaking kingdom, as does their participation in the sacraments. For Galilea, while there is an individual aspect to missional spirituality, for him it is primarily about a corporate spirituality: fraternities of brothers and sisters practising Christianity together in society.[90]

Costas, as an original member of the radical evangelical movement that was more missiologically and mission practice based, always spoke into communal mission-oriented situations. For him, mission was not primarily the task of

---

88. In the first document sent to the Pope for his consideration as to whether to establish an Order, Ignatius wrote the following regarding the Jesuit: "He is a member of a community founded chiefly to strive for the progress of souls in Christian life and doctrine, and for the propagation of the faith by means of the ministry of the word, the *Spiritual Exercises*, and works of charity . . ." Quoted by Ganss in "Introduction," *Ignatius of Loyola*, 45.

89. Ignatius, "Introduction to the Consideration on the States of Life," *The Exercises*, 154.

90. Galilea noted how the foundation of the church is fraternity based on the fact that Jesus calls himself brother to God's people and that Christians have a common paternity in God the Father. He noted that community is and has always been God's way – from the creation of Israel as a people in the Old Testament, to Jesus's apostles, and ongoing through the church. He argued that fraternal communities are called to practice mercy and Godly love. "The Demand of Fraternal Love," *The Way*, 109–24.

the mission agency but Christians as the church.[91] He called for churches to become communities that sought to transform their neighbourhoods. They were to bear witness to God's inbreaking order of life, and work for love, justice, freedom, and peace among people, institutions, and social structures.[92] The applications of his biblical paradigms were always focused on groups such as minority churches within the social periphery of the United States or churches within Latin America.

While Lausanne at the present time is focused on mission practice, I consider it is also communal in its approach. Its guidelines are primarily directed towards evangelical churches and missionary agencies. However, Lausanne's recent emphasis on workplace evangelization, in my view, makes it even more important for Lausanne to consider embracing integrated mission, so that such individual missioners are supported within a framework of spirituality.

Christianity is based on the building of community, often understood as church, but it also embraces other groups, many of which the theological participants represent or helped create. I am thinking of Methodist societies, the Jesuits, and the CEBs, all of which practised both mission and spirituality integrally. Therefore, I aver that the groups of Lausanne evangelicals that follow its respective mission practices also have the potential to enhance their work by incorporating an explicit communal spirituality.

The Participants Refer to "Following Jesus" as a Frame of Reference for Their Missional Christian Life. What Does Each Mean by This? Should Integrated Mission Be Characterised as Incarnational?

Traditionally, the concept of "following Jesus" is a mode of spirituality. This spirituality was a particular focus of Thomas à Kempis's well-known Christian book, *The Imitatio Christi*.[93] Kempis's aim in the book was to promote a life of "becoming like Christ" in terms of inner virtue as an element of sanctification. Maximillian von Habsburg notes how the *Imitatio* embraced a monastic piety

---

91. Costas, *Liberating News*, 133–36. Costas traced from the Old Testament through the New Testament to post-Testament times to show how evangelization is the task of the people of God in community.

92. Costas, *Liberating News*, 144.

93. Thomas à Kempis (1380–1471) grew up within the lay movement known as the Sisters and Brothers of the Common life in the Netherlands and later became an Augustinian Canon.

both for monks and the laity; it sought to nurture a well-ordered pious life.[94] The *Imitatio* was read by both Roman Catholics and Protestants alike and was pivotal in the early Christian life of both Ignatius and Wesley.

Wesley read the *Imitatio* during his initial conversionary period in 1725. It was so significant for him that he re-published it as *The Christian Pattern* and placed it on the reading list for all Methodists. Similarly, the *Imitatio* was influential in Ignatius's early Christian life. He read it at Manresa when he began to write *The Exercises*. In *The Autobiography*, he noted that he read a chapter of it every day throughout his life:[95] in the second week of *The Exercises*, Ignatius recommended it as reading for exercitants.[96] Consequently every Jesuit read it, and the *Imitatio* became central to Jesuit spirituality.[97]

The significance of the *Imitatio* for both Wesley and Ignatius led them to promote a life of inner piety for themselves, the Methodists, and the Jesuits, respectively. In both cases, focusing on inner piety led to missional practices in the form of loving or helping one's neighbour. In other words, for them, following Jesus in piety led to following Jesus in service. Wesley, as I have shown in question two above, perceived "following Jesus" as performing the commands to "love God and neighbour." He therefore integrated the acts of piety and mercy, by revealing that both were means of God sanctifying the Christian, and consequently they were transforming acts towards becoming perfect in love like Jesus. This was God's ordained path of sanctification, namely, "loving God" and "neighbour." In other words, the pattern of "following Jesus" as a means of inner virtue extended to the outward task of missional service; acts of piety and mercy together through the Holy Spirit created disciples.

For Ignatius, the concept of "following Jesus" was fundamental to his understanding of the Christian life. Ignatius's "Meditation on the Two Standards" made it clear that the ultimate election for exercitants is to choose whom they will follow. Further, his identification of the Christian life as a pilgrimage also conveys the same idea of "following Jesus." How one comes to know how to "follow" is through processes of prayer, meditational Bible reading, participation in the sacraments, spiritual exercises, and discernment. It is in these acts that God encounters Christians through experiences of the

94. Maximillian von Habsburg, *Catholic and Protestant Translations of the Imitatio Christi 1425–1650, from Late Medieval Classic to Modern Best Seller.* (New York: Routledge, 2016), 20.

95. Ganss, "General Introduction," *Ignatius of Loyola,* 28.

96. Ignatius, *The Exercises,* 148.

97. See Habsburg, "The Place of Thomas à Kempis *Imitatio Christi* in the Ministry of Jesuit Spirituality," in *Catholic and Protestant Translations,* 219-42.

intellect and emotions that are perceptibly transforming for Christians. It is through such meetings with God, namely the presence of the Holy Spirit, that God's purposes are revealed and the ability to recognise God in the world is given to the Christian. These purposes for Ignatius and the early Jesuits were obviously mission oriented. Habsburg notes: "The *Imitatio* was, in fact, ideally suited to the Jesuit notion of contemplation in action. It encouraged sincere inward preparation before and during their various ministries in the world."[98] In other words, nurturing a pious life led to loving and helping others towards the same life.

Both historical theological participants had a focus on "following Jesus" as a mode of spirituality – a pattern of behaviour that sought an inner life of virtue in order to enable a sanctified mode of living. For both Wesley and Ignatius, following Jesus was doing God's will; this pattern of life was found in their own ways of discipleship and in helping others to become disciples.

More recently, Bosch notes that the liberation movement in Latin America revived the idea of incarnational mission.[99] Liberationists refocused mission so that Jesus's life on earth was included with his death and resurrection as significant for mission practice. They expressed that the concept of "following Jesus" is fundamental to the Christian life; however, liberationists' mode of "following" has different roots than that of the *Imitatio*. Incarnational mission in the liberation movement takes up the ideas of Irenaeus who described Jesus Christ and the Holy Spirit as "the two hands of God": it is through Jesus and the Holy Spirit that God relates to the world.[100] This brings to mission the idea of kenosis, the self-emptying of Christ described in Philippians 2, as a pattern for missioners as well as a movement to be with the poor and outcast on the periphery of society. It is following Jesus in moving downward to be with others and to lift them up. Taking up this missional theme, the WCC in their Melbourne meeting in 1980 endorsed the incarnation as having a significant impact on the nature and content of mission.[101]

Costas also took up the idea of the incarnation in his understanding of how the pattern of Jesus's earthly life affects mission. He considered that the

---

98. Habsburg, *Catholic and Protestant Translations*, 62. He also notes that the interiority of the *Imitatio* at the time of Ignatius was considered "complementary and compatible" to their missionary call. He submits that focusing on the divergent ways of the spiritualities is a "modern distortion."

99. Bosch, *Transforming Mission*, 512.

100. Bevans and Schroeder, *Constants in Context*, 63. They also note how both Leonardo Boff and Jon Sobrino accepted Irenaeus's approach to Jesus in their respective Christologies.

101. Bosch, *Transforming Mission*, 513.

incarnation has three implications for mission. First, it means experiencing the Spirit of Jesus among those with whom Jesus identified, namely, the outcast and poor, and in the places where the poor and outcast are found. This gives the missioner knowledge and understanding of the true nature of Christ. Second, such experiences and understandings of Christ among the poor must be authenticated as in keeping with the Jesus of the New Testament documents. I have already noted how Costas exegeted this theme from Mark's gospel. Third, such experiences and understandings must result in mission that transforms those places, that is, Christians are to bear witness to God's new order of love, freedom, justice, and peace. Costas stated: "To incarnate Christ in our world is to manifest the transforming presence of God's kingdom among the victims of sin and evil. It is to make possible a process of transformation from personal sin and corporate evil to personal and collective freedom, justice and well-being."[102] Like the liberation movement, he combined the pattern of Christ's movement with Jesus's inauguration of God's reign and the consequent work for transformation for both humans and the world through God's power in the Holy Spirit. Thus "following Jesus" in this incarnational pattern is missionizing.

Galilea, as part of the liberation movement, also included this incarnational movement within mission. However, I consider he also sought to synthesize into the movement the *Imitatio* way of "following." For Galilea, "following Jesus" was foundational to his understanding of Christianity. He made it clear, however, that this is not "imitation," but rather "following" by modelling the values and attributes of the kingdom of God already partially present on earth today as well as promised in its fullness in the future.[103] This "following" encompasses Christians – individually and corporately – embodying through the Holy Spirit, faith, hope, love, and the values of the beatitudes in their respective contexts, namely, on the fringes of society. Galilea advocated that in these "fringes" one encounters Jesus through the Holy Spirit as sacrament to bless and enable. "Following is a downward and horizontal movement to love others and embrace God. Speaking to the concept of following, Galilea stated:

> This takes us to the root of Christianity and ought to be the basis of movements of spiritual renewal. To find Jesus in the depths of the disconcerting reality that surrounds us, to follow him in the way

---

102. Costas, *Christ Outside*, 16.

103. Galilea noted regarding this "following": "We are speaking more of identifying with the attitudes, the spirit, and the values that Jesus incarnated in the circumstances of his time and that today we must incarnate (follow) in the circumstances of our own history." *The Way*, 30.

of the gospel until we come face to face with the Father, beyond
all realities, this is the challenge to the faith of our generation.[104]

In bringing together the incarnational practices of outward movement
and inner virtue through "following Jesus," Galilea enriched the practice of
mission by revealing its content of both personal transformation and especial
care for those in need. In so doing, the church bears witness to Jesus's nature
and activity; it speaks to God's concern for both the individual and society.

For me, it is interesting that Lausanne's documents also state that Jesus is
a model for mission in that he was a witness and a servant.[105] *The Manifesto*
also states that mission is incarnational and it defines the term as "moving
humbly into other people's worlds, identifying with their social reality, their
sorrow and suffering, and their struggles for justice against oppressive powers."[106]
This echoes the concept of the aforementioned missiological pattern of the
incarnation. *The Commitment* also strongly endorses embodiment of the
Christian way, noting that:

> Jesus calls us to discipleship, to take up our cross and follow him
> in the path of self-denial, servanthood and obedience . . . We are
> called to live as Christ lived and to love as Christ loved.[107]

> In his life Jesus walked in perfect faithfulness and obedience to
> God. He announced and taught the kingdom of God and modelled
> the way his disciples must live under God's reign.[108]

Within its documents, Lausanne references the idea of "following Jesus"
both in terms of a method of mission and one of inner virtue. The concepts
are not connected as they are within Galilea's texts; however, they are present
in different documents, and I suggest that this concept of "following Jesus"
provides a foundation upon which to proffer a way of integrated mission.

---

104. Galilea, *Following Jesus*, vi.

105. *The Covenant, Making Christ Known*, 11.

106. *The Manifesto*, section A, 4. "The Gospel and Social Responsibility," *Making Christ Known*, 237.

107. *The Commitment*, part 1, 4, B, 24–26.

108. *The Commitment*, part 1, 4, A, 1, 24.

If Integrated Mission Can Synthesise and Ameliorate Modes of Spiritual and Missional Practice Such as "Following Jesus," Are there other Missional and/or Spiritual Concepts That Are Enhanced by Such an Integrated View, Such as the Missio Dei?

The missiological concept of *missio Dei* was brought to prominence in the 1950s by the Protestant theologian Karl Barth.[109] This concept understands mission as belonging to God rather than Christians. In other words, Christians are called to "follow" and "participate" with God in God's mission rather than orchestrate it themselves. For me, the key word here is "participation." The word conjures up the image of Christians working not alone, but with God who takes the lead. However, what does this participation look like?

The inner workings of the Trinity are considered "participatory" in the theological concept of *perichoresis*. James B. Torrance applies this Christian doctrine of the Trinity to the participatory nature of prayer and worship.[110] For him, the patristic understanding of *perichoresis* describes the inner working of the Trinity as "mutual love," "mutual self-giving," and "mutual indwelling."[111] He argues that, in prayer and worship, Christ Jesus through the Holy Spirit draws Christians into participating in this life of communion in the same manner as the Trinity, that is, in mutual love, self-giving, and indwelling.

In my view, Ignatius's description of the spiritual dynamic at work in times of discerning prayer and worship is in keeping with *perichoresis*. Ignatius's *Spiritual Diary* reveals that, for him, these acts are carried out participating with all the members of the Trinity; it is "participatory" prayer and worship.[112]

> But during this Mass I was knowing, or experiencing, or contemplating – the Lord knows – that to speak to the Father was to recognize that he was one Person of that Holy Trinity. This brought me to love that Person's whole self; and that all the more because the other two Persons were by their very essence present

---

109. Karl Barth (1886–1968) was a prominent Swiss Protestant theologian of the twentieth century. He was deeply affected by both world wars, and he was the architect of the Barmen Declaration of the Confessing Church that protested against Adolph Hitler. The concept of *missio Dei* was expressed at the International Missionary Council (IMC) at Willingen in 1952. See Bosch, *Transforming Mission*, 389–93.

110. James B. Torrance, *Worship, Community and the Triune God of Grace* (Carlisle: Paternoster, 1996), 9.

111. Torrance, *Worship, Community*, 20.

112. Harvey Egan affirms my thinking. He considers that Ignatius's explanation of the Trinity in this text encompasses an understanding of the theological concept, "*perichoresis*." *Ignatius Loyola*, 71.

in that One. I experience the same recognition about prayer to the Son, and again about prayer to the Holy Spirit.[113]

I consider that Ignatius's descriptions of worship with the members of the Trinity is *perichoretic*; his prayer was one of mutual love and sharing with the Trinity. In Ignatius's *Exercises*, his "Contemplation to Attain Love" [of God] also affirmed this understanding as he described such love in the context of a relationship between two persons as mutual love and sharing.[114] While Ignatius does not directly speak of mission in terms of this participatory relationship, Torrance extends the concept of *perichoresis* beyond the arena of prayer and worship into mission. He considers that this *perichoretic* relationship is how Christians participate through the Holy Spirit in Christ's mission from the Father to the world.[115]

Wesley did not use the term *perichoresis*, however his explanation of how Christians visit the sick is a good demonstration of how a Christian participates in such a task with the Triune God.[116] Wesley encouraged the visitor to pray to the Father before and during the visit, so that the indwelling Holy Spirit, through God's grace and enabled by Christ, will give the gifts required to perform the task to the missioner. In my view, the relationship between God and the missioner in this task echoes the *perichoretic* understanding of the working Trinity. The missioner participates with God the Creator, through Christ, and in the Holy Spirit in order to serve the sick. It involves mutual love, as one is loving God and neighbour; further, God through the Holy Spirit is sharing the gifts to complete the service as the missioner shares the love of God with the one visited.

In a similar way to Wesley, Costas articulated the importance of "participation" with God in mission also without specifying *perichoresis*. His explanation was similar to that of Torrance's. Costas understood "participation" as the church partaking in the continuing mission of Jesus through the pattern of the incarnation of Christ "because it [the church] is the body of Christ indwelled by his Spirit."[117] In other words, there is *perichoretic* participation as Christian disciples communally incarnate the pattern of Jesus through working with the Holy Spirit in the *missio Dei*.

---

113. Ignatius, *Spiritual Diary*, 247.

114. Ignatius, *The Exercises*, 176.

115. Torrance, *Worship, Community*, 19.

116. Wesley, "On Visiting the Sick," *Works*, 3:389–390.

117. Costas, *Christ Outside*, 13.

Galilea described the interaction of spiritual practices and mission slightly differently. He considered service to be a dialectical movement from being with God in the place of prayer to being with God in the act of mission. In other words, at all times God is present and the Christian is participating with God, in what Galilea determined was a "double encounter" – the first encounter being incarnated in the second. Thus, the spiritual missional life is participatory in all its aspects. There is no segregation between becoming and doing; both are significant and possess a similar nature of participation, integrity and being embraced by God in blessing. For me, this understanding can also embrace a *perichoretic* understanding of participation with the *missio Dei*. The double movement involves participating with God in prayer and participating with God in mission. The constant is the Triune God who is always present. All the theological participants emphasized the importance of participation with God within a relationship of love for the animation of life, including mission. Thus, I suggest the division of mission and spirituality is incongruent and artificial. Both arenas have important practices that are interrelated via a common source and both nurture the other.

Lausanne speaks in terms of mission as being participatory. While not referring directly to the *missio Dei*, it notes that mission is "wholly derived from God's mission, addresses the whole of God's creation, and is grounded at its centre in the redeeming victory of the cross." God's people are called to "participate" in this venture: to be "a blessing and light to the nations," "a community of holiness, compassion, and justice," "to bear witness," "to worship and glorify God . . . and to participate in the transforming mission of God within history."[118] These are statements only; there are no particulars about how these are to be attained, for example, in terms of prayer, participation with God, or modes of sanctification. Nor are there theological concepts of how these connect together. Nevertheless, I do consider that the "bones" of the *missio Dei* are present and linked to the inner virtue of the church which opens up the question of how the people of God "become" what God requires without spiritual practices.

In my view, by connecting a *perichoretic* aspect to participation in the *missio Dei*, one is adding an inner participatory dimension to the outer participatory venture with God. One draws into mission the Trinitarian dynamic of mutual love and sharing. It is a theological description of the missioner's relationship with God attained through both spiritual and mission practices. It also portrays the nature of this relationship as God fills the missioner with grace, gifts, and

---

118. *The Commitment*, part 1, 10, A, 44–45.

direction sending the missioner with the Holy Spirit into the world for the purposes of evangelization. In this way, the participatory nature of missioners working with God is linked and rooted in an understanding of the Trinitarian God who is the source of mission.

A Summary of the Round Table Findings

I aver these theological participants, through the means of a round table, bring helpful insights to both the practices of mission and spirituality in ways that integrate two areas that are currently considered separate. The salient findings are as follows.

First, it is not helpful to divide mission into two separate and distinct activities – namely, evangelism and social practice. None of the theologians in the round table divide mission in this way. Wesley and Ignatius perceived persons as whole beings interrelated with their social settings. Therefore, they worked to remove any obstacles, social or otherwise, that prevented persons from having committed relationships with God. Galilea and Costas, with more contemporary understandings of both personal and structural sin, perceived evangelization as reaching out to transform persons and societal structures with the truth of God's inbreaking kingdom. Lausanne, by not giving priority to evangelism over social responsibility, is currently also moving in this direction and I am assuming that this will continue. Therefore, this book supports the idea of an integral mission practice.

Second, mission practice is a "means of grace" for the missioner as well as the missionized, that is, it is a spiritual task. Via Matthew 25:31–46 and personal experience, Galilea, Wesley, and Costas identified that missional practice, particularly to the poor and outcast, is a sacramental or sanctifying practice. The Spirit of the Risen Christ is present in the place where persons are in need of missional service, and the Holy Spirit is there to aid, help and bless the missioner as well as the missionized. In my view, this is a significant finding; here is a correlation between historical and contemporary understandings of the missional task as a means of grace, that is, helping a missioner to become more like Jesus. This finding also enables comprehension of why Jesus brought the two commands of "loving God and loving neighbour" together (or "works of piety and works of mercy" in Wesley's terms) as both are places where God is available to bless and sanctify. For me, this finding is critical to the re-shaping of mission practice as integrated mission.

Third, integrated mission requires an intimate relationship with God; this is developed through spiritual practices that help a person grow in grace and love for God. Wesley and Galilea both argued that to see God in the sacramental/ sanctifying acts of service, the Christian should first grow in knowledge of God through spiritual practices. Therefore, they both underscored the practices of prayer, meditational Bible reading, and participation in the sacraments, as activities where God is encountered and experienced. Ignatius supported such thinking in this regard. His *Autobiography* and *Spiritual Diary* described his own experiences of encountering and knowing God in these practices and how these enabled him to see God in the world. Further, Ignatius's *Exercises* also assumed that God works affectively within a person through such activities as prayer and meditation; his rules on discernment help exercitants, via a spiritual director, identify the source and meaning of such affects.

While the aforementioned practices lead to "knowing God" through experience, this does not mean that reason and cognitive ways knowing are not also helpful. Costas's hermeneutical biblical interpretation is a rational method that supports incarnational mission; Wesley's sermons are logical and rational; and Ignatius's methods and support of education also embrace reason. Therefore, these theologians encouraged the use of formal education and reason in the pursuit of the knowledge of God. However, for me, the strength in their ways of "knowing" God is in their diversity. They used both experiential encounters and reason to come to know God.

Fourth, integrating mission and spirituality also allows spiritual practices to become practices of mission. In their texts, Costas and Galilea revealed how worship and the practice of the sacraments, particularly the Eucharist, become public prophetic statements. Such thinking broadens the meaning of what is otherwise deemed personal spiritual practice and removes the divide between personal and corporate spirituality and mission.

Fifth, Wesley and Galilea both established that spiritual and mission practices are interdependent and give depth and meaning to the other. They argued that the Christian life is lived in a "to and fro" between these spiritual practices and mission. This is the basis for the command to "love God and neighbour." It is a continual relationship in which God is simultaneously "loving missioner and neighbour" through the Holy Spirit. Ignatius described such a concept as "a relationship of mutual love and sharing." Thus, integrated mission suggests that missioners will live in this to and fro movement, with God as the constant source of their respective lives.

Sixth, integrated mission is both communal and individual. All the theologians affirmed that Christian life is best experienced with others. They all created or promoted communities of Christians practising spirituality and mission together: the Methodist movement, the Jesuit Order, Latin American

CEBs, and churches. Communal life brings accountability to such practices and is in keeping with God's biblical view of community. Lausanne also assumes that mission practice is done through churches or mission agencies; while it does not speak to spirituality, it does acknowledge the corporate nature of the Christian life.

Seventh, "following Jesus" according to Wesley and Ignatius is about Christians becoming like Jesus in their attributes and embodying the values of God's kingdom. For Costas, "following Jesus" is practising the movement of incarnational mission; Galilea and Lausanne underscore both understandings. Lausanne identifies each concept separately, however Galilea blended the aspects of movement and embodiment and thus encouraged Christians to follow Jesus in both being and doing. I consider this synthesis of a spiritual and a missional theological concept affirms the integrated nature of humanity made in God's image.

Finally, integrated mission provides an opportunity to synthesize the concept of the *missio Dei* with the patristic thought of *perichoresis*. Ignatius's spirituality illustrates that in spiritual practices Christians, through Jesus and the Holy Spirit, are drawn into God as Trinity (three persons mutually indwelling); Christians thus participate with the Triune God. Then, as Wesley, Costas, Galilea, and Lausanne all revealed in their respective writings, this continues when Christians partake in the *missio Dei*. Integrated mission brings together "participation" with God in both spiritual and missional practice to underscore that the source of all life, including mission, is God.

I opine that these findings reveal the benefits of integrated mission. Lausanne, therefore, would enrich its mission and strengthen its missioners by adopting such an integrated approach. My final chapter provides proposals for Lausanne to consider.

9

Strategic Practical Theology Part 2

Towards Integrated Mission for Lausanne

Concluding Proposals

I have argued that areas of mission and spirituality are inextricably linked; therefore, to optimise their respective benefits to both the practice of mission and the missioner, they are best synthesized in the form of what I am calling "integrated mission." In so doing, both mission and missioner become rooted in the missional purposes of the Triune God, the *missio Dei*. Moreover, missioners through a sanctifying and/or sacramental process receive from God gifts that animate and empower them to practice mission faithfully and obediently with God and, simultaneously, through God's grace, grow in Christlikeness. In this final chapter, I return to Lausanne which is the focus and beneficiary of my enquiry.

My goal throughout this book has been to reveal to Lausanne the benefits of fully incorporating spirituality into its approach to mission so its missioners and their practice are enriched, sourced and resourced in intimacy with God. My aim in this chapter is to provide Lausanne with concrete suggestions as to how it may redirect its approach towards encapsulating integrated mission within its current mission practice. To be clear, it is not my intent to give a specific framework to Lausanne; this is best achieved by Lausanne itself. However, my proposals will highlight those areas where Lausanne might encourage its churches and mission agencies towards practising integrated mission in their respective contexts and in keeping with Lausanne's ethos.

Generally, I suggest that my recommendations will only make sense if the Lausanne Movement continues to move towards a more integral view of the world and God's provision for it. Lausanne's more open and expansive thinking as evidenced in *The Commitment* must endure as this will help it to embrace spirituality as endemic to mission.

In making various proposals linked with practical outworkings, I am mindful that, first, Lausanne is an evangelical think-tank and a voice regarding mission and its practice to those connected with it and, second, that it accomplishes its purposes primarily through its congresses, committees, and documents. It is also a movement that develops and encourages leaders and networks towards missional transformation of certain geographical regions and areas of concern. Consequently, my proposals are addressed to Lausanne's leadership, its subject groups, and their respective leaders within the Movement.

My Proposals
Proposal One: Embrace a Broader Understanding of the Nature of Mission

One of the critical findings of my work is that the practice of mission is a sanctifying and sacramental act for the missioner. In other words, the missional task, particularly service to those in need as described in Matthew 25:31–46, provides a place for the missioner to experience a transformational encounter with God. The presence of the Spirit of Christ to bless and sanctify means that missional practice is a means of grace and therefore a place of spiritual formation. Hence, mission is more than obedience to God, as central and important as this is. It is simultaneously a work of service and a means of spiritual growth. To date, Lausanne does not embrace such a dynamic within its missional practice; doing so will require a conceptual revision by Lausanne. Therefore, my first proposal is that Lausanne embrace this broader understanding of the nature of mission, that is, that mission is spiritually transformative for the missioner as it promotes growth in Christlikeness or perfect love.

To embrace this proposal, I suggest that Lausanne's theological and scriptural groups work together to reform and expand their views in this matter. I also recommend that specific talks and papers on the subject are prepared and discussed at Lausanne's next global congress. The goal is to ensure that the successor to *The Commitment* recognizes the importance of mission as a place of spiritual formation, thereby enabling this understanding of mission to become an essential constituent of Lausanne's global evangelical voice.

Proposal Two: Identify That Mission Is Sacramental and Sanctifying for the Missioner

Previous chapters have demonstrated that mission practice as a multivalent concept is not only plausible, but also grounded in sound biblical interpretation.[1] As grace for spiritual formation is available for missioners encountering God in missional practice, it has sacramental and/or sanctifying effects. At present the idea of sacramentality is not embraced by many evangelicals, and this includes Lausanne, however change is afoot, with important evangelical theologians, such as Gordon T. Smith and Hans Boersma, advocating for sacramentality within evangelicalism.[2]

Smith reflects that in his youth "evangelical" meant living by faith supported by God's word, that is, the Bible; accordingly, evangelicalism distinguished itself from sacramentalism or Pentecostalism. Smith challenges this perspective and argues that the church should be all three, namely: evangelical, Pentecostal and sacramental. In relation to sacramentality, particularly the partaking of the Eucharist, he argues that in this event participating Christians are drawn through the power of the Holy Spirit into fellowship with Christ and thus "the church is sustained in union with Christ."[3] Simultaneously, the event is a means of grace, which is bestowed upon the Christian partaking in the bread and wine, enabling them to live as Christ lived.[4] Smith further argues that the event of the Eucharist should be tied to the preaching of the Bible for its full effect. He considers that "the Word precedes, informs and sanctifies the sacramental action." [5] Moreover, Smith states: "We remember that the genius of the sacramental vision is that the glory and grace of God is revealed to us and comes to us through materiality and that the incarnation, the embodied Word of God, the real live physical Jesus, is the means by which God's grace is known." [6]

Boersma notes that while young post-modern evangelicals consider that "higher exegesis" and modern methods of biblical interpretation are the cause

---

1. Michael Gorman in *Abide and Go: Missional Theosis in the Gospel of John* (Eugene: Wipf and Stock, 2018), reads John's Gospel with a missional hermeneutic and argues that the Gospel supports the concept of theosis. He suggests that participating with God in mission leads to the transformation of the missioner into the likeness of God.

2. Smith, *Evangelical, Sacramental*; Hans Boersma, *Heavenly Participation*.

3. Smith, *Evangelical, Sacramental*, 85. Here he is influenced by the missiologist, Lesslie Newbigin.

4. Smith, *Evangelical, Sacramental*, 91–92.

5. Smith, *Evangelical, Sacramental*, 88.

6. Smith, *Evangelical, Sacramental*, 87.

of modern and post-modern evangelical issues,[7] he prefers to attribute these issues to "the abandonment of a premodern sacramental mindset in which the realities of this-worldly existence pointed to greater, eternal realities in which they sacramentally shared."[8] Drawing on the theology of Henri De Lubac who sacramentally connected the eucharistic body of Christ and the body of the church, Boersma suggests that Christians, when participating in the Eucharist, allow God's real presence therein to grace the church body with the unity that God intends for it.[9] Boersma advances a reweaving of a sacramental mindset into evangelical Protestant thinking and various practices today so that Christians understand that their activities are also participation with God in the heavenly realm.[10]

For me, both Boersma's and Smith's arguments are important. While neither deal with mission, they both advocate for reincorporating a sacramental worldview so that evangelical Protestant theologizing and thinking is enriched and its practice more participative with God, thereby creating a material link between heaven and earth.

I endorse this view of the Christian life and consider that a sacramental worldview both enhances our understanding of the reality of God in this world and underscores the participative nature of mission with God. A notion of sacramental mission is compelling theologically and only reinforces the relevance of integrated mission. While my desire is for Lausanne to adopt a sacramental view of mission, I do understand that evangelicalism for the most part is deeply hesitant about sacramentality and, therefore, at the present moment this proposal may be rejected. Notwithstanding this possibility, my long-term desire is that Lausanne adopt an understanding of mission as sacramental. In the meantime, I proffer as a first step towards an integrated mission practice that Lausanne re-incorporate into its understanding of mission the well-established evangelical and Protestant concept of sanctification.

Richard Lovelace, in *The Dynamics of the Spiritual Life*, argues that the historical development of Protestant evangelicalism led it to lose sight of the importance of sanctification.[11] He considers that nineteenth century revivalists,

---

7. Boersma, *Heavenly Participation*, 2. He is sympathetic to such arguments.

8. Boersma, *Heavenly Participation*, 3.

9. Boersma, *Heavenly Participation*, 101–16. Chapter 6 entitled "Eucharist as a Sacramental Meal," provides his full argument.

10. Boersma suggests a reweaving of a sacramental mindset into the areas of the Eucharist, time, biblical interpretation, knowledge, and theology.

11. Richard F. Lovelace, *Dynamics of Spiritual Life: An Evangelical Theology of Renewal*, 2nd ed. (Downers Grove: IVP Academic, 2020), 0334.

such as Charles Finney, wrongly encompassed sanctification into conversion, leading conversion to signify both justification and sanctification.[12] He argues this led to what he describes as the "sanctification gap" in which there is no emphasis on growth in the Christian life as part of mission. Lovelace proposes that overcoming the gap requires evangelicals to engage a deeper spirituality based on a biblical view of a Christian spiritual life, one that engages the power of the Holy Spirit, as in the times of revival.[13]

In this book, Wesley, representing early evangelicalism, underscored the importance of sanctification. For him, becoming perfected in God's love through God's grace as gift is the goal of the Christian life. This is an important part of the Christian pilgrimage – that one can love one's neighbour like Christ. For him, it was important to reveal to Christians that sanctifying grace was available not only through works of piety but also through works of mercy. Therefore, he encouraged Christians to serve their neighbours. It is this early evangelical understanding that I propose Lausanne grasp again and integrate into its practice. In so doing, Lausanne would help its missioners and missional practice, it would revive the long view and the integrated understanding of mission, and it would reflect Jesus's call to make disciples rather than converts.

I suggest that Lausanne's theological committee review its understanding of sacramentality and sanctification. Then, as suggested in the first proposal, there can be discussion of the theological understanding of sacramentality/ sanctification and mission at the next global conference, and amendments made in the next congressional document accordingly.

Proposal Three: Root Missional Practice in an Intimate Relationship with God: Bringing Together Loving God and Neighbour.

In *The Commitment* Lausanne bases its mission on the biblical text "to love God and love neighbour." In this commandment Jesus brings together two fomerly individual commands and interlinks them. He underscores that to love one's neighbour, Christians must also love God. In other words, Christian intimacy with God is required to love one's neighbour with God's love. Both Galilea and Wesley underscored this point, each respectively highlighting that to meet God in mission requires Christians to have an existing and enduring intimate relationship with God.

---

12. Lovelace, *The Dynamics*, 336.
13. Lovelace, *The Dynamics*, 339–341.

Lausanne expresses (by means of declarations in *The Commitment*) why evangelicals love God; these declarations are theologically orientated rather than experiential or practical. From my perspective, such declarations of love, while biblical and important, are wanting for they do not provide guidance on how an experiential relationship with God can be developed, one that would lead to loving one's neighbour. In comparison, Wesley, Ignatius and Galilea, in explaining to Christians the importance of a loving relationship with God, each promoted a practice based approach. They each proffered their readers Christian practices that help a person into such a relationship with God that they can receive what they require to perform a missional task.

I suggest that this mode of expression is more helpful. Therefore, with this in mind, my third proposal to Lausanne is to express its approach to "loving God" in a manner similar to its love of neighbour, that is, in practical ways. Doing so would ensure the linkage between God and neighbour is made clear, and missioners are directed not merely in head knowledge, but towards practice. I advocate that Lausanne should create a subject group that deals directly with the interlinking of spirituality and mission, perhaps naming it an "Integrated Mission Group" (IMG). I suggest that its current subject group on "prayer" is then included in this group. The group leader can then network with other subject groups, interested mission agencies, and churches to bring about the integration of spiritual practice and mission, so that missioners can begin practising "loving God and neighbour."

Proposal Four: Loving God: Expressing the Nature of the Relationship

Before suggesting to Lausanne practices that assist missioners to grow in their relationship with God, it is helpful to be reminded how our theologians perceived the nature of this relationship. It is an intimate relationship with the Triune God; one that is akin to the patristic theological concept of *perichoresis*. Therefore, it involves mutual love, sharing, and participation. Missioners are called by God into this loving relationship of participation, but they retain their humanness. It is through this relationship that God sends missioners with the Holy Spirit to participate in mission and provides the gifts that they will require for the task.

In *The Commitment* Lausanne demonstrates it is aware that the nature of missioners' relationships with God in mission is participatory. It also notes it is a relationship of love. However, it does not describe an experiential and intimate relationship of mutual sharing and love like that of *perichoresis*. Lausanne expresses this relationship based on biblical aphorisms that, in my view, give rise to a relationship that is primarily "head" rather than "heart" based.

In this proposal, I recommend that Lausanne conveys to missioners the complete nature of a relationship with God, namely, one that is both biblical and experiential. It leads to participation with the Trinity, understanding God's will for mission, and receiving gracious love and gifts as God wills, for all God's purposes. It is a relationship that moves notions in one's head to the heart and then into practice.

It would surprise me if there are not stories of such experiential knowledge within Lausanne's leaders and associated mission agencies and churches. However, leaders and participants require an opportunity to speak of these "experiences" and place them within a theological framework. I suggest that at its next global conference Lausanne, through its "new" Integrated Mission Group, encourage such opportunities. This will help the experiential side of spirituality to gain a voice and legitimacy. In tandem, Lausanne's theological and scriptural groups might want to expand their understandings of the Trinity so that "perichoretic" fellowship is promoted and thereby experiential knowledge has a theological framework.

Proposal Five: Enhance Mission by Integrating Spiritual Practices for Individuals and Communities

Once Lausanne has explained the full nature of the relationship, it can proceed to identify the practices that cultivate one. This book distinguishes that the common practices of prayer, meditational Bible reading, and corporate worship (including participation in the Eucharist) lead participants into greater intimacy with God. None of these practices are new; they are traditional biblical practices that have endured through time. Many of these practices are both communal and individual. I opine that it is these traditional practices that help persons form a loving relationship with God and the ones that Lausanne should promote with a missional focus, so that an integrated way of mission is achieved.

Contextualization is key in missiological practice today. In arguing for contextual theology, Stephen Bevans notes that it is "imperative" that a theology takes into account "human experience, social location, particular cultures, and social change within those cultures."[14] I consider that this is also true for

---

14. Stephen B. Bevans, *Models of Contextual Theology*, 2nd ed. (Maryknoll: Orbis Books, 2015), 15.

missiology and missional practice, and this makes praxis (theological reflection on practice) significant. Therefore, these traditional spiritual practices give missioners the opportunity to cultivate their relationships with God into one's of mutual love, sharing, and participation. In such practices, they can bring the questions from their contexts to God for the discernment of God's will. In this way, spiritual practices with a missional focus become productive and relevant to contemporary life. They lead to an acknowledgement and participation in the *missio Dei;* they help the missioner to discover and receive God's love for the task and help to contextualise mission practice with God.

The Practice of Contemplative Prayer

One of the main ways that Christians come to "know" God is through prayer. As would be expected, Lausanne encourages its missioners to pray in terms of intercessory prayer and thanksgiving and, of course, I affirm such practices. However, I contend that the practice of contemplative prayer provides missioners with an opportunity to enrich and deepen their relationships with the Triune God. Hans Urs von Balthasar on contemplative prayer states the following:

> [F]irstly, prayer is a conversation between God and the soul, and secondly, a particular language is spoken: God's language. Prayer is dialogue, not [hu]man's monologue before God . . . speech implies reciprocity, the exchange of thoughts and of souls, unity in a common spirit, in a common possession and sharing of the truth . . . prayer is a conversation in which God has the initiative and we, for the moment, can be nothing more that listeners. The essential thing is for us to hear God's word and discover from it how to respond to him.[15]

I recommend that Lausanne includes contemplative prayer in its guidelines, as it is a practice that provides a way for missioners to deepen their relationship with the Triune God. It promotes a mutual relationship of knowing and loving God and, consequently, God's will, and gives missioners the ability to respond in practice. Thus, missioners are called to attentive listening to God first, rather than a missional practice manual. All the theologians in this book ascribed to this contemplative, deeper, receptive, Spirit-led approach to prayer which accompanies their missional practice. Costas, in his interpretation of biblical

---

15. Hans Urs von Balthasar, *Prayer,* trans. Graham Harrison (San Francisco: Ignatius Press, 1986), 14–15.

obedience encouraged such listening which he described as: "[to] incline one's ear, to listen in faith, and respond by faith to God's word".[16] This is not prayer that is entirely "inward" for personal growth; it is prayer that leads one into the world empowered by and with God. Ignatius attested to this consequence: he submitted that such a prayerful relationship with God enabled him to love God more, perceive God in the world, know God's will in particular circumstances, and led him to a life animated and strengthened by God to "help people."

The Practice of Meditational Bible Reading

Lausanne underscores that the authoriative source of their knowledge of mission is the biblical text. Consequently, Lausanne lays emphasis on didactic methods for missioners and ministers so they can learn to interpret the Bible and, in the case of ministers, instruct congregations in their understanding of Scripture on mission. In my view, this is Lausanne's strength. However, where does this leave other methods of reading Scripture? My argument highlights that meditational Bible reading is a means of grace and therefore a way of encountering God – which benefits the missioner.

Lausanne does not refer to such types of reading, yet their value historically and in contemporary society should not be understated. Wesley's Methodist groups read the Bible together and their practices transformed both individuals and society around them, as did the CEBs in Latin America. Galilea's instruction on contextualizing such reading, by bringing questions from readers' respective contexts to the text, enabled those readers to relate the Bible to their present reality and find biblical help for contextual mission. He also emphasized such reading to help Christians with embodying the values and attitudes of Jesus in one's mission.

Such reading is different from exegesis and interpretation. It does come with certain risks as Carlos Mesters indicates in *Defenseless Flower*.[17] While lauding the overall effects of such reading, he expressed certain concerns about its nature, such as its potential for subjectivity even within the boundaries of a collective interpretation and the ability of those with a power position to participate and influence such reading to promote their own agenda. He proffers that scientific exegesis and interpretation also has an important role to play, but at the same time acknowledges that integrating this approach with popular interpretation is difficult. Despite such concerns, I consider the

---

16. Costas, *The Integrity of Mission*, 22.

17. Carlos Mesters, *Defenseless Flower*. This book is grounded in Mester's research into the contextual Bible reading of the CEB's in Brazil.

many contextual and personal benefits resulting from these reading practices make a compelling case for Lausanne encouraging such practices among its missioners, particularly when communal reading groups are led by experienced and spiritually-formed leaders.

Further, as Mesters asserts, the better approach entails both exegetical and meditational reading. Lausanne is strong in the arena of exegetical and hermeneutical interpretation and, of course, this focus should continue. However, from a contextualization perspective, I would add that Costas's hermeneutical process, whereby he also read social scientific material to aid practical application in a particular context, would be a welcome addition to any method of interpretation that Lausanne uses.

Therefore, I propose that Lausanne promote both methods of reading the Bible as complementary to one another. It should underscore that meditative reading has advantages for the missioner in terms of "knowing" God, participation in the *missio Dei,* and incarnational embodiment. It also aids in incarnational mission practice and contextualization.

Practices of Worship (Including Participation in the Eucharist)[18]

Wesley, Galilea and Ignatius all state that participation in the Eucharist is important as a means of grace. For them, through participation in this practice, God meets with Christians to sanctify, strengthen, and bless. There are varied views on the efficacy of the Eucharist among evangelicals and, without evidence of Lausanne's views on this issue, it is difficult to ascertain what Lausanne would advocate in terms of Eucharistic practice. I advocate for its inclusion in missional spiritual practices as a means of grace and strength for the missioner. At minimum, I proffer that Lausanne promote its practice together with the general worship of the church community as missional prophetic practices. As I noted in the previous chapter, one of the advantages of integrating mission and spiritual practice is that communal church practices, which are often perceived as beneficial only to the Christian community, are also missional. In future statements Lausanne could reveal how such practices bear witness to the attributes and values of God's kingdom – values that include equality, justice, grace, and love for all.

---

18. In this context, by worship, I mean public church services of worship. This includes the sacrament whereby bread and wine is taken in accordance with New Testament instructions. Different denominations call this event by differing names, the Lord's Supper, Holy Communion, the Eucharist. I have referred to it as the Eucharist throughout this book. It is the event rather than its name that is important to me.

The Communal Nature of Spiritual Practices

All four theologians examined in this work affirmed the importance of living the Christian life collectively, having created or participated in communal life themselves. Lausanne has the benefit that it speaks to a communal audience, that is, churches and mission societies. It is therefore primed to highlight the strength of communal, missional, Christian life. Further, my arguments in this book have identified that Trinitarian life provides a framework for missional life together.

Communal life provides accountability, support, and allows for a process of discernment. It also allows for the wisdom of experience and the acuity of the neophyte to be heard. Robert Schreiter, in his volume *Constructing Local Theologies,* asks the question, "Who is the local theologian?"[19] He advocates that "to ignore the resources of the professional theologian is to prefer ignorance over knowledge. But to allow the professional theologian to dominate the development of a local theology seems to introduce hegemony into often already oppressed communities." He asserts that Christian communities have an important part in the theologizing process. They raise contextual issues and provide local experience; they implement solutions as they deal authentically with the difficulties at hand. Moreover, by being part of the solution, they are more likely to accept and partner in it.[20] I aver that this is also true for practising integrated mission. The group dynamic is significant; it can help particularly with the interpretation of prayer, meditational Bible study, and biblical exegesis and hermeneutics in context, that is, communal practices help create contextual integrated mission.

I opine that Lausanne's failure to expressly acknowledge the importance of spiritual practices, both individually and corporately, deprives missioners of the life blood of mission. Therefore, I recommend that Lausanne proffers such spiritual acts as significant for establishing a relationship with God, reorienting missioners towards God, and, thereby, benefitting mission.

I consider Lausanne can promote such practices through its new IMG by encouraging churches and missional agencies to form and cultivate groups of mission strategizers and missioners. These groups, like those of Wesley, can then practice spiritual and missional activity together. In this experiential life, they can also identify how these practices interrelate to each other. For example, they could bring together factual data with prayer and Bible study to enable God-led contextual mission. They could also provide opportunities to

---

19. Robert J. Schreiter, *Constructing Local Theologies* (Maryknoll: Orbis Books, 1985).
20. Schreiter, *Constructing Local Theologies,* 17–18.

speak of experiencing God in the places of their respective activity. For me, the creation of such groups would form the grassroots foundation of an integrated mission movement. I also suggest that Lausanne establishes a clear channel for feedback from such groups so that it receives information and knowledge to inform its ongoing theologizing and voice.

Proposal Six: Underscore the Nature of Mission as Incarnational

The biblical record of God incarnating in Jesus, particularly his outreach in word and deed, is considered by many Christians as a pattern for carrying out God's mission in the world; that is, mission is incarnational. Many Christian spiritualities through the centuries have supported this approach, referring to it as "following Jesus." As discussed earlier, this is not an "imitation" of Jesus, as humans are not God, but rather "resembling" or "following" Jesus and radiating the values of God's kingdom that Jesus inaugurated. This "following" requires reliance on the Holy Spirit for connection to God and empowerment. All the theologians in this book, including Lausanne, considered that the nature of mission is incarnational; "following Jesus" is a recurring theme in all their works.

I have noted that there are two streams in this incarnational approach. One stream focuses on the directional movement of mission; this is the idea that like Jesus, who moved downward towards those in need to raise them up, Christians must move towards the poor and outcasts of society with whom Jesus, through the Holy Spirit, is found. Costas highlighted this approach in his biblical missiology and proffered application by suggesting that the church become a sojourning community in those peripheral areas. There, it can work for the transformation of both individuals and society, in keeping with God's inbreaking new order of life. This was also the modus operandi of the incarnation employed by the liberation movement in Latin America, of which Galilea was part. The second stream's focus is upon embodying the virtues and values of the human Jesus such that missioners' ways of being and activities reflect the attributes and ways of the human Jesus and God's inbreaking kingdom.

Lausanne's congressional documents embrace both these streams of incarnation, namely movement and embodiment. In my opinion, this is one of Lausanne's strengths. Its earlier documents proffer the movement of the incarnation while The Commitment suggests the way of embodiment. In both cases, however, Lausanne does not attend to the practical necessities of such approaches. I aver that, if Lausanne embraces integrated mission and outlines means for missioners to live this out, it will enable its missioners to synthesize movement and embodiment, as Jesus did in his life.

Incarnational mission from an embodiment perspective requires Lausanne to underscore intimacy with the Triune God. As such, my proposal to encourage Lausanne to promote spiritual practices and mission in smaller groups helps here, particularly where the focus is upon coming to "know" Jesus both cognitively and experientially, so that missioners receive the gifts from God for their tasks, such as the fruit of the Holy Spirit and the love of Christ for their neighbour. The fuller understanding of mission also aids incarnational mission by further emphasizing that God is present in locations of service to provide the attributes that the missioner requires for the missional task. Therefore, Christians, through both practices, become more like Christ and able to perform mission like Jesus.

For these incarnational movements to take place, Lausanne will need to challenge associated churches and mission societies to become kenotic and locate themselves on the periphery of society before challenging the centres of power, as this was Jesus's own pattern. However, it can also affirm the Spirit of Christ's presence in such places to bless, give insight, and love.

I aver that to follow Jesus in mission requires movement and embodiment. Giving priority to missioners' relationship with God through spiritual practices and service enables missioners to attend to God, to do God's will, and to become like Christ in participating with God in mission. In this mode, Christians can "follow" Jesus, in both becoming and doing. This, in my view, is integrated mission. Thus, it is important that the IMG promotes spiritual formation within small groups, mission agencies, and churches, taking into account within their respective contexts the demands of both incarnational movement and embodiment. This may require encouraging leaders of such groups to be educated in the ways of spiritual formation so that they and the members of their groups are appropriately guided in incarnational practice, for example, they could learn to lead Ignatius's *Exercises* in a group setting.

While clearly my proposals require change on the part of Lausanne, the benefits gained would be significant; they would also keep Lausanne moving in the current direction of those missioners and academics calling for direct spiritual input within mission.

Conclusion

This book, as a piece of practical theology, participates in the conversation between the disciplines of Christian spirituality and practical theology. It reveals how the work of the former can inform and partner with practical theology to further and enhance both arenas. Like Wofteich, moving forward, I hope such participation continues as, in my view, Christian spirituality and practical activity are enhanced by each other.

More particularly, in this book, I set out to establish that what I term "integrated mission" is credible and that mission practice, such as that promoted by Lausanne, will be enriched by its implementation. To this end, I have provided proposals for Lausanne that can help it move towards such integration.

I have revealed the importance of mining Christian history for important insights that can help contemporary missioners revitalize evangelization. I have also demonstrated the usefulness of methods such as a Gadamerian process in doing this. Through retrospection, I have disclosed that Wesley and Ignatius both realized there is an inextricable link between spiritual and mission oriented practices; their respective missional practices were animated and rooted in their life with the Triune God.

I have promoted the work of contemporary theologians writing in contexts alien to my own. In reviewing the work of Costas and Galilea, I revealed how challenging circumstances can lead to renewal. Both Costas and Galilea, confronted by a world of injustice, had to reflect on their respective understandings of Christianity to discern God's will in such circumstances. Costas re-read the biblical story with new eyes, giving us a new biblical paradigm. Galilea refreshed traditional Christian practices so that the work of liberation could be properly ascribed to the Triune God and Christian social justice workers could find their strength and purpose in this God.

Further, in reflecting upon these theological participants' perspectives, I chose to use Tracy's concept of "similarities in difference"; I am challenged by how in very different circumstances, the theologians with missional hearts lived similarly. All viewed the integration of spiritual practices with mission as essential. Simple practices that connected them to God revitalized each respectively, enabling them to work with others and, ultimately, with the Triune God to implement change.

This work underscores that the Triune God's mission is more than a way of bearing witness to this world of God's provision of a kingdom and a way of salvation; it is also a process that God uses to form God's people. God's mission is multivalent. I opine that this finding is critical; it challenges our understanding of mission. It reconceives the *missio Dei* as a place of being, participating (*perichoresis*), and growing in grace with God. Lausanne has an ever-broadening mission practice and I welcome its recent changes. However, there is a need for Lausanne to regrasp the spiritual importance of mission and I suggest that this is best done by interweaving missional and spiritual practices explicitly, so that its missioners and mission are sourced and animated by the Triune God of grace.

Integrated mission is a movement: a process through which God embraces missioners and the world. It commences with missioners in their context and community, in a posture towards God, seeking to grow in their relationship with God through various spiritual practices and attending to the Triune God's will and the *missio Dei.* As God meets with them, missioners move in a way of mission that is incarnational and *perichoretic,* participating with God in the peripheral areas of the world. Here God in Christ and through the Holy Spirit continues to embrace the missioners, to give them the love, strength, and gifting they require to be channels of God's transforming grace to persons and the world. In so doing, through God's grace, missioners are also changed into the likeness of Christ. I aver this movement integrates and revitalizes the biblical, spiritual, and traditional practices of the past with the innovative realities of the present. It is a dynamic movement, characterized by continual love and participation with the Triune God in the concrete reality of the world.

Bibliography

à Kempis, Thomas. *The Imitation of Christ.* Edited by Harold C. Gardiner. Garden City: Doubleday, 1955.

Abraham, William J. "Saving Souls in the Twenty-First Century: A Missiological Midrash on John Wesley." *Wesleyan Theological Journal* 38, no. 1 (Spring 2003): 7–20.

Albrecht, Ruth. "We Kiss Our Dearest Redeemer through Inward Prayer: The Mystical Traditions in Pietism." In *The Wiley-Blackwell Companion to Christian Mysticism,* edited by Julia A. Lamm, 473–88. Oxford: Blackwell, 2013.

Amalraj, John, Geoffrey W. Hahn, and William D. Taylor, eds. *Spirituality in Mission: Embracing the Lifelong Journey.* New York: World Evangelical Alliance Mission Commission, 2018. Kindle.

Andinach, Pablo, R., and Alejandro F. Botta, eds. *The Bible and the Hermeneutics of Liberation.* Atlanta: Society of Biblical Literature, 2009.

Balthasar, Hans Urs von. *Prayer.* Translated by Graham Harrison. San Francisco: Ignatius Press. 1986.

Barth, Karl. *Church Dogmatics* Vol. 4, pt. 1, *The Doctrine of Reconciliation.* Edited by Geoffrey. W. Bromiley and T. F. Torrance. Translated by Geoffrey W. Bromily. New York: T&T Clark, 2009.

———. *Church Dogmatics* Vol. 4, pt. 4, *The Foundation of Christian Life.* Edited by Geoffrey W. Bromiley and T. F. Torrance. Translated by Geoffrey W. Bromily. Edinburgh: T&T Clark, 1981.

Bebbington, David W. *Evangelicalism in Modern Britain: A History from the 1730s to the 1980s.* London: Routledge, 1989.

Bell, Daniel M., Jr. *Liberation Theology After the End of History: The Refusal to Cease Suffering.* New York: Routledge, 2001.

Bennett, Zoë, Elaine Graham, Stephen Pattison and Heather Walton. *Invitation to Research in Practical Theology.* New York: Routledge, 2018.

Bernard. *Bernard of Clairvaux: Selected Works.* Translated by G.R. Evans, New York: Paulist, 1987.

Bevans, Stephen B. "Life, Joy, and Love: Together towards Life in Dialogue with *Evangelii Gaudium* and *The Cape Town Commitment,*" *International Review of Mission* 104, no. 2 (2015): 193–202.

———. *Models of Contextual Theology.* Maryknoll: Orbis Books, 2002.

Bevans, Stephen B., and Roger P. Schroeder. *Constants in Context: A Theology of Mission for Today.* Maryknoll: Orbis Books, 2004.

Bibby, Reginald W. *Beyond the Gods & Back: Religion's Demise and Rise and Why It Matters.* Lethbridge: Project Canada Books, 2011.

Boersma, Hans. *Heavenly Participation: the Weaving of a Sacramental Tapestry.* Grand Rapids: Eerdmans, 2011.

Boff, Clodovis. "Epistemology and Method of the Theology of Liberation." In *Mysterium Liberationis: Fundamental Concepts of Liberation Theology*, edited by Ignacio Ellacuría and Jon Sobrino, 57–85. Maryknoll: Orbis Books, 1993.

———. *Theology and Praxis: Epistemological Foundations.* Maryknoll: Orbis Books, 1987.

Boff, Leonardo, and Clodovis Boff. *Introducing Liberation Theology.* Translated by Paul Burns. Maryknoll: Orbis Books, 1987.

Boff, Leonardo. *Church: Charism and Power: Liberation Theology and the Institutional Church.* Translated by John W. Dierksmeier. Eugene: Wipf and Stock, 2012.

———. *Ecclesiogenesis: The Base Communities Reinvent the Church.* Translated by Robert R. Barr. Maryknoll: Orbis Books, 1994.

———. "The Need for Political Saints: From a Spirituality of Liberation to the Practice of Liberation." Translated by Linde Rivera and Leon King. *CrossCurrents* 30, no. 4 (1980): 369-84.

———. *Trinity and Society.* Maryknoll: Orbis Books, 1988.

Bosch, David J. *Transforming Mission: Paradigm Shifts in a Theology of Mission.* Maryknoll: Orbis Books, 1991.

Brendlinger, Irv. *Social Justice Through the Eyes of Wesley: John Wesley's Theological Challenge to Slavery.* Peterborough: Joshua Press, 2006.

Briggs, Richard S. "Biblical Hermeneutics and Practical Theology: Method and Truth in Context," *Anglican Theological Review* 97, no. 2 (2015): 201-17.

Brown, Sally. A. "Hermeneutical Theory." In *The Wiley-Blackwell Companion to Practical Theology*, edited by Bonnie J. Miller-McLemore, 112–22. Malden: Wiley-Blackwell, 2012.

Browning, Don S. *A Fundamental Practical Theology: Descriptive and Strategic Proposals.* Minneapolis: Fortress, 1991.

———, ed. *Practical Theology: The Emerging Field in Theology, Church, and World.* San Francisco: Harper & Row, 1983.

Brueggemann, Walter. *The Prophetic Imagination.* Minneapolis: Fortress, 1978.

Buber, Martin. *Between Man and Man.* New York: Macmillan, 1967.

Cabestrero, Teófilo. "A Conversation with Segundo Galilea." In *Conversations with Contemporary Theologians*, edited by Teófilo Cabestrero, 63–67. Translated by Donald Devenish Walsh. Maryknoll: Orbis Books, 1980.

Cahalan, Kathleen A., and James R. Nieman. "Mapping the Field of Practical Theology." In *For Life Abundant: Practical Theology, Theological Education, and Christian Ministry*, edited by Dorothy C. Bass and Craig Dykstra, 62–85. Grand Rapids: Eerdmans, 2008.

Caraman, Philip. *Ignatius Loyola: A Biography of the Founder of the Jesuits.* San Francisco: Harper & Row, 1990.

Castro, Emilio. "Liberation, Development, and Evangelism: Must We Choose in Mission?" *International Bulletin of Mission Research* 2, no. 3 (July 1978): 87–91.

Chan, Simon. *Spiritual Theology: A Systematic Study of a Christian Life.* Downers Grove: InterVarsity Press, 1998.

Clark, J. C. D. *English Society, 1688–1832: Ideology, Social Structure and Political Practice during the Ancient Regime.* New York: Cambridge University Press, 1985.

Collins, Kenneth J., ed. *Exploring Christian Spirituality: An Ecumenical Reader.* Grand Rapids: Baker Books, 2000.

———. "John Wesley's Assessment of Christian Mysticism." *Lexington Theological Quarterly* 28, no. 4 (Winter 1993): 299–318.

———. "Wesley's Life and Ministry." In *The Cambridge Companion to John Wesley,* edited by Randy L. Maddox and Jason E. Vickers, 43–59. Cambridge: Cambridge University Press, 2010.

Conner, Benjamin T. *Practicing Witness: A Missional Vision of Christian Practices.* Grand Rapids: Eerdmans, 2011.

Cook, A. William, Jr. "Base Ecclesial Communities: A Study of Re-evangelization and Growth in the Brazilian Catholic Church." *International Bulletin of Mission Research* 4, no. 3 (July 1980): 113–17. DOI 10.1177/239693938000400304.

Coote, Robert T. "Lausanne II and World Evangelization." *International Bulletin of Missionary Research* 14, no. 1 (January 1990): 10–17.

Costas, Orlando E. *Christ Outside the Gate: Mission Beyond Christendom.* Maryknoll: Orbis Books, 1982.

———. *The Church and its Mission: A Shattering Critique from the Third World.* Wheaton: Tyndale House, 1974.

———. "Conversion as a Complex Experience: A Personal Case Study." In *Down to Earth: Studies in Christianity and Culture,* edited by John R. W. Stott and Robert T. Coote, 173–91. Grand Rapids: Eerdmans, 1980.

———. "Ecumenical Experiences of a Hispanic Baptist." *Journal of Ecumenical Studies* 17, no. 2 (Spring 1980): 118–24.

———. "Evangelism and the Gospel of Salvation." *International Review of Mission* 63, no. 249 (January 1974): 24–37.

———. "Hispanic Theology in North America." In *Struggles for Solidarity: Liberation Theologies in Tension,* edited by Lorine M. Getz and Ruy D'Costa, 63–74. Minneapolis: Fortress, 1992.

———. *The Integrity of Mission: The Inner Life and Outreach of the Church.* New York: Harper & Row, 1979.

———. *Liberating News: A Theology of Contextual Evangelization.* Grand Rapids: Eerdmans, 1989.

———. "The Missiological Thought of Emilio Castro." *International Review of Mission* 73, no. 289 (January 1984): 86–97.

———. "Missiology in Contemporary Latin America: A Survey." *Missiology* 5 no.1 (January 1977): 89–114.

———. "The Mission of Ministry." *Missiology* 14, no. 4 (1986): 463–472.

———. "Mission Out of Affluence." *Missiology* 1, no. 4 (1973): 405–423.

———. "The Subversiveness of Faith: Esther as a Paradigm for a Liberating Theology." *Ecumenical Review*, 40, no. 1 (January 1988): 66–78.

———. "Tradition and Reconstruction in Mission: A Latin American Protestant Analysis." *Occasional Bulletin of Missionary Research* 1, no. 1 (January 1977): 4–8.

Coupeau, Carlos J. "Five Personae of Ignatius of Loyola." In *The Cambridge Companion to the Jesuits*, edited by Thomas Worcester, 32-51. Cambridge: Cambridge University Press, 2008.

Croatto, J. Severino. "Biblical Hermeneutics in the Theologies of Liberation." In *Irruption of the Third World: Challenge to Theology*, edited by Virginia Fabella and Sergio Torres, 140-70. Maryknoll: Orbis Books, 1983.

———. *Exodus: A Hermeneutics of Freedom.* Translated by Salvator Attanasio. Maryknoll: Orbis Books, 1981.

Cunningham, Lawrence S., and Keith J. Egan. *Christian Spirituality: Themes from the Tradition.* New York: Paulist Press, 1996.

Dawsey, James, M. "The Lost Front Door into Scripture: Carlos Mesters, Latin American Liberation Theology and the Church Fathers." *Anglican Theological Review* 72, no. 3 (Summer 1990): 292–305.

Demeterio, F. P. A., III. "Introduction to Hermeneutics." *Diwatao* 1, no. 1 (2001). https://www.geocities.com/philodept/diwatao/introduction_to_hermeneutics.htm.

Douglas, J. D., ed. *Let the Earth Hear His Voice: International Congress on World Evangelization, Lausanne, Switzerland.* Minneapolis: World-Wide Publications, 1975.

———., ed. *Proclaim Christ Until He Comes: Calling the Whole Church to Take the Whole Gospel to the Whole World. Lausanne II in Manila.* Minneapolis: World Wide Publications, 1990.

Dreyer, Frederick. "Faith and Experience in the Thought of John Wesley." *The American Historical Review* 88, no. 1 (February 1983): 12–30. https://www.jstor.org/stable/1869343.

Egan, Harvey D. "Christian Apophatic and Kataphatic Mysticisms," *Theological Studies* 39, no. 3 (September 1978), 399–42.

———. *Ignatius Loyola the Mystic.* The Way of the Christian Mystics. Wilmington: Michael Glazier, 1987.

———. *The Spiritual Exercises and the Ignatian Mystical Horizon.* St. Louis: Institute of Jesuit Sources, 1976.

Endean, Philip. *Karl Rahner and Ignatian Spirituality.* Oxford: Oxford University Press, 2001. doi: 10.1093/acprof:oso/9780198270287.001.0001.

Escobar, Samuel. *Christian Mission and Social Justice.* Scottsdale: Herald Press, 1978.

———. "The Legacy of Orlando Costas." *International Bulletin of Missionary Research* 25, no. 2 (April 2001): 50–56.

————. *The New Global Mission: The Gospel from Everywhere to Everyone.* Downers Grove: InterVarsity Press, 2003.

————. *In Search of Christ in Latin America: From Colonial Image to Liberating Savior.* Downers Grove: InterVarsity Press, 2019.

Farley, Edward. *Theologia: The Fragmentation and Unity of Theological Education.* Philadelphia: Fortress, 1983.

Ferm, Deane William. *Third World Liberation Theologies, An Introductory Survey.* Maryknoll: Orbis Books, 1981.

Field, David N. "John Wesley as a Public Theologian: The Case of Thoughts Upon Slavery." *Scriptura* 114, no. 1 (2015): 1–13. https://scriptura.journals.ac.za.

Finn, Nathan A., and Keith S. Whitfield. "The Missional Church and Spiritual Formation." In *Spirituality for the Sent, Casting a New Vision for the Missional Church,* edited by Nathan A. Finn and Keith S. Whitfield, 9–29. Downers Grove: IVP Academic, 2017.

Foster, Richard J. *Celebration of Discipline: A Pathway to Spiritual Growth.* Rev. ed. San Francisco: Harper & Row, 1988.

————. *Prayer: Finding the Hearts True Home.* New York: HarperCollins, 1992.

Franklin, Kirk. "Mission and Spirituality." In *Spirituality in Mission, Embracing the Lifelong Journey,* edited by John Amalraj, Geoffrey W. Hahn, and William D. Taylor. New York: World Evangelical Alliance Mission Commission, 2018. Kindle.

Frei, H. W. "Conflicts in Interpretation." *Theology Today* 49, no. 3 (1992): 344–56. http://theologytoday.ptsem.edu/oct1992/v49-3-article5.htm

Frostin, Per. "The Hermeneutics of the Poor: The Epistemological 'Break' in Third World Theologies." *Studia Theologica* 39 (1985): 127–50.

Gadamer, Hans-Georg. *Truth and Method.* Edited and translated by Joel Weinsheimer and Donald G. Marshall, 4th ed. London: Bloomsbury Academic, 2013.

Gaines, Timothy R. "Politics, Participation and the *Missio Dei* in the thought of Miroslav Volf and the Wesleyan Tradition." *Wesleyan Theological Journal* 47 (April 2012): 72–89.

Galilea, Segundo. *The Beatitudes: To Evangelize as Jesus Did.* Translated by Robert R. Barr. Quezon City: Claretian Publications, 1984

————. "Between Medellín and Puebla." *CrossCurrents* 28, no.1 (Spring 1978): 71–78.

————. *The Challenge of Popular Religiosity.* Quezon City: Claretian Publications,1988.

————. *Following Jesus.* Translated by H. Phillips. Maryknoll: Orbis Books, 1981.

————. *The Future of Our Past: The Spanish Mystics Speak to Contemporary Spirituality.* Notre Dame: Ave Maria Press, 1985.

————. "Liberation as Encounter with Politics and Contemplation." In *The Mystical and Political Dimension of the Christian Faith,* edited by Claude Geffré and Gustavo Gutiérrez. Concillium 6, no. 10; Theology of Liberation. New York: Herder & Herder, 1974.

———. "Liberation Theology and New Tasks Facing Christians." In *Frontiers of Theology in Latin America*. Edited by Rosino Gibellini. Translated by John Drury. Maryknoll: Orbis Books, 1979.

———. *Spirituality of Hope*. Translated by Terrence Cambias. Quezon City: Claretian, 1988.

———. *Temptation and Discernment*. Translated by Stephen-Joseph Ross. Washington, DC: ICS. Publishers, 1996.

———. "The Theology of Liberation, A General Survey." In *Liberation Theology and the Vatican Document*. Translated by Olga Prendergast and Alberto Rossa. Quezon City: Claretian, 1985.

———. *The Way of Living Faith: A Spirituality of Liberation*. Translated by John W. Diercksmeier. San Francisco: Harper & Row, 1988.

Gallagher, Robert. "Inner and Outer Dimensions of Mission: A Historical Survey of the Role of Spirituality in Latin American Protestant Missiological Writings." *Journal of Latin American Theology* 8, no. 2 (Fall 2013): 87–101.

———. "Mission from the Inside Out: An Integrative Analysis of Selected Latin American Protestant Writings in Spirituality and Mission." *Missiology: An International Review* 40, no. 1 (January 2012), 9–22.

Getz, Lorine M. and Ruy O. Costa, eds. *Struggles for Solidarity, Liberation Theologies in Tension*. Minneapolis: Fortress Press, 1992.

Gittings, Anthony J. *Bread for the Journey*. Maryknoll: Orbis Books, 1993.

Graham, Elaine, Heather Walton, and Frances Ward. *Theological Reflection: Methods*. London: SCM Press, 2005.

Green, Thomas H. *A Vacation with the Lord*. San Francisco: Ignatius, 2000.

Guder, Darrell L., ed. *Missional Church: A Vision for the Sending of the Church in North America*. Grand Rapids: Eerdmans Publishing, 1998.

Guibert, Joseph de. *The Jesuits: Their Spiritual Doctrine and Practice; A Historical Study*. Edited by George E. Ganss, Translated by William J. Young. Chicago: Institute of Jesuit Sources, 1964.

Gunter, Stephen, Scott J. Jones, Ted A. Campbell, Rebekah L. Myles, and Randy L. Maddox. *Wesley and the Quadrilateral: Renewing the Conversation*. Nashville: Abingdon, 1997.

Gunther, John. *Inside South America*. New York: Harper & Row, 1966.

Gutiérrez, Gustavo. "The Prophetic Role of the Church in Latin America." *The Christian Century* 100, no. 30 (October 1983): 931–35.

———. *The Theology of Liberation*. Maryknoll: Orbis Books, 1973.

———. *We Drink from Our Own Wells: The Spiritual Journey of a People*. Maryknoll: Orbis Books, 1984.

Hammond, Geordan. "John Wesley and 'Imitating' Christ." *Wesleyan Theological Journal* 45, no. 1 (Spring 2010): 197–212.

Hardy, Douglas S., and William L. Selvidge. "Review Essay of Some Recent Work of Spirituality and Mission." *Journal of Spiritual Formation & Soul Care* 6, no. 1 (2013): 109–21.

Hartnett, Daniel. "Remembering the Poor: An Interview with Gustavo Gutiérrez." *America: The Jesuit Review*, February 3, 2003. https://www.americamagazine.org/faith/2003/02/03/remembering-poor-interview-gustavo-gutierrez.

Heaney, Sharon E. *Contextual Theology for Latin America: Liberation Themes in Evangelical Perspective.* Paternoster Theological Monographs. Eugene: Wipf and Stock, 2008.

Heath, Elaine A. *The Mystic Way of Evangelism: A Contemplative Vision for Christian Outreach.* Grand Rapids: Baker Academic, 2008.

Heitink, Gerben. *Practical Theology: History, Theory, Action Domains: Manual for Practical Theology.* Translated by Reinder Bruinsma. Studies in Practical Theology. Grand Rapids: Eerdmans, 1999.

Heitzenrater, Richard P. *The Elusive Mr. Wesley, John Wesley as Seen by Contemporaries and Biographers. Volume 2.* Nashville: Abingdon, 1984.

Helland, Roger, and Len Hjarlmarson. *Missional Spirituality, Embodying God's Love from the Inside Out.* Downers Grove: InterVarsity Press, 2011. Kindle.

Hennelly, Alfred, T. "Theological Method: The Southern Exposure." *Theological Studies*, 38, no 4 (1977): 709–735.

Hindmarsh, D. Bruce. *The Spirit of Early Evangelicalism: True Religion in a Modern World.* New York: Oxford University Press, 2018.

Holt, Bradley, P. *Thirsty for God: A Brief History of Christian Spirituality.* Minneapolis: Fortress, 1993.

Holterman, Bart. "Pilgrimages in Images: Early Sixteenth-Century Views of the Holy Land with Pilgrims' Portraits as Part of the Commemoration of the Jerusalem Pilgrimage in Germany." Master's thesis, Utrecht University, 2013. https://www.info:eu-repo/semantics/open access.

Homza, Lu-Ann. "The Religious Milieu of the Young Ignatius." In *The Cambridge Companion to the Jesuits*, edited by Thomas Worcester, 13-31. Cambridge: Cambridge University, 2008.

Howells, Edward. "Spanish Mysticism and Religious Renewal Ignatius of Loyola, Teresa of Avila, and John of the Cross." In *The Wiley-Blackwell Companion to Christian Mysticism*, edited by Julie A. Lamm, 422-36. Malden: Blackwell, 2013.

Hudson, Rex A. *Chile: A Country Study.* Washington, DC: Federal Research Division, Library of Congress, 1994.

Hunsberger, George. "Journey in the Spirit." In *Spirituality for the Sent, Casting a New Vision for the Missional Church*, edited by Nathan A. Finn and Keith S. Whitfield, 217-36. Downers Grove: IVP Academic, 2017.

Hunter, George G. "The Legacy of Donald G. McGavran," *International Bulletin of Missionary Research* 16, no. 4 (October 1992): 158-62. https://doi.org/10.1177/239693939201600404.

Hynson, Lyon. *To Reform the Nation: Theological Foundations of Wesley's Ethics*. Grand Rapids: Francis Asbury Press, 1984.

Ignatius. *Ignatius of Loyola: The Spiritual Exercises and Selected Works*, edited by George E. Ganss. The Classics of Western Spirituality. New York: Paulist Press, 1991.

Irwin, Kevin. "Liberation Theology." *Theological Studies* 55, no. 4 (1994): 675–84.

Jeffrey, David Lyle, ed. *English Spirituality in the Age of Wesley*. Vancouver: Regent College Publishing, 2000.

Jensen, L. Paul. *Subversive Spirituality: Transforming Mission through the Collapse of Space and Time*. Princeton Theological Monograph Series. Eugene: Pickwick, 2009.

Jenkins, Philip. *The New Faces of Christianity: Believing the Bible in the Global South*. New York: Oxford University Press, 2006.

———. *The Next Christendom: The Coming of Global Christianity*. New York: Oxford University Press, 2011.

John of the Cross. *Selected Writings: The Classics of Western Spirituality*. New York: Paulist, 1987.

Johnson, Luke Timothy. *Living Jesus: Learning the Heart of the Gospel*. San Francisco: Harper, 1999.

———. *The Real Jesus Is the Christ of Faith*. San Francisco: Harper, 1996.

Johnston, William. *Mystical Theology: The Science of Love*. Maryknoll: Orbis Books, 1995.

Joling-Van der Sar, Gerda J. "The Controversy between William Law and John Wesley." *English Studies* 87, no. 4 (August 2006): 442–65. https://doi.org/10.1080/001383 80600757810.

Kaiser, Walter C. "Evangelical Hermeneutics: Restatement, Advance or Retreat from the Reformation." *Concordia Theological Quarterly* 46, no. 2–3 (April–July 1980): 167–18.

Kim, Kirsteen, and Andrew Anderson, eds. *Edinburgh 2010: Mission Today and Tomorrow*. Oxford: Regnum Books International, 2011.

Kinnamon, Michael. "Scripture and Mission." In *Unity in Mission: Theological Reflection on the Pilgrimage of Mission*, edited by M.J. Budde and D. Thorsen. New York: Paulist Press, 2006.

Kirkpatrick, David C. *A Gospel for the Poor: Global Social Christianity and the Latin American Evangelical Left*. Philadelphia: Pennsylvania University Press, 2019.

Langmead, Ross. *The Word Made Flesh: Towards an Incarnational Missiology*. Dallas: University Press of America, 2004.

Lausanne Movement. *The Cape Town Commitment*, 2010. Lausanne Missional Content Library. https://www.lausanne.org/content/ctc/ctcommitment#capetown.

———. *The Lausanne Covenant*, 1974. Lausanne Missional Content Library. https://www.lausanne.org/content/covenant/lausanne-covenant.

———. "The Statement from the Consultation on Evangelism and Social Responsibility." In *Making Christ Known: Historic Mission Documents from the*

Lausanne Movement, 1974–1989 edited by John Stott. Grand Rapids: Cambridge: Eerdmans, 1996.

———. *The Manila Manifesto*, 1989. Lausanne Missional Content Library. https://www.lausanne.org/content/manifesto/the-manila-manifesto.

———. *Transformation: The Church in Response to Human Need*, 1983. Lausanne Missional Content Library. https://www.lausanne.org/content/statement/transformation-the church-in-response-to-human-need.

Leonard, Gregory. "The Long Eighteenth Century." In *The Cambridge Companion to John Wesley*, edited by Randy L. Maddox and Jason E. Vickers, 13–42. Cambridge: Cambridge University Press, 2010.

Locher, Frances C., ed. *Contemporary Authors: A Bio-Bibliographical Guide.* Vol. 5. Detroit: Gale Research, 1982.

Lovelace, Richard F. *Dynamics of Spiritual Life: An Evangelical Theology of Renewal.* 2nd ed. Downers Grove: IVP Academic, 2020.

———. "The Sanctification Gap." *Theology Today* 29, no. 4 (January 1973): 363–69. https://doi.org/10.1177/004057367302900402.

Maddox, Randy. *Responsible Grace: John Wesley's Practical Theology.* Nashville: Abingdon, 1994.

———. "Visit the Poor: Wesley's Precedent for Wholistic Mission," *Transformation* 18, no.1 (January 2001): 37–50.

Maddox, Randy L., and Jason E. Vickers, eds. *The Cambridge Companion to John Wesley.* Cambridge: Cambridge University Press, 2010.

Maryks, Robert A., ed. *A Companion to Ignatius of Loyola: Life, Writings, Spirituality, Influence.* Brill's Companions to the Christian Tradition, 52. Leiden: Brill, 2014.

McGinn, Bernard. *Foundations of Mysticism, Origins to the Fifth Century*, New York: Crossroad, 1991.

———. "The Future of Past Spiritual Traditions." *Spiritus* 15, no. 1 (2015): 1–18.

———. *The Foundations of Mysticism.* Vol 1 of *The Presence of God: A History of Western Christian Mysticism.* New York: Crossroad, 1997.

McGrath, Alister E. *Christian Theology: An Introduction* 2nd ed. Malden: Blackwell, 1997.

McIntosh, Mark A. *Mystical Theology: The Integrity of Spirituality and Theology.* Oxford: Blackwell, 1998.

Mesters, Carlos. *Defenseless Flower: A New Reading of the Bible.* Translated by Frances McDonagh. Maryknoll: Orbis Books, 1989.

Metz, Johann Baptist. *Faith in History and Society: Toward a Practical Fundamental Theology.* Translated by David Smith. New York: Seabury, 1980.

———. *A Passion for God: The Mystical-Political Dimension of Christianity.* Translated by J. Matthew Ashley. New York: Paulist Press, 1998.

"Melbourne Conference Section Reports." *International Review of Mission*, 69 no. 276–277, 388-436. https://doi.org/10.1111/j.1758-6631.1980.tb01362.x.

Miller-McLemore, Bonnie. "Five Misunderstandings About Practical Theology." *International Journal of Practical Theology* 16, no. 1 (2012): 5–26.

————. "Introduction: The Contributions of Practical Theology." In *The Wiley-Blackwell Companion to Practical Theology*. Edited by Bonnie J. Miller-McLemore. Malden: Blackwell, 2012.

Nava, Alexander. *The Mystical and Prophetic Thought of Simone Weil and Gustavo Gutiérrez*. Albany: State University of New York Press, 2001.

Nichols, Alan, ed. *The Whole Gospel for the Whole World: The Story of the Lausanne Congress on World Evangelization*. Charlotte: LCWE and Regal Books, 1989.

Nicholls, Bruce J., ed. *In Word and Deed: Evangelism and Social Responsibility*. Grand Rapids: Eerdmans Publishing, 1985.

Noll, Mark A. *The Rise of Evangelicalism: The Age of Edwards, Whitefield and the Wesleys*. Downers Grove: InterVarsity Press, 2003.

Olin, John C. "The Idea of Pilgrimage in the Experience of Ignatius of Loyola." *Church History* 48, no. 4 (December 1979), 387–97.

O'Malley, John W. *The First Jesuits*. Boston: Harvard University Press, 1993.

Osmer, Richard R. "Practical Theology: A Current International Perspective," *HTS Teologiese Studies/Theological Studies* 67, no. 2 (2011). https://doi.org/10.4102/hts.v67i2.1058.

Outler, Albert C., ed. *John Wesley*. Oxford University Press, 1964.

Padilla, C. René. "The Future of the Lausanne Movement." *International Bulletin of Missionary Research* 35, no.2 (April 2011): 86–87.

————. *Mission Between the Times: Essays on the Kingdom*. Grand Rapids: Eerdmans, 1985.

————, ed. *The New Face of Evangelicalism: An International Symposium on the Lausanne Covenant*. Downers Grove: InterVarsity Press, 1976.

Padilla DeBorst, Ruth. "From Lausanne III to CLADE V." *Journal of Latin American Theology* 6, no. 1 (January 2011): 7–13.

————. "Who Sets the Table for Whom? Latin American Congresses on Evangelization (CLADE) 1969–2012: A Revision with Eyes Toward a New Celebration." *Journal of Latin American Theology* 5, no. 2 (2010): 107–124.

Paul VI (pope). *Evangelli Nuntiandi*. December 8, 1975. https://www.vatican.va/content/paul-vi/en/apost_exhortations/documents/hf_p-vi_exh_19751208_evangelii-nuntiandi.html.

Pembroke, Neil. "Outsiders and Insiders: Personal Reflections on Methodology in the Studies of Religion at The University of Queensland, 1986–2010." *Crossroads* 5, no. 2, (2011): 123–126. 61UQ_eSpace.

Principe, Walter H. "Broadening the Focus: Context as a Corrective Lens in Reading Historical Works in Spirituality." In *Minding the Spirit: The Study of Christian Spirituality*, edited by Elizabeth A. Dreyer and Mark S. Burrows, 42-48. Baltimore: John Hopkins University Press, 2005.

Provan, Iain. "How Can I Understand, Unless Someone Explains It to Me? (Acts 8:30–31) Evangelicals and Biblical Hermeneutics." *Bulletin for Biblical Research* 17, no. 1 (2007): 1–36.

Radler, Charlotte. "Actio et Contemplatio/Action and Contemplation." *The Cambridge Companion to Christian Mysticism*, edited by Amy M. Hollywood and Patricia Z. Beckman, 211-24. Cambridge: Cambridge University Press, 2012. https://doi.org/10.1017/CCO9781139020886.015.

Rahner, Hugo. *Ignatius the Theologian*. Translated by Michael Barry. London: Geoffrey Chapman. 1968, 1990.

Rahner, Karl. *Further Theology of the Spiritual Life*. Vol 7 of *Theological Investigations VII*. Translated by David Bourke. New York: Seabury, 1977.

———. *Ignatius Speaks*. Translated by Annemarie S. Kidder. Bend: Augustine Press, 2013.

———. *The Mystical Way in Everyday Life: Sermons, Prayers and Essays*. Translated by Annemarie S. Kidder. Maryknoll: Orbis Books, 2010.

———. *The Practice of Faith: A Handbook of Contemporary Spirituality*. Edited by Karl Lehman and Albert Raffelt. New York: Crossroads, 1992.

———. *Visions and Prophecies*. Translated by Charles Henkey and Richard Strachan. Montreal: Palm Publishers, 1963.

Rakoczy, Susan. *Great Mystics and Social Justice: Working on the Two Feet of Love*. New York: Paulist, 2006.

Randall, Ian M. "A Missional Spirituality: Moravian Brethren and Eighteenth-Century English Evangelicalism." *Transformation* 23, no. 4 (October 2006): 204–14.

Ranly, Ernest, W. "Latin American Spirituality." *CrossCurrents* 39, no. 4 (1989): 458–62.

Ratliff, Therese L. "Educating for a 'Spirituality of Dialogue': Theological Foundations, Hermeneutical Invitations, and Pedagogical Directions." *Religious Education* 105, no. 4 (2010): 430–443. https://doi.org/10.1080/00344087.2010.493408.

Reel, Monte, and J. Y. Smith, "A Chilean Dictator's Dark Legacy." *Washington Post* (Washington, DC), Dec. 11, 2006. https://www.washingtonpost.com/archive/politics/2006/12/11/a-chilean-dictators-dark-legacy/596e14a3-d86c-496f-8568-05f81c199a81/.

Ricoeur, Paul. *Essays in Biblical Interpretation*. Philadelphia: Fortress, 1980.

———. *From Text to Action: Essays in Hermeneutics, II*. Translated by Kathleen Blamey and John B. Thompson. Evanston: Northwestern University Press, 1991.

Ringma, Charles R. *Gadamer's Dialogical Hermeneutic: The Hermeneutics of Bultmann, of the New Testament Sociologists, and of the Social Theologians in Dialogue with Gadamer's Hermeneutic*. Heidelberg: University of Heidelberg, 1999.

Rivers, Isabel. "John Wesley as Editor and Publisher." In *The Cambridge Companion to John Wesley*, edited by Randy L. Maddox and Jason E. Vickers, 144-59. Cambridge: Cambridge University Press, 2010.

Root, Andrew. *Christopraxis: A Practical Theology of the Cross*. Minneapolis: Fortress Press, 2014.

Rowland, Christopher J., ed. *The Cambridge Companion to Liberation Theology*. Cambridge: Cambridge University Press, 1999.

Ruffing, Janet K., ed. *Mysticism and Social Transformation*. Syracuse, New York: Syracuse University Press, 2001.

———. "The World Transfigured: Kataphatic Experience Explored through Qualitative Research Methodology." *Studies in Spirituality* 5 (1995): 232–59.

Runyon, Theodore, ed. *Sanctification and Liberation: Liberation Theologies in Light of the Wesleyan Tradition*. Nashville: Abingdon, 1981.

Samuel, Vinay, and Chris Sugden, eds. *Mission as Transformation*. Oxford: Regnum Books International, 1999.

Schneiders, Sandra. "Biblical Spirituality." *Interpretation* 56, no. 2 (2002): 133–43. https://doi.org/10.1177/002096430005600202.

———. "Hermeneutical Approach to the Study of Christian Spirituality." In *Minding the Spirit: The Study of Christian Spirituality*, edited by Elizabeth A. Dreyer and Mark S. Burrows, 49-60. Baltimore: John Hopkins University Press, 2004.

———. "Spirituality in the Academy." In *Exploring Christian Spirituality: An Ecumenical Reader*, edited by Kenneth J. Collins. Grand Rapids: Baker Books, 2000.

———. "The Study of Christian Spirituality: Contours and Dynamics of a Discipline." In *Minding the Spirit: The Study of Christian Spirituality*, edited by Elizabeth A. Dreyer and Mark S. Burrows, 38-57. Baltimore: John Hopkins University Press, 2004.

Schreiter, Robert J. *Constructing Local Theologies*. Maryknoll: Orbis Books, 1985.

———. "From Lausanne Covenant to the Cape Town Commitment: A Theological Assessment." *International Bulletin of Missionary Research* 35, no. 2 (April 2011): 88–91

Sheldrake, Philip. "A Critical Theological Perspective." *The Wiley-Blackwell Companion to Christian Mysticism*, edited by Julia A. Lamm, 531-49. Malden: Blackwell, 2013.

———. *Spirituality: A Brief History*. Blackwell Brief Histories of Religion Series. Malden: Blackwell, 2007.

———. *Spirituality: A Guide for the Perplexed*. London: Bloomsbury Academic, 2014. http://doi.org/10.5040/9781472594532.ch-001.

———. "What is Spirituality?" In *Exploring Christian Spirituality: An Ecumenical Reader*, edited by Kenneth J. Collins. Grand Rapids: Baker Books, 2000.

Sider, Ronald, J. "An Evangelical Theology of Liberation." *Christian Century* (March 19, 1980): 314–18.

Sluhovsky, Moshe. "Loyola's Spiritual Exercises and the Modern Self." In *A Companion to Ignatius of Loyola: Life, Writings, Spirituality, Influence*. Leiden, Brill: 2014. https://doi.org/10.1163/9789004280601_014.

Sobrino, Jon. *Christ the Liberator*. Maryknoll: Orbis Books, 1978.

———. *Christology at the Crossroads: A Latin American Approach*. Translated by John Drury. Maryknoll: Orbis Books, 1978.

———. *Spirituality of Liberation: Toward Political Holiness*. Translated by Robert. R. Barr. Maryknoll: Orbis Books, 1988.

Smith, Gordon T. *Evangelical, Sacramental, and Pentecostal: Why the Church Should Be All Three*. Downers Grove: IVP Academic, 2017.

Snyder, Howard A. "Pietism, Moravianism, and Methodism as Renewal Movements: A Comparative and Thematic Study." Ph.D. dissertation, University of Notre Dame, 1983.

———. *The Radical Wesley and Patterns for Church Renewal*. Downers Grove: InterVarsity Press, 1980.

Stott, John, ed. *Making Christ Known: Historic Mission Documents from the Lausanne Movement, 1974–1989*. Grand Rapids: Eerdmans, 1996.

———. "The Significance of Lausanne." *International Review of Mission* 64, no. 255 (1975): 288–94.

Stott, John, and Christopher J. H. Wright. *Christian Mission in the Modern World*. 2nd ed. Downers Grove: InterVarsity Press, 2015.

Teevan, Donna. "Philosophical Hermeneutics and Theological Education." *Teaching Theology and Religion* 3, no. 2 (2000): 62–70.

Tejirian, Eleanor, and Reeva Spector Simon. "Disintegration, Revival, Reformation, and Counter-Reformation 1450–1800." In *Conflict, Conquest, and Conversion: Two Thousand Years of Christian Missions in the Middle East*. New York: Columbia University, 2012.

Teresa of Avila. *The Interior Castle*. Translated by E. Allison Peers. New York: Doubleday, 1989.

Thiselton, A. C. *New Horizons in Hermeneutics*. London: HarperCollins, 1992.

Tizon, Al. *Transformation After Lausanne: Radical Evangelical Mission in Global-Local Perspective*. Eugene: Wipf and Stock, 2008.

Torrance, James B. *Worship, Community, and the Triune God of Grace*. Carlisle: Paternoster Press, 1996.

Tracy, David. *The Analogical Imagination: Christian Theology and the Culture of Pluralism*. New York: Crossroad, 1981.

———. "A Correlational Model of Practical Theology Revisited." In *Religion, Diversity and Conflict*, edited by Edward Foley. New Jersey: Transaction Publishers, 2008.

———. *Dialogue with the Other: The Inter-Religious Dialogue*. Grand Rapids: Eerdmans, 1990.

———. "The Foundations of Practical Theology." In *Practical Theology: The Emerging Field in Theology, Church and World*, edited by Don S. Browning, 61-82. San Francisco: Harper & Row, 1983.

———. "God, Dialogue and Solidarity: A Theologian's Refrain." *Christian Century* (October 1990): 901–904.

———. "Traditions of Spiritual Practice and the Practice of Theology." *Theology Today* 55, no. 2 (1998): 235–41. https://doi.org/10.1177/004057369805500208.

Tuttle, Robert G. *Mysticism in the Wesleyan Tradition*. Grand Rapids: Francis Asbury Press, 1989.

Tyler, Peter. *The Return to the Mystical*. London: Continuum, 2011.

Van Gelder, Craig. "The Future of the Discipline of Missiology: Framing Current Realities and Future Possibilities." *Missiology: An International Review* 42, no. 1 (2013): 39–56. https://doi.org/10.1177/0091829613507027.

Von Habsburg, Maximillian. *Catholic and Protestant Translations of the Imitatio Christi 1425–1650, from Late Medieval Classic to Modern Best Seller.* New York: Routledge, 2016.

Vatican II. *Decree Ad Gentes: On the Mission and Activity of the Church.* https://www.vatican.va/archive/hist_councils/ii_vatican_council/documents/vat-ii_decree_19651207_ad-gentes_en.html.

Wall, John. "The Creative Imperative: Religious Ethics and the Formation of Life in Common." *The Journal of Religious Ethics* 33, no. 1 (2005): 45–64. https://doi.org/10.1111/j.0384-9694.2005.00182.x.

———. "Phronesis as Poetic: Moral Creativity in Contemporary Aristotelianism." *The Review of Metaphysics* 59, no. 2 (December 2005): 313–31. http://www.jstor.org/stable/27504272.

———. "Phronesis, Poetics, and Moral Creativity." *Ethical Theory and Moral Practice* 6 (2003): 317–41. http://www.jstor.org/stable/27504272.

Walton, Heather. "Poetics." *The Wiley-Blackwell Companion to Practical Theology*, edited by Bonnie J Miller-McLemore 173-82. Malden: Wiley-Blackwell, 2012.

Ward, W. Reginald. *Early Evangelicalism: A Global Intellectual History, 1670–1789.* New York: Cambridge University Press, 2006.

———. *The Protestant Evangelical Awakening.* New York: Cambridge Press, 2006.

Watson, Kevin M. *Pursuing Social Holiness: The Band Meeting in Wesley's Thought and Popular Methodist Practice.* New York: Oxford University Press, 2014. DOI: 10.1093/acprof:oso/9780199336364.001.0001.

Webber, Robert E. "Narrating the World Once Again: A Case for an Ancient-Future Faith." *Criswell Theological Review* 3, no. 2 (Spring 2006): 15–28.

Wesley, John. *The Holy Spirit and Power*, edited by Clare Weakley. Alachua: Bridge-Logos, 2003.

———. "Sermons 1872 Edition." *Wesleyan Holiness Digital Library.* https:/www.whdlorg.

———. *The Works of John Wesley: The Bi-Centennial Edition*, edited by Albert C. Outler. Nashville: Abingdon, 1984–1992.

West, Gerard. "The Bible and the Poor: A New Way of Doing Theology." In *Cambridge Companion to Liberation Theology*, edited by Christopher Rowland, 129–52. Cambridge: Cambridge University Press, 1999.

Whaling, Frank, ed. *John and Charles Wesley: Selected Writings and Hymns.* The Classics of Western Spirituality. New York: Paulist Press, 1981.

Wolfteich, Claire. "Animating Questions: Spirituality and Practical Theology." *International Journal of Practical Theology* 13 (2009): 121–143. https://doi.org/10.1515/IJPT.2009.7.

———. "Practices of Unsaying: Michel de Certeau, Spirituality Studies, and Practical Theology." *Spiritus* 12, no. 2 (Fall 2012): 161–71. https://doi.org/10.1353/scs.2012.0031

———. "Spirituality." In *The Wiley-Blackwell Companion to Practical Theology*, edited by Bonnie J. McLemore, 328-36. Malden: Blackwell Publishing, 2012.

Worcester, Thomas, ed. *The Cambridge Companion to the Jesuits*. Cambridge: Cambridge University Press, 2008.

Wright, Christopher J. H. *The Cape Town Commitment: A Confession of Faith and a Call to Action*. Peabody: Hendrickson, 2011.

———. *The Mission of God: Unlocking the Bible's Grand Narrative*. Downers Grove: IVP Academic, 2006.

Wrogemann, Henning. *Theologies of Mission*. Translated by Karl E. Bohmer. Downers Grove: IVP Academic, 2018.

Wulf, Friedrich. *Ignatius of Loyola: His Personality and Spiritual Heritage, 1556–1956: Studies on the 400th Anniversary of His Death*. Series II – Modern Scholarly Studies About the Jesuits in English Translations, no. 2. St. Louis: Institute of Jesuit Sources, 1977.

Zeiden, Adam. "Mamluk." *Encyclopædia Britannica*. https:/www.Britannica.com/topic/Mamluk.

Zscheile, Dwight J., ed. *Cultivating Sent Communities: Missional Spiritual Formation*. Missional Church Series. Grand Rapids: Eerdmans, 2012.

About Langham Partnership

Langham Literature and its imprints are a ministry of Langham Partnership.

Langham Partnership is a global fellowship working in pursuit of the vision God entrusted to its founder John Stott –

> *to facilitate the growth of the church in maturity and Christ-likeness through raising the standards of biblical preaching and teaching.*

Our vision is to see churches in the Majority World equipped for mission and growing to maturity in Christ through the ministry of pastors and leaders who believe, teach and live by the word of God.

Our mission is to strengthen the ministry of the word of God through:
- nurturing national movements for biblical preaching
- fostering the creation and distribution of evangelical literature
- enhancing evangelical theological education

especially in countries where churches are under-resourced.

Our ministry

Langham Preaching partners with national leaders to nurture indigenous biblical preaching movements for pastors and lay preachers all around the world. With the support of a team of trainers from many countries, a multi-level programme of seminars provides practical training, and is followed by a programme for training local facilitators. Local preachers' groups and national and regional networks ensure continuity and ongoing development, seeking to build vigorous movements committed to Bible exposition.

Langham Literature provides Majority World preachers, scholars and seminary libraries with evangelical books and electronic resources through publishing and distribution, grants and discounts. The programme also fosters the creation of indigenous evangelical books in many languages, through writer's grants, strengthening local evangelical publishing houses, and investment in major regional literature projects, such as one volume Bible commentaries like *The Africa Bible Commentary* and *The South Asia Bible Commentary*.

Langham Scholars provides financial support for evangelical doctoral students from the Majority World so that, when they return home, they may train pastors and other Christian leaders with sound, biblical and theological teaching. This programme equips those who equip others. Langham Scholars also works in partnership with Majority World seminaries in strengthening evangelical theological education. A growing number of Langham Scholars study in high quality doctoral programmes in the Majority World itself. As well as teaching the next generation of pastors, graduated Langham Scholars exercise significant influence through their writing and leadership.

To learn more about Langham Partnership and the work we do visit **langham.org**

Milton Keynes UK
Ingram Content Group UK Ltd.
UKHW020025040624
443552UK00014B/554

9 781839 737626